Rod Serling and The Twilight Zone:

The 50th Anniversary Tribute

DOUGLAS BRODE
AND
CAROL SERLING

BARRICADE
BOOKS

FORT LEE, NEW JERSEY

Published by Barricade Books Inc.
185 Bridge Plaza North
Suite 308-A
Fort Lee, NJ 07024

www.barricadebooks.com

Library of Congress Cataloging-in-Publication Data
A copy of this title's Library of Congress Cataloging-in-Publication
Data is available on request from the Library of Congress.

ISBN 13: 978-1-56980-358-5
ISBN 1-56980-358-7

10 9 8 7 6 5 4 3 2 1

Manufactured in the United States of America

To the Memory of Rod Serling

CONTENTS

Chapter 7

THE UNDISCOVERED COUNTRY: Death in the Fifth Dimension   113

Chapter 8

DEALS WITH THE DEVIL: Dr. Faustus in the Fifth Dimension   131

Chapter 9

Chapter 10

Chapter 11

Chapter 12

Rod Serling
and
The Twilight Zone

Foreword
by Carol Serling

Man consists of body, mind and imagination.
His body is faulty
His mind untrustworthy,
But his imagination has made him remarkable.
—John Masefield

SUBMITTED FOR YOUR approval, as Rod would have said, HERE is a book that for the first time goes behind the TV cameras to dissect and examine the mysterious, provocative, seductively terrifying stories that make up the body of *The Twilight Zone* world.

If you watched *The Twilight Zone* as a child, you might have been thoroughly frightened, though in actuality only a few of the programs were intended to scare. If you were a teenager back then, you might have enjoyed the fables as electronic-age campfire folktales. Now, as an adult, it's likely that you have learned that the stories can be viewed on many different levels. Entertainment? Yes. But enlightenment, too. For there is a morality to those episodes; a message, if you will. And that is what this book is all about.

Through parable and suggestion, Rod commented on the state of the world and man's eternal search for self. He often wrote of the dread of the unknown, the loss of identity, and the subtle destruction of human freedoms. But there were stories, too, that dealt with the dignity of man, his treatment of his fellows, his need for commitment, and the importance of love.

The TV sponsors and network bigwigs didn't wield the black pencil of censorship because they either failed to understand what Rod was saying or just figured that he was off somewhere in outer space. But in truth, Rod was writing about the problems and issues of the day. Think of *The Twilight Zone*, then, as a thinly veiled call to public consciousness. Strange, but unfortunately true, the issues we encountered back then are not so very different from those we face fifty years later. Perhaps that partly explains the show's continued relevance over the past half century.

The Twilight Zone continues to thrill audiences decades after it first aired on television in the late 1950s and early 1960s. No other television series has surpassed *The Twilight Zone* for sheer excitement and wealth of ideas. Those original 156 episodes still play in reruns around the world, proof of the power and timelessness of intelligent stories well told. Individual episodes deal with all aspects of the human condition, past, present and future, and are as varied as man's dreams and fears. But all reveal a deep concern for taste and adult sensibilities.

I know that Rod would approve of Douglas Brode's remarkable book and the insight that he offers into Rod's work. *The Twilight Zone* lives on in the twenty-first century and will entertain and provoke as long as the art of storytelling exists.

I hope that you enjoy your journey through these pages.

Carol Kramer Serling
September 25, 2008

INTRODUCTION:
THE WORLD ACCORDING TO ROD

"I DON'T HAVE THE imagination most writers have," Rod Serling once claimed. Anyone hunting for proof that the worst place to go for an understanding of an author is his own words need look no further! *Zone*'s still-potent stories attest to Serling's stellar reputation as the most imaginative of all American writers since Edgar Allan Poe. So . . . was Serling merely being humble? Did he fail to grasp the full enormity of his gift? Might he have hoped that his non-fantasy work, *Patterns* (1955) and *Requiem for a Heavyweight* (1956) most notable among them, might be more vividly recalled if he downplayed his contribution to the under-appreciated imaginative-fantasy genre? Likely, Serling's words derived from a combination of all the above. And, truth be told, other elements that tormented this deeply conflicted man.

On other subjects, Rod spoke truthfully and fearlessly. One early observer of TV hailed him as the medium's "angry young man." The only other contender: Edward R. Murrow, whose interview show followed *Zone* on Friday nights (1959–1960). What Murrow achieved in CBS's newsroom—*integrity!*—Serling pulled off at that network's entertainment arm.

Earlier in the decade, Serling and other top talents openly addressed important issues during TV's brief "golden age." Colleagues included Reginald Rose (*Twelve Angry Men*), Paddy Chayefsky (*Marty*), and J. P. Miller (*The Days of Wine and Roses*). All turned out smart scripts for "live" anthologies that dominated TV drama from 1948 to 1955. Then the price of sets lowered and TV became big business for mass entertainment. Serious drama was out; predictable potboilers were in. From that point on, Serling necessarily presented politics and philosophy in a foxier manner. Yet present them he did, initially as a haunting off-screen voice. Then, beginning with the first show of *Zone*'s second season (Fall 1960), he spoke directly into the camera. Eyeballing the audience, Serling charmed the nation with his charismatic presence, uniquely alliterative way with words, and the ideas, largely of a liberal-progressive order, he so deeply believed in.

Casting a seductive smile, Serling alone continued to convey on TV what every other serious writer wanted to say but wasn't allowed to. High-profile sponsors now acted as self-appointed censors, making certain that their products were presented in a context that offended no one. So Serling "said something" by doing so indirectly, dropping confrontational realism for parable. During *The Twilight Zone*'s five-year run (1959–1964), he employed imaginative/allegorical fiction to comment on (and sharply criticize) postwar America. "On *Zone*," Peter Kaplan claimed, "the nightmare side of American life was opened up." What initially seemed to be out-of-this-world dreams of darkness reflected a shadow-world existing on the edge of our brightly lit suburbs.

But where did such a politicized view of drama come from? Serling's early surroundings appear unlikely to lead to an intellectual approach. Born on December 25, 1924, young Rod (age two) moved with his family (parents Sam and Esther; older brother Robert) from Syracuse, New York to the smaller city of Binghamton. As a child growing up in a provincial area, Rod remained blissfully unaware of John Steinbeck or Clifford Odets, the era's great realists. "Upstaters" might have the opportunity to catch an occasional touring company, but Manhattan's live "theatre of ideas" was not easily accessible. Movies had emerged as an average American's source of drama and comedy. An avid fan, Rod memorized dialogue from his favorite film, *Adventures of Robin Hood* (1936), then performed the story for family and friends. Likewise, he enjoyed *Flash Gordon* and *Buck Rogers*.

In time, *Zone* would offer the next generation an open door to an alternative universe. Serling's approach transformed the time/space fantasies he'd adored as an impressionable boy into sophisticated fantasy, his configured paradigm of imaginative fiction, appropriate for a brave new world in which a trip to the moon or an invasion from Mars suddenly seemed a likely possibility.

But back to the beginning . . . friends recall young Rod as a red-blooded American boy, fascinated by pretty girls, all sports, model airplanes, and Hollywood movies. *Dr. Jekyll and Mr. Hyde* left an indelible impression with its vision of dual identities. Such movies were special, a once a week treat. Radio, on the other hand, existed as a part of the emergent twentieth century environment. Listeners discovered seductive realms of music, sports, and chatter. Rod, like most everyone else, devoured it all. Best of all, he listened to drama everyday. Not serious stuff, mostly: *The Shadow* and *The Green Hornet* took troubled minds off the Depression. Rod best loved *Lights Out*. This aural spook-fest had been created by innovative author/producer Arch Oboler. In an anthology format, qualifying *Lights Out* as predecessor to **Zone**, Oboler experimented with strange stories introduced by the sound of a slowly opening door. Just such a doorway (now visual and floating through space) would eventually open many excursions into the fifth dimension on commercial TV, still a seemingly far-off dream in the thirties.

Mostly, *Lights Out* had been just for fun. As such, and however much the youth who would become Rod Serling enjoyed it, he already grasped Oboler's limitations. Then by chance, at age thirteen, Rod encountered something important. Spinning the dial, he happened upon *The Fall of the City*, the inception of serious writing for radio by already established playwrights and poets. Penned by Archibald MacLeish, *Fall* dealt with the heavy issue of fascism, emotionally involving its audience, then intellectually challenging listeners much as **Zone** would a generation later. So key influences that shaped the Serling vision and his artistic approach piled up: movies, an anthology format, the lure of a good scare, a highly politicized play presented as fable . . .

Shortly, Norman Corwin began broadcasting his legendary liberal-crusader pieces. Corwin, whom Rod Serling would idolize all his life, pushed beyond MacLeish's political parable into fantasy. One December eve, Corwin enthralled the nation with *The Plot to Overthrow Christmas*. Broadcast on CBS, the piece left its mark, particularly on one boy eagerly awaiting his birthday. Serling later referenced that play in *Night of the Meek*, a second season **Zone**, and *Carol for Another Christmas* (1964), a U.N. special. From Corwin, Serling inherited the coda to which he would remain true, a variation on what critic Kenneth Rexroth once tagged "literature as equipment for living." Art, and for that matter commerce and entertainment, ought never be empty, style without substance. Their reason for existing is to make better people of us; teaching the masses, through positive examples and cautionary fables, how we ought to live our lives, what we must avoid at all costs.

Not surprisingly, then, Rod's editorials in *Panorama*, his high school paper, were overtly didactic. When chosen to address his graduating senior class of 1943, he quoted Goethe! How the All-American Boy discovered that German poet, even his most influential teacher, Helen Foley, could not guess. Passionately and persuasively, the intense youth implored fellow graduates to do the right thing after they left their sheltered enclave. "The writer's role is to *menace* the public's conscience," **Zone**'s creator insisted a quarter-century later, addressing the Library of Congress. Though Rod might not have been able to articulate that idea so precisely at age nineteen, the Serling sensibility was in place even at that early age.

Also, Rod always wanted to write. Initially, he tried his hand at conventional literary genres. Poetry, the most exalted form, he tenuously delved into during the war years. Serling enthusiastically signed up for active duty, originally hoping to be a tail-gunner, settling for the paratroopers. Big brother Robert took one glance at a Tennyson-like military ode Serling mailed him and scribbled back: "Forget about it!" Their father brought one such piece to seasoned Syracuse journalist Leo Kosoff; the old pro lamented, "Better he should be a butcher" (Sam's occupation). Rod sensed that they were correct. Not that he couldn't write; verse just wasn't his natural outlet. What, then, was? By fate or accident, Rod would soon happen upon the proper medium. Serving in the South Pacific, he had the opportunity to pen his first radio playlet. Serling was about to engage in the battle of the Mahonag foothills on Leyte Island. To relieve tension at the 511th's headquarters, Jack Benny flew over for a morale-boosting show performed live in the jungle. Broadcast over AFR, the partly scripted, partly improvised performance went out to servicemen about to participate in Manila's recapture. Serling, who would shortly be reassigned to demolitions, was attached to his outfit's communications team. Contributing to this show allowed a budding talent to reach an immense audience for the first time. Already enthralled by radio, Serling now grasped its full potential.

Despite these rich and varied experiences, Serling did not encounter the tradition of "serious" stage drama until 1946. Following discharge, he took advantage of the new G.I. Bill and traveled to Yellow Springs, Ohio, enrolling at Antioch College. His initial major was, of all things, phys. ed. (How intriguing to imagine Serling as the beloved gym teacher at some small-town high school, perhaps in a place called Willoughby or Homewood?) Under the guidance of the college's English department, Serling switched to liberal arts. Now he was exposed to the famous dictum Henrik Ibsen, father of modern drama, had in 1877 scrawled over the entrance to his theatre of revolutionary ideas: "*Not* for entertainment only!" A good story brings in the masses; once they were seated, a writer could employ theatre magic to challenge any existing prejudices.

At Antioch, Serling encountered such work . . . when not slipping off to make a much-needed buck by testing new parachute technology, "hitting the silk" for the army air force. He also knew how to relax. If art struck Serling as serious, sports offered a great escape. He played intramural football and loved to listen to a Sunday afternoon baseball game on the radio. Meanwhile, his desire to write increased. Forsaking poetry, Serling tried his hand at hard-bitten prose. Several times, he turned to the subject of boxing, a gifted flyweight himself. The short stories, which appeared in the campus literary magazine, fared better than had his brief fling with verse. His most successful piece, "The Good Right Hand," concerns a KO'ed fighter, serving as a primitive prelude to and dry-run for *Requiem for a Heavyweight.*

Because Serling attended a leading liberal arts college, he sensed that to be academically correct, he ought to at least try and become a novelist. Yet personal instincts insisted otherwise: Radio was where he wanted to go. Here was the medium in which Serling's talent could run free. And where he could earn a living! Want-ads in the local paper didn't contain job offerings for a poet. Radio, however, had work aplenty, for both writers and announcers. Serling qualified as a double threat. In addition to his authorial way with words, there was that mesmerizingly grainy voice. Fortunately, Antioch qualified as a progressive school with a work-studies approach to higher education. To fulfill this commitment, Serling found employment at several local stations and, in time, at Manhattan's public radio outlet, WNYC. While there, he composed an on-air tribute for the first-ever Veterans Day celebration, a deep commitment to the men who fight our wars always as basic as his anti-war philosophy.

In November 1948 Serling was named manager of the campus radio station. Immediately he formed his own troupe. Now he commanded an academic variation on Orson Welles' *Mercury Theatre of the Air*, which Serling recalled from childhood. Like that legendary group, Serling's company of writers, actors, and directors mounted a weekly dramatic anthology. "There was a lot of Welles in Rod," Rudy Ruderman, who worked with Serling at Antioch, later recalled. It's worth noting that in 1958, while **Zone** was in the planning stages, Serling agreed to narrate only after Orson Welles, his first choice, passed. And that the most famous of all Mercury Theatre broadcasts had been science fiction: H. G. Wells' *War of the Worlds*.

Not that all Serling's energies went into radio. Always a magnetic figure to women, diverse attractive objects of his temporary affection slipped into the background the moment he met and fell in love with co-ed Carol Kramer. A brainy beauty, Carol's lineage included former President Taft. Despite such social status, her immediate family took a liking to this brash beau, obviously a highly talented as well as attractive young man. Still, they felt that Carol ought to complete her studies. She honored that request from her mother's side of the family. The one exception to acceptance was her father, who objected to her marrying a Jew. She stood by her man; the two were married on June 30, 1948.

The couple moved into married student housing, nicknamed "Trailertown" by war veteran residents and their brides, for the final two years of her education. Carol's influence on her husband's career cannot be overstated. She learned that ABC had initiated a scriptwriting contest for their *Dr. Christian Show*, and insisted that her husband mail in an entry. Serling's play *To Live a Dream* tied for second. Acceptance of a $500 check transformed a gifted amateur into a professional. Another prize went to Earl Hamner, Jr., who before creating *The Waltons* in 1971 would pen many a *Zone*. Shortly afterward, Serling accepted a full-time job as staff writer at WLW-AM radio in Cincinnati. Far more intriguing to him was a newly created sister station, WLW-T(V). Initially, Serling took a liking to this evolving medium as it allowed him to watch, as well as listen to, sports. Gradually, his desire to emerge as the next radio auteur gave way to a reconfigured dream.

To try for a career in radio, Serling would have to compete with established writer-stars. On the other hand, well-known scribes hesitated to risk their reputations on an untried form. In television, then, the field remained wide open. With myriad time slots, TV boasted an immense appetite for fresh talent, particularly young writers who instinctually understood the uniqueness of TV/video. Serling grasped this as fully as Corwin and Welles had the specific demands of aural storytelling. Also, the yet open book of TV might turn out to be the serious populist venue radio should have become.

Network head William Paley had scuttled Corwin's serious dramas for silly comedies and overwrought soaps. In Serling's words, radio now offered "writing and thinking downward at the lowest possible common denominator." Though this pattern would be repeated by television once it passed a pioneering stage, no one could have predicted that at the time. If only some young turks might seize power from the onset, TV could become a Group Theatre of the airwaves—an emergent popular art form. Sensing this, Serling hoped to be among that company. He quit his day job at WLW to freelance for regional venues, turning out scripts for *The Storm*, produced at Cincinnati's WKRC. Without that steady paycheck the Serlings had come to depend on, however small, "it was tuna casserole time," Carol recalls. Eager, ambitious, and quite irresistible, Serling persuaded New York agent Blanche Gaines to send his scripts around to Manhattan TV producers. These were grabbed up for shows like

Danger, Studio One, Lux Video Theatre, and *Hallmark Hall of Fame.*
Then as always, Rod's best work derived from personal experience.
He had killed and been wounded during the war; he was awarded
a Purple Heart with Oak Leaf clusters; he now drew on lingering
memories of that period in his life.

By writing about what happened, Serling discovered, he could
put events into proper perspective; popular art proved therapeutic as
well as financially rewarding. Now, though, the realities of life at its
most intense (that is, in war) rubbed up against the fantasies in the
Hollywood movies he had been drawn to earlier. The mentality of
John Wayne vehicles (*Sands of Iwo Jima,* 1949) struck Serling as dishonest, dangerous. A naive pro-war kid had become a battle-scarred
pacifistic adult. This burning desire to set the record straight would
eventually turn up in some of **Zone**'s most poignant episodes, *The
Purple Testament* among them. That had been the case sans imaginative fiction's devices in plays he penned for NBC's *Armstrong Circle
Theater.* Most notable among them: *The Sergeant,* broadcast live on
April 29, 1952. A mini *Lord Jim* set during WWII, the tale concerned
a conscience-stricken soldier, unable to resolve his self-image as a
hero with stark reality: During an enemy attack, his sudden shriek of
fear caused the death of squad members. So what was he . . . really?
The brave hero of his own imagination? Or a craven figure who in
actuality betrayed, however unwittingly, his comrades? Is the self
as each of us sees himself more or less "real" than the way the world
views any one person?

The tricky nature of identity, first encountered years earlier in
Jekyll and Hyde, would be raised in such early TV plays—eventually
reaching full fruition with **Zone**, most strikingly in *Mirror Image*—as
would the notion that all reality finally exists, for a modernist, in
the human mind.

Meanwhile, with considerable sales under his belt and the pressures
of small-town radio/TV finally getting to him, Serling decided that it
was time to head for the east coast. Carol agreed. The timing couldn't
have been more perfect, since network TV remained headquartered
there. At that moment, the industry was still "dominated by creative
people," producer Jerome Hellman later recalled, "to whom New York

represented a kind of creative Mecca." As to television in those final hours of infancy, producer Fielder Cook added: "We had no rules, so we in effect created the medium ourselves." An insistent Serling broke into *Kraft Television Theatre*, at that moment the best of all live dramas. *Playhouse 90* would shortly seize that distinction due to Serling's contributions, including *Requiem* (1956). That masterpiece remained two years away. In 1954, Serling wrote *The Strike*, his most vehement anti-war play yet. The piece received rave reviews when aired on *Studio One*, making his name more widely known.

Serling set to work on *Patterns*, detailing the dehumanizing aspects of a Madison Avenue career. When ABC telecast this on January 12, 1955, on *Kraft Television Theatre*, the country discovered a new writer-star. According to the *New York Times'* Jack Gould, *Patterns* rated as "one of the high points in the TV medium's evolution." Only the *Wall Street Journal* had something nasty to say. That bastion of conservative values attacked his politics. In an era of McCarthy-inspired red-baiting, the businessman's newspaper labeled Serling a "Marxist." The irony was that he remained one of the more conventional, if politically left of center, among the era's writers. Following the first sweet smell of success, the Serlings had moved to upscale Westport, Connecticut, there beginning a traditional family: kids and pets everywhere, neighbors invited over for backyard barbeques.

Many other writers set out on different trips. This was the period when Jack Kerouac and Neal Cassidy went "on the road." Beatniks became dharma bums in search of Zen-like truth, subterraneans inhabiting an underground existence in Greenwich Village cellar clubs. Bearded rebels wore dirty jeans and burly sweaters, but Rod Serling always looked clean-cut in a natty suit. The Beats scorned suburbia for its homogeneity. Folksinger Malvina Reynolds complained about "little houses made of ticky-tacky, and they all look just the same."

If the Serlings enjoyed an upscale lifestyle, they saw through its hypocrisies. Whereas Kerouac and his ilk dropped out of a mainstream they detested, hurling angry insults backward, Serling attacked its limitations from the inside. Later, after he and Carol had moved to the west coast, Serling insisted (with a tinge of guilt) that he did indeed "like" the lifestyle: "We had a swimming pool and a tennis court. Got a little work done, too." Some old friends and critics claimed that he had sold out. In truth, first Westport and later Pacific Palisades allowed Serling the necessary experiences to write about split-level traps with a knowing eye, not the blind contempt of the Beats. Had he never "gone Hollywood," how could Serling have penned his brilliant indictment of that place, *The Velvet Alley*?

"I was a strange, haunted middle of-the-roader trying to find his way," Serling confessed. Not so different from Franz Kafka in Europe a generation earlier, Serling was likewise a physically small man in an unassuming suit. As Kafka stated in 1920, "I have lost my way among my own thorns." Many **Zones** have been described as "Kafka-esque," most notably *The Obsolete Man*.

Why did Serling leave the New York scene? Out of necessity! His euphoria after winning a well-deserved Emmy for *Patterns* proved short-lived. 1955, the year in which Serling rose to the top of the talented writing heap, also marked a juncture as the industry began its move to California. TV executives had gradually grasped that film allowed them greater control over the product, also providing larger revenues through reruns. Overnight, TV became the entertainment form for people who couldn't afford to leave the house. In response to this reality, the networks lowered their aim, afraid to offend anyone, including extremists on the far left or right. Serling was stunned to learn that *The Arena*, his biting analysis of political infighting for CBS's *Studio One*, would be watered down to make it "palatable," precisely what he did not want. Later, he recalled that "to say a single thing germane to the current political scene was absolutely prohibited."

The result, as FCC Chairman Newton Minnow would shortly note, constituted "a vast wasteland," all but devoid of the innovation and creativity that characterized TV only half a decade earlier. For a writer of social conscience, the choice became painfully evident: Drop out of TV to concentrate on the higher level of movies and Broadway plays, or join the migration to "the coast" and try to somehow survive in an industry now obsessed with achieving the highest ratings by playing to a lowest common denominator. Chayefsky chose the former route; Serling, the latter. In Hollywood Serling would continue to fight the good fight for quality TV, if now necessarily going "underground" to do so.

The result: *The Twilight Zone*. What could possibly sound less controversial to a network head or wary sponsor than science fiction, perceived by those who fail to comprehend it as superficial escapism? But Serling employed the genre as a means to take a video-inspired weekly walk on the wild side. *Zone* crystallized menacing alleys and badly lit back streets of what people in retrospect chose to recall as a simpler, more prosperous time: our "happy days." In truth, this had been a difficult era: The cold war, fear of nuclear oblivion, ever-escalating violence over civil rights, supposed infiltration of our government and military by subversives, and an economic recession that dimmed the brief postwar boom. As Stephen King noted, one TV writer "had put none of his cudgels away but was now wielding them in the name of fantasy." Within the context of amazing stories, Serling created a forum that freed him to say anything he wanted while, by implication rather than direct statement, he then addressed immediate problems.

Understandably, then, when Minnow delivered his damning speech about TV in May 1961, he hastened to point out that there remained one last oasis in the desert this once-potent medium had degenerated into: *The Twilight Zone*.

TV's age of live experimentation (1948–1955) now over, the industry began an imitative approach that would last for three decades: tagging along behind whatever was new at the movies by several years. *The Thing (from Another World)* and *The Day the Earth Stood Still* in 1950 paved the way for high-impact movies appealing to America's first youth audience. When initial ratings were tabulated (decent, if never huge), Serling had been surprised to learn that a great many *Zone* viewers were teenagers. He needn't have been: This was the only show that equaled the impact of the daring films they loved best. Like those films (*Invasion of the Body Snatchers* the ultimate example), *Zone* often opened with a deceptively calm tableau. During the following thirty minutes (sixty in the fourth season), this semblance of normalcy gradually twisted up into something terrifying.

The vision proved as true as it was terrible. Many of its wondrous epiphanies occurred as fans were entranced by turnabouts during any episode's final seconds. *Zone* was not the only dramatic anthology that offered such a powerful, if unexpected, conclusion. *Alfred Hitchcock Presents* (1955–1965) preceded Serling's show by four years, likewise raising audience expectations for a final revelation. The Master of Suspense insisted on a distinction between a "trick" ending (which he disparaged) and a true "twist." A trick feels arbitrary, tacked on at the last moment, leaving a viewer unsatisfied; we sense there was, after all, nothing in the unfolding drama to imply that this alone had been coming. A twist succeeds because it simultaneously delights and frustrates. We take ourselves to task for not guessing at once that this would (must!) be the conclusion. In the great *Zones*, Serling dutifully followed Hitchcock's dictum, thus the similarity between TV's two finest filmed dramas.

More significant was the difference. Hitch's work (with the possible exception only of *The Birds* in 1963) derived from an attitude expressed by a character in *The Lady Vanishes* (1937): "I'm half-inclined to believe," one ordinary chap confides to another as their lives turn without warning into a nightmare by daylight, "there's a perfectly logical explanation behind all of this." In Hitchcock, however bizarre things may seem, they ultimately can be explained as part and parcel of the everyday world. In *Zone,* characters not only momentarily feel as if they've been pulled into an alternative dimension (or visited by denizens of other worlds) but, at the end, realize that they have been. Here, Serling was inspired by his single favorite line in Shakespeare: "There are more things in heaven and earth," the metaphysically minded Hamlet informs his realist friend Horatio, "than are dreamt of in your philosophy."

Week after week, *Zone* offered modern Grand Guignol, the theatre of horror, a freak show that forced its audience to gaze back into its collective psyche and admit the existence of something disturbing (all the more frightening because it proved inexplicable) there. Still, the initial grounding was often, as in Hitchcock, everyday reality. *Zone* shocked and scared because stories usually took place close to home rather than in distant Transylvania. Frankenstein, Dracula, and the Wolfman, once blood-curdling visages, now appeared (to borrow from Poe) quaint and curious, particularly after their joint encounter with Abbott and Costello (1949). The book now closed on what horror had once meant. A new volume opened for the likes of Rod, Richard Matheson, and Ray Bradbury to fill.

A theatrical movie like *Body Snatchers* or a *Zone* might begin in a seemingly average corner of our world. Then its odd, unsettling vision stretched further, rippled outward, turning that image of ordinariness into an exaggeration, revealing a deeper, more profound truth just beneath the surface vision. Between *Zone*'s initial conception and its premature demise, the series survived the Eisenhower era's final years and pushed into Jack Kennedy's New Frontier. However brief-lived, at the time (and on the show) a spurt of youthful optimism emerged, only to be shattered that day in November 1963 when the global community learned of the president's blood spilling out onto a Dallas street.

Zone not only existed during that era of transition from gray days to blinding psychedelic colors, but reflected all that happened. "Of all the dramatic programs which have ever run on American TV," King noted, *Zone* "is the one which comes closest to defying any overall analysis." Serling's series included science fiction and horror, Westerns and comedies, arch melodrama and serious social commentary without being limited to any of them. The whole was always greater than the sum of its parts, explaining why those episodes that do not work (Serling admitted that there were plenty) don't trouble us. We emphasize the positive by recalling the best. This volume will concentrate on those *Zones* which did touch a common core, focusing on classics written by Serling himself. Key episodes by other contributors will be discussed in passing so *Zone*'s full impact will be fully represented.

Note, then, that this is not an encyclopedia with an entry on every episode. That has already been provided by Mark Scott Zicree in *The Twilight Zone Companion*. Rather, consider this an in-print equivalent to the pre-title sequence in *Twilight Zone—The Movie* (1978). On a starry, starry night, two guys drive down a lonesome highway. The passenger, Dan Aykroyd, is a hitch hiker whom the driver, Albert Brooks, picked up to relieve boredom. Initially, they sing college drinking songs, then swap favorite *Zone* plots. As the two relate these tales with great passion and vividness, viewers grasped the incredible impact this series had on an entire generation. That will be the approach here: to try to capture what we all loved most about the best *Zones*, those that live on in what Jung tagged our "collective unconscious."

To conclude as we began, here's yet another quote that reveals how little Serling grasped the enormity of what he had accomplished. In an interview weeks before his death at age fifty (Serling's passing occurred on June 28, 1975, following open-heart surgery), he said; "When I look back over thirty years of professional writing, I'm hard pressed to come up with anything that's important. Some things are literate (and) some are interesting . . . but very damn little (seems) important." Au contraire: If there is one word that best describes his output, that word is important.

Zone was never subtle; elitist sophistication was not Rod's way. Nor is it for popular entertainers, influenced by him, such as Stephen King and Steven Spielberg. Let others worry about the literary/arthouse crowd; here's a work that, in the tradition of Shakespeare, may just move the masses. And alter them for the better!

Yes, Rod Serling and *Twilight Zone* were important. The purpose of this book will be to reveal how and why.

THE WAY WE WERE:
The Lure of Nostalgia

DURING THE POSTWAR years, average Americans in ever greater numbers deserted small towns and big cities to embrace the emergent concept of suburbia. Rod and Carol Serling made that move, following commercial success, to a notably upscale aspect of the new American paradigm. But like so many other young adults of the 1950s, Serling experienced an uneasy sense of dislocation. Something essential, however hard to define, had been lost en route; some aspect of innocence, perhaps, that at least to a romantic imagination, once existed in our towns. Each such place had been unique, organically created over decades, taking on a shape and style all its own. Suburbia, in comparison, was defined by Pulitzer-prize winning author David Halberstam as "the new social contract according to Bill Levitt." Reacting to rampant blandness, residents began to yearn for the good old days, if less the reality of a bygone lifestyle than what Richard Schickel called "an imagined past." Our growing hunger for this mythic America shortly informed "much of the new popular culture." What would eventually come to be called The Nostalgia Craze would prove essential to *Zone* from its earliest episodes.

You Can't Go Home Again:

WALKING DISTANCE (10/30/59)

The opening image of the fifth *Zone* broadcast offers what had already become a Friday night ritual: A slow descent from primordial darkness punctuated by dots of light. The camera's downward tilt then highlights the tops of trees in daylight, suggesting a romantic vision in which nature serves as a positive element. As our viewpoint lowers to a rural service station where a young attendant works, a modern sports model tears down the road. From the moment we first see Martin Sloan (Gig Young), he appears angry, on the verge of losing control. The character is not now, and never will be, provided with any clear motivation for simmering hysteria, though such details will be supplied in a follow-up, *A Stop at Willoughby*. Sloan isn't running from a single incident like the one we'll encounter there but from the lifestyle: high-powered board meetings, underhanded deals, cocktail lunches with men he neither likes nor respects.

An executive in charge of media relations for a New York City advertising firm, Sloan engages in an irrational flight from unsatisfying conformity. His vaguely understood (for Sloan as for us) departure from all he's become mired in is clear from erratic behavior: driving furiously, then beeping the horn like a crazy person once he screeches to a halt. The weekend allows Sloan furtive attempts to escape an everyday schedule filled with ennui. His (implied) work-week existence is not the one that, in his idealistic youth, he planned on. A creative person who sold his talent for commercial success in a consumer-driven society, Sloan is posited as a contemporary Everyman for white-collar, button-down types. He might be considered typical of those who, according to Thoreau, lead "lives of quiet desperation:" consumed by an inner angst that derives from a gnawing sense of self-betrayal not unlike the author's own.

"This is not just a Sunday drive," Rod's voice-over informs us. "He is looking for an exodus," hinting at a Biblical dimension. Sloan's odyssey provides an entrance into the imaginative realm he will return from, if in a notably altered state. A believable plot development (his car needs a lube job, requiring several hours work) provides Sloan with incentive to walk to the aptly named "Homewood." A rural town, this is where Sloan grew up. Relocated in its leisurely streets, this visitor steps into the drugstore. There, he learns an ice-cream soda (three scoops) still costs a dime. That we must deal with two Sloans (his once-idealistic self and the cynical creature he has become) is established by director Robert Stevens's use of a mirror, set behind the counter, allowing us to view a dichotomized Martin. One aspect is glimpsed to the right of Charlie (Byron Foulger), an elderly fellow behind the counter in the mirror image, the other to the left. "As if I left yesterday," Sloan notes of a place that appears identical to warm memories of it. Sloan even notes that the soda jerk looks vaguely familiar. "I have that kind-a face," Charlie softly replies.

Early in the decade, Jack Kerouac titled his first novel *The Town and the City*. That narrative focused on a growing distinction in American lifestyles, suggesting a split between the positive ambience of small towns and the glitzy, superficial appeal of modernity. Sloan's problem, we grasp, has less to do with spending most of his time in New York (the place) as that Manhattan (the idea) now exists inside him and cannot be left behind. Learning how cheap a soda is here, he expresses not delight but concern as to profit margin: "You're gonna lose your shirt!" His flight to freedom is doomed to failure; how can you run away from the contemporary money culture when you carry it around inside? Nobody sells sodas for a dime anymore. Then again, this is not anymore, or anywhere . . . but the fifth dimension.

We learn this before Sloan does. He speaks of the long-deceased owner, Mr. Wilson (Pat O'Malley), before stepping back out onto the street. Violating the established point of view (Sloan's) for a single shot, the camera remains inside. Charlie ascends rickety stairs and speaks to his elderly boss, fanning himself in a stuffy office. If we have guessed that Mr. Wilson awaits before Charlie arrives at the dark at the top of these stairs, our shared premonition adds to the impact. We are allowed the sensation of collaborating with Serling, of being in on a grim joke before it's actualized. We're invited to stand alongside Serling, sharing his detached vision on this mid-twentieth century American Faust who furtively dreams of winning his soul back from the modern Mephistopheles of corporate greed and suburban existence.

A series of anecdotes gradually make Sloan aware that he hasn't arrived in Homewood circa 1959, but the town as it existed twenty-five years earlier. A little boy (Ron Howard) playing marbles knows an eleven-year-old Marty Sloan. A teen (Buzz Martin) polishing a new '34 roadster forces Sloan into a growing cognition of his situation.

The single incident that cinches Sloan's understanding occurs in a park. "Wonderful," he sighs, finding the grassy area more appealing than the town. He helps a distraught mom (Nan Peterson) coax her son down from dangerously high branches. (Trees, benign in most *Zones*, are something we'd be unwise to take lightly.) He is, at this moment, J. D. Salinger's *Catcher in the Rye*, the rare sensitive adult who knows that children must connect with nature, then stations himself nearby to prevent a hard landing. After the boy safely reaches the ground, Sloan recalls how he once climbed up a post, carving his name there. Glancing in that direction, he spots himself (as a boy) doing precisely that and tries to confront his eleven-year-old alter-ego, causing the frightened Marty (Michael Montgomery) to run away.

Sloan does not know what to say. Words written by William Wordsworth in 1802 might serve his purpose:

> *O blessed vision! Happy child!*
> *Though art so exquisitely wild,*
> *I think of thee with many fears*
> *For what may be thy lot in future years.*

Ironically, Martin Sloan will later that day inadvertently create a physical incapacity that will form Marty's lot in life. For the time being, this experience leaves Sloan with one option: to confront his parents. He approaches the house where he was raised only to be rejected by his father and mother. She (Irene Tedrow) and he (Frank Overton) cringe behind the screen door, its hazy surface lending an other worldliness to their presence. Like the figures in Grant Wood's *American Gothic*, these small-towners fearfully glance at a deranged stranger. At the dramatic midpoint, Martin Sloan will return, as he must, to again try. In Serling's words, Sloan has a "resolve to put in a claim to the past": to redeem a wasted life by recapturing a golden summer. But that's not possible without forcing out his youthful self.

The inability of two versions of one person to coexist in a juncture of the time/space continuum will be referenced in Robert Zemeckis's *Zone*-influenced *Back to the Future* (1985). Here, Sloan must accept the impossibility of returning to the lovely dream of an idealized past while realizing such a situation can lead to a positive view:

> *Here I stand, not only with the sense*
> *Of present pleasure, but with pleasing thoughts*
> *That in this moment there is life and food*
> *For future years . . .*
> *—William Wordsworth—*

For Sloan, as for the poet's nineteenth-century narrator and upcoming Marty McFly (who shares Sloan's first name), that conclusion must be understood, accepted. Sloan, like a Greek mythic hero, must face a set of parents who emerge from out of the past to seal his fate. Martin Sloan will not, Oedipus-like, violate the primal taboo, though Marty McFly nearly does!

As to namesakes: why did Serling name the man "Sloan"? Another writer had a few years earlier offered a similar vision in a non-fantastical context. Sloan Wilson's book *The Man in the Gray Flannel Suit* (1953), filmed in 1956, offered an unsparing portrait of upwardly mobile fellows who shop for suits at Brooks Brothers. The book encapsulated the common experience of a generation; in Tom and Betsy Rath (Gregory Peck and Jennifer Jones on screen), several million upwardly mobile couples were treated to a nightmare scenario of their lives. In *Walking Distance*, Serling brought that vision home to those who had overlooked both the book and movie, knowing only what they saw on television. "Their dreams seemed to be about material progress," *The Fifties* tells us about the Raths and their real-life counterparts. This preoccupation led to a "narrowness" among men who, in their adolescence, dreamed of becoming poets or playwrights only to turn out advertising tripe. Their talent with words had, if for a considerable price, been co-opted to manipulate members of a new consumer culture into purchasing items they neither wanted nor needed, yet couldn't resist after a marketing campaign by those whom Vance Packard tagged "the hidden persuaders." After a full day's debasing work, these junior executives retreated to an upscale enclave on Long Island or Connecticut to wash down depressions with Chivas Regal while trophy wives gazed on, confused. What was wrong with their husbands?

Rod delivers as imaginative fiction what Sloan Wilson realistically documented. Like the narrator of Wordsworth's "Lines" (1789), Martin Sloan is

> . . . *More like a man*
> *Flying from something that he dreads, than one*
> *Who sought the thing he loved.*

Temporarily, Sloan has rediscovered just that: the Main Street, USA of his lost youth. Still, he's now

> . . . *Changed, no doubt, from what I was when*
> *First I came among these hills . . .*
>   *—Wordsworth—*

Sloan senses this as he touches the baseball mitt his dad gave him or rings the bell on his beloved bike. "I belong here," he desperately tells his father as the concerned man steps out from the screened porch and accuses this thirty-six year-old of delusions. "I'm Martin," the protagonist insists to his mother when she joins them. "You've got to believe!" The act of believing, in defiance of all rational thought, will underline the entirety of *Zone*. But in fear and panic, she slaps him as Sloan attempts to offer proof (his driver's license). Her simple act might seem like minor stuff compared to the incessant din of machine gun fire on *The Untouchables* every Thursday night during that 1959 season. Yet her slap remains a classic moment of televised violence.

Context, in art and entertainment, is everything. The gesture happens so unexpectedly, yet seems so right in its wrongness that it never fails to shock a first-time viewer. This loving mother never before struck her son. But this vaguely familiar stranger threatens the fragile order of her world. She does so not because she still believes him to be an imposter, but because, on some unconscious level, Mrs. Sloan senses that he speaks the truth. At that moment,

Sloan is shocked into a recognition that his presence is dangerous. Simultaneously, he hears the sound of the calliope and turns away from them: nostalgic chords invoke an entire era via a tune emanating from the predecessor of a modern theme park.

Sloan is drawn to the well-lit amusement pier that in the 1930s offered simple wholesome entertainment. By 1959, such spots had fallen into disrepair. *Walking Distance* now segues into a perfect resolution. The style alters as Sloan notices his youthful self on the merry-go-round; director Stevens shifts from simple camera set-ups to oblique angles, turning a relatively realistic setting into something quite surreal. The shots grow more disconcerting as Sloan hops on and is glimpsed by Marty, who falls off, injuring a leg. At that moment Sloan is gripped with pain. "I only wanted to tell you," he whimpers as people rush to the boy, "that this is a wonderful time of life for you. Don't let any of it go by without enjoying it." From personal experience, Sloan can grasp the essential truth to a time-worn adage: How tragic that youth is wasted on the young. There won't be any more merry-go-round rides, the mature Martin Sloan knows; young Marty can't, in his innocence, imagine the shape of things to come: no more cotton candy or band concerts.

"The boy will be all right," Pop Sloan confides after tracking down Martin. Checking the dropped I.D., Pop now knows that this is an older incarnation of his son. "But he will limp some." Pop grasps what Sloan, clinging to the pathetic hope he can return to a paradise lost, must accept: It's time to leave. "Maybe there's only one summer to every customer," he wistfully sighs. Sad news! Yet we experience a sense of guarded optimism. "Maybe when you go back," Pop suggests, "you'll find there are merry-go-rounds and band concerts where you are." The problem is not that they no longer exist—Martin has merely been looking in all the wrong places. Or perhaps not searching hard enough.

Initially, Sloan is not convinced by his father's words, fearing (as Wordsworth did) that

> *The things which I have seen I now can see no more. ("Ode,"*
> *1804)*

Gradually, though, as he slouches out of town, Sloan draws hope from the possibility that his father may be right.

> *Nothing can bring back the hour*
> *Of splendor in the grass, of glory in the flower*

Like Wordsworth's narrator, Sloan will grieve not; rather, he will find strength in what remains behind. Even when youth has left us, gilded memories of that final summer may be enough to see us through the winters of our adult discontent.

The (contemporary) soda jerk asks whether Sloan's limp is the result of a war wound. No, he confides, a freak accident when as a kid he fell off a merry-go-round. Serling concludes with a statement worthy of Wordsworth: "Like all men, on occasion, maybe some summer night, he'll look up from what he's doing and listen to the distant music of a calliope. And feel a melancholy yearning," stirred by

> *. . . that primal sympathy,*
> *Which having been must ever be;*
> *In the soothing thoughts that spring*
> *Out of human suffering*
>   *—Wordsworth—*

Man in the Gray Flannel Trap:

A STOP AT WILLOUGHBY (5/6/60)

The first season's thirtieth episode served as a follow-up to *Walking Distance*. Like other **Zones**, *Willoughby* opens with a shot of twinkling stars on a black night, the camera then drawing us down to an incident in progress. In a Madison Avenue office, the aptly named Mr. Misrell (Howard Smith) dominates a silent scene, the capitalist king perched on an overstuffed throne, pompously puffing a cigar. A window frames the vulgar fellow from behind; above and beyond, we notice a line of high-reaching Manhattan office buildings.

Misrell faces but does not directly eyeball an assortment of suited executives, seated on either side of the meeting room's long table. Director Robert Parrish sets up his mise-en-scene so that the hapless men appear to spread outward in the manner of a half-open fan. At last, Gart Williams (James Daly) is revealed as a marginalized figure on the far right. The positioning proves ironic since Williams will shortly be revealed as the only radical present. Like the others, Gart wears the costume of choice for the era's rising executive. Yet we're visually informed that this man is different. Williams relentlessly taps a pencil against his hand while the others remain in a state of stony silence. Shortly, we learn the reason for anxiety. Misrell and his staff impatiently await the arrival of Williams's protege, 35 minutes late. The first physical action surprises us after such stasis: Williams leaps up to use the phone. He's the only group member regularly seen in action, whether bolting from his seat or reaching under his jacket to apply pressure on an irritated ulcer. Williams's abrupt movements foreshadow that climactic moment when he leaps forward to embrace his fate.

For the time being, Williams confronts a secretary (Mavis Neal) who delivers disastrous news: the protégé has quit, taking an automobile account worth $3 million. This leads to an excoriation as well as repetition of the boss's mantra: "This is a push! push! push! business, Williams!" four times during the berating. Such excessive repetition, when effectively applied, partakes of a time-tested tradition, reaching back at least to Shakespeare. Most notable: Lear's squeal upon entering the ruined scene of ancient England with dead daughter Cordelia in his arms: "Howl, howl, howl, howl." Serling takes this approach with another elderly (in status, kingly) man to make the audience despise rather than empathize with him. "Push! Push! Push!" renders any question as to the wisdom of Williams's business decision irrelevant. The group watches in pity and fear; there but for the grace of God goes any of them!

Williams asserts himself as a man unlike any of the others. We assume that if any of his colleagues found himself in such an awful position (each capable of making a bad business call on a down day), he'd silently accept the tongue lashing. Yet Williams explodes: "Fat boy, why don't you shut your mouth?" Each junior exec inwardly cheers Williams on for breaking with the pack. Not that the others don't think and feel the same way; each also once harbored creative desires, only to now find himself part of a pack of overpaid hacks. Williams alone retains a modicum of the "primal sympathy" that sustained Sloan in *Walking Distance*. We know at once that Williams alone will act on dreams and desires common to the others.

One other element in the opening demands consideration: the visualization in the master shot of the office. Obvious (for some viewers, painfully so) is that the city behind Misrell is an artist's rendering. The mock-up (calling a viewer's attention to its artificiality) initially appears less than effective. If, that is, the intent had been to lock the show into a realist sensibility. The absence of an authentic verisimilitude at first seems a flaw; shortly, the opposite proves to be the case. In minutes, Williams slips into the fifth dimension, encountering a fantasy-land which proves more real to him than New York or his upscale Connecticut suburb. That other universe—"Willoughby"—will be actualized in documentary fashion to convey how "true" it is for him. How necessary, then, for Serling and Parrish to make us experience how unreal the "real" world is for Williams.

Serling's intro occurs as Gart Williams darts into his sad sanctuary of an office. Frantic, he serves as representative for a generation of early-middle-aged WWII vets who believed (naively) that the postwar era, as the title of a 1946 William Wyler film ironically hinted, would be the best years of their lives. The bright future that appeared within easy reach (their variation of the American Dream, to achieve happiness through commercial success) swiftly degenerated into a glitzy hell on earth. We witness in Williams's plight the apotheosis of what had become a new national nightmare: the modern male with no option but a frantic escape into an idealized America left behind during the frenzied scramble to "better" our lives via a handsome split-level trap.

Rod notes that this man will shortly enter into *The Twilight Zone*. His narrative line provides a specific reason why: "a desperate search for survival," similar to (if more intense than) the one that motivated Martin Sloan's flight. In the upscale reaches of our asphalt jungles, spiritual survival becomes the last great hope for our new American Everyman. Williams's physical journey—here as in many episodes—an emblem for the protagonist's inner odyssey, takes place on a commuter train. Beginning in the 1950s, that travel venue brought executives home each evening. We alternately see Williams as one member of the men who constitute this lifestyle and as an individual, distinct from the others via rapid cross-cutting between long shots (the mass) and close angles (a stranger worthy of Camus). The men say nothing. Each allows for a notable amount of space between himself and the next. They are rugged (in attitude, not appearance) individualists rather than members of a community. Or, as a telling expression that emerged from the era put it, they form a lonely crowd.

Thoreau argued that "most men lead lives of quiet desperation." The mass cannot be easily dramatized; inertia is antithetical to theatre, live or on the screen. What sets Williams apart is his depth. He can, when his conscious mind closes down, re-experience that original innocence which, for Wordsworth, "having once been, must ever be," however dormant. Williams, like Camus's rebel, "says no!" A heretofore closeted iconoclast, his desperation can no longer remain quiet. Williams is the face that emerges from the crowd, demonstrating a potential for heroism that will prove tragic. The window to Williams's left reveals a starry night as dazzling—if intimidating—as the one in Van Gogh's painting. That Dutch artist's on-the-edge-of-hysteria vision served as a key predecessor to expressionism. Another of course was the Norwegian Munch's *The Scream*, paving the way for a style that would become all the rage in early twentieth century Germany. Serling brought such a paranoid sensibility to the modern audience as general consensus gradually caught up with what had once been the vanguard.

Williams pulls down the shade much like William Shatner aboard a plagued airplane in Richard Matheson's *Nightmare at 20,000 Feet*, and momentarily dozes off. A dissolve suggests the dislocation of time and space essential to what pundits have tagged modernism. When Williams opens his eyes again, we can't be sure if he remains asleep, dreaming that he is now awake, or if Williams has emerged from a dream that seemed real into a reality that feels like a dream.

Like the equally confused narrator of Proust's *Remembrance of Things Past*, Gart Williams cannot be sure. He's emblematic of us all: living embodiments of neurotics who scurry down menacing city streets, wishing the shadow world at least remained rich with meaning and magic. The whole point of the piece (here we encounter a theme that's traceable to Shakespeare, particularly *A Midsummer Night's Dream*) is that such distinctions are irrelevant. The dream may be more real than reality, at least for the dreamer. If all reality exists (in a modern view) in the mind, does it matter whether the dream is real or not? (See Chapter 2.)

Yet there's nothing modern in what Williams sees when he lifts the shade and, for the first time, peers out at Willoughby. Shortly, Williams describes the place to the (1959) conductor (Jason Wingreen) as embodying the way we were. When the commute is over, he says much the same thing over an obligatory cocktail with aloof wife Janey (Patricia Donahue) at a tellingly central bar in the huge home they've sold their souls to mortgage. Willoughby encapsulates a mythic memory of the way we want to believe America was "right around 1888." Williams had glimpsed "a lovely little village" where eternal sunshine beams down on happy people—or so we disoriented moderns believe—a bygone world displaced by the disillusioning postwar existence: terribly cold, not only in the snowy November months Williams currently passes through.

He had spotted an incarnation of a dreamy land where band concerts are still a regular occurrence, where people slowly make their way along dirt paths and neat brick roads via unicycles and horse-drawn carriages. Tom Sawyer (Billy Booth) and Huckleberry Finn (Butch Hengen), complete with straw hats, were about to head off for a day of fishing. (Disneyland Park which, according to Carol, Rod adored, includes both a Main Street USA and a Tom Sawyer's Island.) With Willoughby, as with Homewood, Rod Serling provided full artistic throttle to a significant strain then developing in our national psyche. WWII ended with the nuclear bombing of Hiroshima. In the atomic age, something important in our collective past seemed missing in action from everyday life. In what had turned out to be grey days, we as a people fell in love with a gorgeous dream-image of the past.

Moderns fantasized of revisiting the water-color world of Norman Rockwell's *Saturday Evening Post* illustrations, or, in an even earlier form, Currier and Ives magazine covers. They longed for a world where, as in Disneyland, band concerts are always on view in the Victorian pavilion while a calliope plays in the background; a place where cops are of the Keystone variety and everyone magically knows your name. But the real world, as Wordsworth insisted, is too much with us. So Williams must return to where he lives.

Here, we see, he inhabits a space, not a place; his house represents anything but a home. Serling popularizes what Sloan Wilson earlier offered in a popular bestseller. Gart and Janey Williams are identical to Tom and Betty Rath:

> *Without talking about it much they both began to think of the house as a trap, and they no more enjoyed refurbishing it than a prisoner would delight in shining up the bars of his cell.*

This is the house that Janey had wanted. "A wife (with) an appetite," Williams says of her, after admitting he's "sick"—in the head, of course. "You're in the right ward," Janey replies, making cynically clear that Williams's problem is common to everyone. Though Williams blames her for his problems, Serling does not. Janey berates her husband for "heart-bleeding sensitivity." Yet when he whines that "you tried to make me that person, Janey," we sense his dishonesty. They both knew precisely what they were getting into. The marriage emerged as a fittingly forlorn metaphor for the new social contract then developing between women and men, together forging a shared agenda of socio-economic upward mobility.

When Janey insists, mid-argument, "Where would you be if not for my appetite?" there's no trace of venom in her voice. Williams can't articulate a comeback since he (like we) knows that she's right. Janey did the lion's share of work behind their worldly ascension that dictated his spiritual decline. In Serling's variation, what we encounter plays less as a war between men and women, James Thurber style, than a conflict involving the polar sensibilities of two mismatched people. This becomes clear as each character speaks his/her piece:

> **WILLIAMS:** I've never seen such serenity . . . the way people lived a hundred years ago.
>
> **JANEY:** You were just born too late.

She sarcastically (if correctly) tags Williams as "a man whose big dream in life is to be Huckleberry Finn"—an understandable, if not entirely acceptable, complaint. Likely, Williams won this beautiful woman by promising to

> *Wear the gold hat, if that will move her;*
> *If you can bounce high, bounce for her, too.*
> *'Till she cry, "Lover, gold-hatted, high-bouncing lover,*
> *I must have you!"*

F. Scott Fitzgerald may have written that ditty in an entirely other era, but his words still ring true.

It's worth determining Williams's distinctive flaw. Janey points to this in their scene together; Serling mentions it in the opening narration. He possesses "sensitivity," qualifying Williams as at once superior and inferior to other executives. In the home they share, books (so significant a symbol in *Time Enough at Last* and other *Zones*) are everywhere. In a post-literate world of TV addicts, here is a man who still reads. Had he not fallen into the gray flannel trap, Williams might have enjoyed life as a tweedy professor. Sensitivity is why he breaks with the crowd and earns our admiration. On a sadder note, it's what will do him in.

Why must Williams die when Martin Sloan was allowed to live? This has to do with age: Sloan, thirty-six; Williams, thirty-eight. Williams is what Sloan will become in two years if he doesn't mend his ways. Or, as Joseph Campbell might have put it, if he doesn't follow his bliss by writing/teaching.

Williams wishes for "a place in time where (a person) can live his life full measure." But what makes that move difficult is that he *isn't* fired following his outburst! A business-world reprieve comes across as believable; Misrell kept Williams on not out of compassion but owing to an understandable fear that this experienced employee would take several accounts with him to any competing PR firm he might join. Though we don't at this point see Williams at work again, he (and we) are at once back on the train as set-up gives way to conflict. In yet another segue from the modern car to the one with old-fashioned ceiling lights, a kindly old conductor (James Maloney) appears to negate the earlier words of his counterpart. "Willoughby? No such place, far as I could see," the modern man tells Williams. "Next stop, Willoughby," the charming codger announces. Following a moment's hesitation, Williams decides to disembark, but instinctually turns to grab his attaché case. This would bring his sophisticated (in the negative sense) world with him into this sweet, simple all-American Shangri-La, violating the essence of his dream. So Williams misses his opportunity. Understanding that he who hesitates is lost, Serling's alter-ego makes a solemn promise to himself: "Next time, I'm going to get off!"

Now, we do return to Williams's office, where he pops pills (likely, the first time such behavior was dramatized on TV) while attempting to deal with simultaneous calls. The story takes place before the age of multiple channels for conference calls, so Williams must hold two phones, one to each ear. One complainer howls about the low ratings for a series Williams convinced him to sponsor; the other whines about scratched film on an advertising reel. Williams reaches his breaking point: Peering into a mirror, he smashes an imagined vision of Misrell only to realize, as he's drawn back to an ever more tenuous reality, that he's only shattered his own image. Here is the episode's theme, crystallized in one potent shot. What Williams hates is not the boss, but what he's allowed himself to become. Life in our time, and his acquiescence to it, is what Williams despises. He only thinks he'd like to kill Misrell; actually, that's what he wants to do to himself.

Or perhaps he'd like to kill what he's become as the only remaining means to free his inner child before losing all contact with that better incarnation of himself. When, desperate, Williams calls Janey in Westport, he can only gasp, "I'm coming home." But Thomas Wolfe's dictum rings true: You can't go there again. Janey's response is to hang up; the front door will likely be locked when/if he arrives, not unlike the fate awaiting John Cheever's similarly lost soul in *The Swimmer*. As we already know, and Williams is about to realize, home is where the heart is. Williams' sensibility is stuck in Willoughby. Shortly, his soul will be there, too. Next time the dream recurs, he vows, Hamlet-like, not to "lose the name of action."

Our protagonist's name sounds notably similar to the place: Williams, Willoughby. This pastoral setting proves universal, owing to its appeal to many like-minded Americans. Still, Willoughby is also Williams custom made version of the broader American fantasy, one specifically suited to him. Leaving his attaché case behind this time (emphasized via a close shot), he steps down from the train and into a village where Tom and Huck hurry up to greet him, as does everyone else, all dressed in a turn-of-the-century style. Here is the Main Street, U.S.A., we all wish we could return to. But that's impossible (other than at a Disney theme park, which also allows us to ferry over with the boys to Tom Sawyer's island), because what he and we experience is a melange of mythic icons, hailing from differing periods (the 1840s, 1910s, etc.), running together in the modern imagination, forming a generalized notion of the "good old days."

Here then is the essence of an emergent nostalgia movement, with us still. Then comes the denouement: a segue back to reality, managed through the concept of time. A pendulum (a clock fading into a waving lantern) carries us from one dimension to the next. Similar transitions involving time pieces will reappear often. We learn that Williams leaped off his train during a raging blizzard, screaming about a place called Willoughby. The final O. Henry-style twist, redeemed from mere superficial cleverness owing to philosophic import, appears as the limo carrying away Williams's body reveals its logo: "Willoughby Funeral Service." Serling's voice-over imports that Willoughby may be "wishful thinking," or an actuality which remains "nestled in a part of man's mind." Or, at least, in our uniquely American imagination. Our brief glimpse of the corpse reveals Williams smiling. As in Greek myth, death is not negative, but a happy release from life's suffering; as in Sophocles, the worldly fall (we watched as Williams was stripped away of his possessions in the physical arena) is accompanied by a spiritual rise.

The luck/pluck Horatio Alger coda from the century's early years now makes way for a postwar American hunger: to find one's self in an inhumane arena of complacency and conformity. That this man died to achieve salvation offers a vivid realization of the tragic element in our modern life. This vision initially seems pessimistic. Yet as Serling earlier indicated, there is an alternative to Williams's fate, if only a man seizes the day in time. If, like Martin Sloan, we accept with bittersweet honesty that nothing can bring back the hour of splendor in the grass, perhaps like him we can learn to grieve not. Rather, as romantics from Wordsworth to Serling insist, we should find strength in what remains behind: an understanding heart, a philosophic mind. And, while there's still time, we ought to recall that carousels and calliopes may still exist in our grim world, then set out on the redemptive quest of searching them out.

Nostalgia Ain't What It Used to Be:

THE INCREDIBLE WORLD OF HORACE FORD (4/18/63)

As *Zone* moved toward endgame, Serling sensed the need to provide a corrective to his sentiments. He called upon one of the other great talents from television's golden age, then collaborated (if without credit) with the man who had penned *Twelve Angry Men*. Together, they created an antidote that would assuage any guilt on Serling's part about overselling the past as preferable to the present. Reginald Rose's play had been presented on June 13, 1955, as a *Studio One* starring Art Carney. Pat Hingle took the lead for this filmed version. His title character designs toys. Middle-aged, Horace Ford has grown older without growing up, continuing his job owing to considerable skills despite outbursts that resemble an eight year-old's temper tantrums. Horace has a friend, Leonard (Phillip Pine), and a sympathetic wife Laura (Nan Martin), as well as his job of choice. Yet he despises his life. Always, Ford dreams of the great times he had on Randolph Street, his old neighborhood, where kids ran around with cap guns and hot dogs sold for three cents.

This being *Zone*, Ford leaves his apartment heading back to that rough section of the lower East Side to see things have changed. Director Abner Biberman depicts the return from a down angle, visually suggesting the experience will not turn out well. Ford does join "that old gang of mine" in an alley on what, in the real world, ought to have been his thirty-eighth birthday. A surprise party awaits Ford at home, but he's absent, with "the fellas" on a previous birthday thirty years earlier. In truth, though, they had not been invited to his (then) party, and turn on him (one of *Zone*'s many dreaded mobs). The boys beat little Horace (Jim E. Titus) to a pulp. His wife (the antithesis of *Willoughby*'s Janey) hurries to help, carrying Horace home. As the child transforms back into a man he, sobered by experience, admits: "When I was a kid, it was an ugly, sad, unbearable nightmare." Ford has undergone a catharsis; he can at last put the fabled past behind him and, for the first time, appreciate just how good he (as compared to Williams or Sloan) has it in the present. Laura comforts her shaken husband: "We're all like that. We remember what's good and blank out what's bad. Because we couldn't live if we didn't."

She speaks for the audience as well, tempering the good old days of previous episodes via strong verbal medicine. Nostalgia (like alcohol in *A Passage For Trumpet* or gambling in *The Fever*) can, if over indulged, become a dangerous addiction, as Serling realized. He proves his authorship of the series by re-imagining Rose's piece. The original version ended on a darker note. Little Hermy Brandt (Jerry Davis in *Zone*), a childhood friend, regularly appears at the apartment to return a watch that adult Ford had dropped. Here also is the Time Theme, as important a motif as nostalgia.

The final image might have been Hermy, doing this one last time, after young Horace has been beaten (to death!) in the alley, lost to a deadly past. In Rose's original, Hermy shows up again, hands Laura the watch, and rushes away. When Laura glances down, she's shocked to realize that she's holding not the adult Ford's watch but the Mickey Mouse one her husband loved as a child. That image is included, but Serling persuaded Rose to add an epilogue in which Laura hurries to the past herself. Through her courage and dedication, she is able to drag her husband home to the loving enclave of here and now. Things, we grasp, will be better. Not in a "happy ending" sense; Ford still has a long way to go. But, like other *Zone* protagonists, he has been given what, according to Serling, every man has a right to ask for: A second chance. That is the essence of Serling's cautious optimism; an element basic even to those *Zones* he did not himself write.

WHAT DREAMS MAY COME:
Nightmares at Noon

WHILE A STUDENT at Antioch, Rod Serling had the opportunity to study the precepts of Freudian psychology, which would have a major impact on his writing, as well as for his first time the full Shakespeare canon. Years later, he recalled just how much he enjoyed *The Taming of the Shrew*. Most classmates were taken with the battle of the sexes conflict between the original man-woman odd couple, Petruchio and Katharina; Serling found far more fascinating the brief induction scene in which two bored noblemen play a cynical trick on drunken lout Christopher Sly. While he sleeps, they carry Sly off and dress him in finery. When Sly awakens, they pretend to be his servants, insisting that he's a great lord who had a bad dream in which he spent his life as a lowly rogue. The existence Sly remembers was merely a nightmare, at last, they say, he has returned to genteel reality. Stunned, Sly calls out: "Do I dream? Or have I dream'd till now?" The audience, like the lords, wait for the terrible denouement. At that moment, *Zone* began to bud in the ever-expanding imagination of Rod Serling.

One Is the Loneliest Number:

WHERE IS EVERYBODY? (10/2/59)

"The place is here," Serling intones as we beam down from our first image of twinkling stars to a seemingly normal daylight situation, "the time is now." An average-looking fellow (Earl Holliman) wanders along a country road as Serling sets the modus operandi for most **Zones** to follow. Though some installments would sweep us off into other, distant worlds, most begin in our immediate reality. The protagonist, Mike Ferris, soon grasps that he's an amnesiac while Serling sets up a "perfectly logical explanation" via Ferris's air force fatigues. Spotting a café and hearing a jukebox playing inside, Ferris heads in that direction. Although no one is around, coffee perks in the pot while the grill sits ready for a short-order cook to fix eggs and home fries. Ferris requests just that, but his words go unanswered. In his monologue, Ferris admits "there's some question as to my identity." In so doing, he introduces a theme to be developed in future shows: Characters attempt to determine who they are, but realize that self-knowledge may not be possible when other people aren't present.

Where Is Everybody? introduces key recurring concepts. Moments later, Ferris adds: "I woke up . . . actually, I didn't wake up . . . I just found myself out on the road, walking." Dreaming (including somnambulism) and its relationship to reality plays a role in dramas and comedies to come over the next five seasons, as it did in Shakespeare. When Ferris wanders into town, the place we see is middle-America, exaggerated. Director Robert Stevens shot the sequence on an old standing studio set. In 1959, these were used ever less frequently for theatrical films as moviemakers in the postwar years filmed on location for heightened realism. Here the use of a retro set, one that viewers vaguely recognize from 1930s movies, provides a sense of déjà vu. Serling later recalled his inspiration for this script came while he strolled through an MGM back lot shortly after reading a newspaper account of experiments to test an astronauts' ability to survive while in isolation, revealing **Zone**'s germination: the author's individual experiences blended with topical news stories.

In *Where Is Everybody?* the manner in which we discover our identities by watching movies is introduced when Ferris wanders into a theatre. The film playing is *Battle Hymn*. As the feature shows a plane ascending, Ferris recalls that he is in the air force. An autobiographical element emerges here, as few of Serling's own life experiences defined him as thoroughly as did his years in the service. *Zone*'s first protagonist shares this with the author; so will many other characters.

Earlier in this episode, Ferris believed that he had discovered another person when he noticed what appeared to be a woman sitting in a pick-up. As he speaks while crossing the street, Ferris reveals a need for companionship as his voice grows less controlled, more desperate. When the woman fails to respond, Mike pulls open the passenger seat door and a mannequin falls to the ground. In *The Lonely*, the series' second episode, the character (if that's the correct term) of Alisha will cause Jack Warden's anti-hero to grow equally confused, re-establishing how easy it is to mistake a faux person for the real thing. *The Mighty Casey*, *After Hours*, and *The Dummy* will extend that theme.

Another key sequence, one that connects Serling to Alfred Hitchcock, occurs when Ferris hears a phone ringing in a booth across the street; here the Long-Distance Call theme debuts. Ferris darts over; even as he arrives, the ringing stops and the lonely theme emerges. Ferris shoves a coin into the slot and dials the operator to speak with a person and make that human connection. But *Where Is Everybody?* takes place on a tip of the iceberg of emergent technology. Ferris, devastated to realize that the voice on the other end is prerecorded, is the first of many *Zone* heroes whose identity will be shattered by a strange, inhuman voice on the telephone. The Hitchcock connection is cinched by a statement from that legendary director: "I'd like to shoot an entire film in a phone booth." Though Hitch never did attempt that, the 2003 film *Phone Booth* was inspired by his words. Among Hitch's most memorable sequences is Tippi Hedren's desperate retreat into a phone booth midway through *The Birds* (1963). In *Zone*, such a bit rates as autobiographical. Once, Serling became panicky when at an airport he couldn't force the door of a booth open, and called for help before realizing that it had to be pulled inward. Mike Ferris's situation may be fictional, but the first *Zone* rates as emotionally autobiographical.

Earlier, director Robert Stevens visualized a major distinction between Serling's show and Hitch's via a point-of-view shot from

Ferris's perspective. He glances across the road to that phone. A formidable wire fence separates Ferris from the booth. As he turns to walk away the onscreen image is objective (what we see) rather than subjective (what Ferris sees). Then the phone rings. Ferris turns, runs toward it. As he does Stevens cuts to a far/high angle: No wire fence is in sight. Most viewers become so involved in Ferris's plight they don't notice its disappearance. Those few who do write it off as a continuity "film flub." Here is the one incident during Ferris's mental odyssey that isn't explained when we reach the final revelation. Such a theory (some things can't be logically justified), antithetical to Hitchcock, provides *Zone* with its unique identity.

After the episode aired, Serling realized there ought to have been more of the "inexplicable," but a tight budget precluded re-filming. Ferris is revealed to be an astronaut, dreaming in isolation as doctors watch closely. They do this via a TV screen. The team is presented as an audience and Ferris is seen as the "show," (the first time a TV program referenced its own medium, deconstructing the home viewer's experience). After *Zone* achieved success, Serling rewrote several of his best episodes for an anthology, *Stories From The Twilight Zone* (Bantam). When Ferris enters the theatre, Serling added a bit of business: absent-mindedly, Ferris picks up a ticket and slips it into his shirt pocket. Later, after all has been revealed as a nightmare Ferris experienced after cracking (food and water was pumped into his system, waste similarly removed), he discovers that stub. So, was "the dream" (and the town) real after all? If we dream a situation rather than live it in the real world, does that imply that it's any less real for the dreamer? Happily, Serling learned from his mistake. Almost every *Zone* to follow contains some element that violates everyday reality providing a metaphysical element.

Setting the image for those semi-surreal towns in *Walking Distance* and *A Stop at Willoughby* is this place's name: Oakwood, suggesting traditional values and an old-fashioned lifestyle. Here, though, Serling appears at odds with his upcoming visions of such places. Half-forgotten hamlets usually prove preferable to contemporary suburbs and cities. Oakwood is described by Ferris, after regaining consciousness, as "a place I don't want to go back to," even though it appears to be nearly identical to the one Martin Sloan steps into in *Walking Distance*. The key distinction between horrifying Oakwood and charming Homewood is that there are no people here. Humanism, a firm belief in the goodness of man, proves essential to Serling's philosophy. He will offer scathing portraits of people at their worst, as in *The Masks*. Even terrible people, he implies, are ultimately better than no people at all. Serling's heroes always love mankind, warts and all. As we shall see, any character who does not feel this way cannot elicit Serling's sympathy.

The "doubling" concept, so basic to Hitchcock, is introduced here. The first incident happens when Ferris calmly talks to his mirror image in the ice cream parlor; the second when, in sudden panic owing to isolation, Ferris runs into a full-length mirror, colliding with a precise image of himself. Human identity, the fear that each of us may be two people, will be developed in episodes including *Mirror Image* and *The Mirror*; as will the notion of time. Ferris glances at wall clocks and hears the hour solemnly announced from a stately old town hall. Finally, when Ferris cracks under the pressure of prolonged isolation, he's revealed to be clutching the second of two broken clocks. When an Air Force Captain (James Gregory) instructs his men to remove Ferris, the number-one subject of conversation is time. An attempt to comprehend time in relationship to man's earthly existence (particularly after the Einstein formula $E=mc^2$ revolutionized twentieth-century thinking) is among the most significant *Zone* themes.

In the epilogue, when Ferris expresses disappointment that he failed to hold up, Serling references his earlier (realistic) teleplay, *The Rack*. "A nightmare that your mind manufactured for you," one caretaker tells Ferris, explaining how Oakwood came into being. *Where Is Everybody?* emphasizes Serling's belief in "man's need for a companion," the inability of even sophisticated science to overcome "the barrier of loneliness." This constitutes "the pit of man's fears"; human contact, "the summit of his knowledge." Together, they form "the dimension of imagination," an area we collectively have called, for half a century now, *The Twilight Zone*.

My Brother's Keeper:

KING NINE WILL NOT RETURN (9/30/60)

Serling's dissatisfaction with *Where Is Everybody?* helped him grasp how to best structure future episodes. *King Nine* offers a redux of *Where Is Everybody?*: Unique enough in story elements, character, and setting that viewers did not consider this an unnecessary recycling of previous material. As in the earlier episode, *King Nine* has a basis in then-current events which Serling combined with personal experience. *King Nine* derived from a news account, released in the spring of 1959, detailing the discovery of an old WWII B-24 bomber, *Lady Be Good*, by Englishmen searching for oil on the Libyan desert. Other than expected damage from sun and sand, *Lady Be Good* remained intact after sixteen years. Although the water tanks remained full inside the hull, no sign of the crew turned up. The air force labeled the discovery "one of the greatest mysteries in aviation history." In fictionalizing this incident, Serling (like Hitch) assumed, "There must be a perfectly logical explanation behind all of this!" Yet Serling goes Hitchcock one better. After providing a rational explanation, he delivers what was missing from *Where Is Everybody?*: A final detail that cannot so easily be explained.

King Nine opens on a desert. Captain James Embry (Robert Cummings) regains consciousness and gazes around realizing that he's stranded in Africa. "War spits out violence overhead," Serling's narration informs us; "the sandy graveyard swallows it up." An anti-war attitude is implied. As Embry wanders in search of other survivors, we hear his thoughts as a second voice-over. This eliminates the need to have a character talking out loud to himself, an element that damaged the impact of *Where Is Everybody?* This opening tableau left a lasting impression on a future filmmaker: Here is the basis of that WWII fighter squadron discovered on the desert in Steven Spielberg's *Close Encounters of the Third Kind*.

Embry is one more of The Lonely. Of all such visitors to the *Zone,* he most resembles Serling's original lonely man, Mike Ferris. That young member of the air force called out, "Where is everybody?";

this similar serviceman shouts "Where are they?" Yet in *King Nine*, Rod brings a moral dimension to the plight not found in that first *Zone*. The great problem for Embry, as for earlier officers whom Rod Serling wrote about, is not his own survival, but a sense of duty to his comrades in arms. "I'm responsible for the crew," Embry insists half-a-dozen times. Finding water to keep himself alive is barely mentioned. "I'm in charge," he mutters guiltily, consumed less by oppressive heat than by the weight of command.

That this will turn out to be a dream episode is not withheld from us; doing so would have constituted an unforgivable trick. Rather, Serling states this outright. "Maybe I'm asleep," Embry muses, and "I'll wake up and be back at the base." That's precisely what does occur, if not quite the way Embry guessed. Then he spots crew members. Instead of running from their ghost-like visages, Embry rushes to them, partly to relieve loneliness, largely because he cares more for them than himself. Embry embodies Serling's humanist hero because of sincere concern for the other guys and we want him to come out of this okay. In the *Zone*, we (like Serling) can forgive almost anything except man's inhumanity to man. The opposite of Cain, Embry accepts his role as "my brother's keeper," though these are brothers in every sense but the biological one. Three times, Embry runs through a litany of names, making clear that he does not simply care about the crew as a collective to which he, as an officer, had a responsibility—but as individuals. Names, not numbers!

We need some hint as to what's coming, a detail that prepares us for the eventual turnabout. Embry spots several jet aircraft overhead. The problem, as Embry notes, is less that these are flying machines from the future than that he knows the term—*jets*—by which they'll be called. How is that possible? The finale must (and will) offer a logical explanation. "Perhaps I don't exist," Embry wonders. If a man reaches a point of isolation so extreme he can no longer be certain he is real because there can be no confirmation . . . and if we accept the notion that reality ultimately exists only in the mind . . . then Embry is right. As such, he serves as the small screen's first modernist/solipsistic protagonist.

As to the religious/spiritual element, Embry's dream appears end-less until he falls to his knees and, in an act of humility, cries: "Oh, God! . . . What's happening? Oh, God! . . . Please let me in on it, God! . . ." Apparently, someone was listening, since Embry's ordeal abruptly comes to an end. The scene cuts, precisely as in *Where Is Everybody?*, to an air force base where a doctor (Paul Lambert) and a psychiatrist (Gene Lyons) care for this fellow. The logical explanation is offered: More than fifteen years earlier, Embry was assigned to command a B-25 departing Tunisia to bomb Italy's southern tip. But Embry fell sick and so another man filled in. The plane crashed and was never located. Embry afterwards suffered from "survivor guilt," repressing this by shoving self-loathing thoughts down a trap door into the lower levels of his psyche. One day (1959) Embry spotted a newspaper headline: *King Nine* had been found. The shock proved too much for him; long-repressed emotions rose to the surface caus-ing Embry to suffer a breakdown.

Even as Embry regains consciousness, he wonders if he might have been a coward. Neither doctor believes that: He got sick at the wrong (or right) time and should not feel personally responsible. Tenuously he tries to accepts this. There's no easy ending, though guarded optimism appears; since in therapy, the truth may set him free. As to Embry's feeling that he had actually gone there, today? "All in your mind," the others assure him. They leave the room, pass-ing a nurse (Jenna McMahon) carrying Embry's clothes. She drops a shoe. As doctor and psychiatrist look on, it falls to the floor. Sand pours out. Not dirt, found outside the hospital. Sand! The kind that only exists on an African desert. Here is the "missing ticket" from Mike's pocket. Was Embry's mind so strong that, even if what we have witnessed happened only there, the dream was powerful enough to transform fantasy into reality? Was it the other way around? Did he go there, via a dream, bringing the sand back (reality impact-ing on the mind?) That, in 1950s parlance, is the *$64,000 Question*. Importantly, it's the one question Serling will never, during the show's five-year run, answer. That would be akin to explaining how a magic trick works, ruining its appeal.

What a Way to Go!:

PERCHANCE TO DREAM (11/27/59)

One of Charles Beaumont's best remembered episodes, adapted from his own short story and directed by Robert Florey, reveals that *Zone* was constantly autobiographical for Serling, even when he was not the author of a particular installment. Also, two themes, dreaming and death, always interrelate. The concept here is powerfully simple: Edward Hall (Richard Conte), referring to himself as "the tiredest man in the world," staggers into the office of psychiatrist Dr. Rathmann (John Larch). Crashing on the couch, Hall weaves a weird web of a tale. All his life, he has had to avoid excitement owing to a rheumatic heart. Lately, he's dreamed of a beautiful woman who lures him to passionate action and likely demise. Deciding that the doctor won't be able to help, Hall rises and leaves the way he came in. When he spots the receptionist, Miss Thomas (Suzanne Lloyd), Hall recognizes her as "Maya, the Cat Girl" from his dark dreams. Hysterical, he darts back into the office, rushes across the room, and leaps out a high window. Rathmann then calls his secretary in: his latest patient lies dead on the couch. What we have witnessed was a dream within a dream. Then, the final twist; though sorry for this poor man who never uttered a word, Rathmann tells Miss Thomas: "At least he died peacefully." If all reality, including death, does exist in the mind, Hall's end was anything but peaceful.

The title derives from Hamlet's "to be or not to be" speech, that melancholy Dane's reason for not committing suicide: "to sleep: perchance to dream: ay, there's the rub; For in that sleep of death what dreams may come . . . must give us pause." Why take one's life only to hasten an eternity of nightmares? Before Hall heads inside the skyscraper, key continuing themes are introduced. A stranger (Ted Stanhope) expresses concern for a deeply troubled man. He's a Good Samaritan worthy of the Bible. Hall brushes by, failing to even utter "thank you." This interchange colors our reaction to all that happens. Hall did nothing to make us believe that he deserves

his horrible fate, yet neither do we feel particularly bad about it. He
lacks a humanistic aura.

With his unique but pressing problem, Hall represents what
Baudelaire once declared to be the essence of Poe's genius. Hall is
"the exception to the moral order"; we empathize with the distraught
man's plight yet never are we asked to sympathize with this autobiographical figure—for Serling! Like the show's producer, Conte
appears short, darkly handsome, here nattily dressed. Conte's voice
and clipped mode of delivery seem Serling-esque. Hall chain-smokes
through the episode. He's obsessed with death and connects death
with eroticism. Maya brings him close to end game when, in his
delirium, Hall believes that she's cornered him in a horrific carnival
funhouse where Maya angles for a kiss of death, la petite mort—the
irresistible experience from which a man will not survive.

Here Serling's idea of perception as reality, actualized in the here
and now via the act of looking, comes into play. "Did you ever really
look" at the picture of a boat on the wall, Hall asks Rathmann. This
is less "seeing is believing" than believing is seeing: If Hall concen-
trates, he detects that the boat and waves move. If this is real to him,
then it doesn't matter that, like his lurid dreams (half-nightmare,
half-wish-fulfillment), it's the work of a human imagination. As to
those dreams, Hall tells us that Mara's most spellbinding feature is
her eyes, reviving a recurring image that in *Zone*, as in ancient myth,
signifies perception. Though we visit an old-fashioned amusement
park, no calliope plays in the backdrop. A carousel appears threatening rather than charming. "Imagination is strong," Rathmann
admits. Hall responds: "The mind is everything!"

Some critics note a supposed flaw. Near the beginning, Hall passes
through the secretary's corridor between a main hallway and the doctor's
private office. En route he gets a look at the secretary (indeed, he
eyeballs her), while we see her only from behind. Later, when Hall
makes ready to exit, he steps back toward her desk, spots her again,
then notices that she is Maya from his dreams. If she were Maya, or
a look-alike, why wouldn't he have noticed this earlier? Yet this isn't a
mistake but the set-up. Everything that happens from the moment Hall
rests on the couch, including the second time he views the secretary

and his subsequent leap, is but a dream that takes us twenty minutes to watch, less than a second to be dreamt. Important information was not withheld, the ending something other than a cheap trick.

The moment Hall closes his eyes, an eerie light, which will consistently be associated with death, passes over him, providing us with necessary visual information to understand that he was dead from that moment. This should come as no great surprise at the end, though it does. Hall didn't recognize Maya from past dreams because he never had them! He notices the secretary's face before closing his eyes. In the split-second before death, Hall has a dream in which he dreams he's had those dreams, recreating the quiet secretary as a cat girl. Understandably, he would not recognize her when entering, but would while leaving. In truth, though, this too was a dream within a dream within a dream . . . leading not to a false trick ending, but to a legitimate Hitchcockian twist.

The Good Seed:

NIGHTMARE AS A CHILD (4/29/60)

This dreaming-by-daylight story takes place inside an apartment house where Helen Foley (Janice Rule), a late-twenties single career woman, resides. We are never allowed to see her on the street; this chamber drama's first shot reveals Foley stepping inside the lobby and closing the door behind her. There, she discovers Markie (Terry Burnham), a pretty if eerie child, sitting on the staircase, patiently waiting. Foley, we learn, is a schoolteacher. Her greatest pleasure comes from helping young people mature positively, though she cannot remember anything at all about her own youth. That will alter as a result of a conversation which ensues after Foley invites Markie in for some hot chocolate.

In time, Foley will also be visited by Peter Selden (Shepperd Strudwick), who knew her during that period Foley can't recall. Some 26 minutes later, this mini-tragedy ends with Foley's catharsis. As a result of facing a dark act from childhood, Foley is cleansed. Freud's modernist notions of the need to face and overcome childhood trauma before an adult can possibly become whole thankfully emerges as Foley's situation at the end. Serling opens the narration: "Month of November, hot chocolate, and a small cameo of a child's face, imperfect only in its solemnity." Why begin with a reference to the time of year if we will not be allowed to see Foley's world? To paraphrase Melville, this is a bleak November in Foley's soul. Her existence, when we meet her, can be described as an imitation of life. Foley goes about her daily business and attends to details, large and small. This provides a means for her to live in denial of her terrible truth: Without any sense of her past, she suffers from the identity crisis underlining so many *Zones*. This story draws to its conclusion later that day. The lighting choices of director Alvin Ganzer and cinematographer George T. Clemens make clear that, although the season's first snowstorm encroaches, Foley's mind enters into spring-like brightness. Perhaps even early summer, the preferred season for Serling.

An autobiographical element is reinforced by the lead's name. Helen Foley was the teacher whose love of literature influenced young Rod Serling. The author relates this episode to the series itself by including another key word: "Fear!" As Serling said in 1960, fear is "universal. There are maybe eight different types. I think you could categorize them and put them in a textbook." One avenue of approach to *Zone* is as a televised textbook in which those subgenres are alternately dramatized. Of those eight, one stands out: "The worst fear of all is the fear of the unknown working on you," he said; the fear "which you cannot share with others," relegating you to one of The Lonely. "To me," Serling concluded, "that's the most nightmarish." No *Zone* better captures this specific fear better than his script for *Nightmare*.

As a result of this seemingly chance meeting, Foley now "understand(s) the properties of terror" that cleanse rather than destroy her. Cursed by Shakespeare's idea that "life is but a dream," Helen Foley is finally freed from that and able to enter the real world. At the finale, Foley's earlier affected smile of grim hopefulness is replaced by a sincere grin of self-acceptance. She knows (for the first time) who she is. Only by facing fear dead-on can we too become free. Serling, a child of the Depression, absorbed Franklin Delano

Roosevelt's memorable advice: We have nothing to fear but fear itself. This is what Helen Foley learns in the *Zone*.

The theme of mind over matter, so basic to turning darkness and ignorance into knowledge and light, reappears. Following Selden's arrival, Markie slips away. Foley can hear the child singing a ditty outside; Selden cannot. We guess what will take Foley the entire episode to grasp: Markie is Helen Foley as a child. She has come to warn the intellectually mature, emotionally under-developed adult of imminent danger. To begin this woman's belated understanding of what happened long ago, the necessary first step resides in coming to grips with who she is today. Selden is why Foley blocked out her past, explaining why she doesn't remember that as a child her own nickname was Markie. Selden killed Foley's mother in a brutal incident that the child, rising from sleep, witnessed; Foley was later unsure whether she dreamed the violent act or observed it. To rid herself of confusion and a sense of threat, she repressed the intolerable memory. Selden, who planned to kill her, too, darted away when people ran to help. Later, he did not track down the child because he learned that she suffered amnesia as a result of trauma. Now, worried that with the passage of time Foley would eventually recall the events and name him, Selden has returned to finish the job.

Serling dared suggest that the true reason for memory loss may have been something more horrific even than murder. Just before Selden reveals his true intention, he speaks of the past. While he leaves out the murder, we have no reason to believe anything he does say is a lie. One line stands out: "I had quite a crush on you, you know." It was the child whom, in flashbacks, he confronts. In her bedroom! Serling pushed the boundaries of TV at that time. By implication, this was the first-ever TV drama about what can be openly portrayed today: the impact of child molestation.

"After the tragic thing happened," Selden says at one point. Tragedy is employed by Selden (in the sense that it's misused) as any incident that leads to the death of an innocent. The episode itself is not the tragedy of Helen Foley's mother but of Foley herself, in the Greek sense. Though most everyone else might die during the course of an ancient tragedy, the hero (or heroine) does not, cannot. Foley's inner journey is accompanied by a dual reaction on the part of the viewer: pity (for her) and fear that but for fate, there could go you or I. These simultaneous emotions lead to a cleansing of our soul(s) and spirit(s) that parallels Helen's.

In addition to tragedy, which Serling came to appreciate at Antioch, he also fell under the spell of the Romantic poets. One basic idea, as advanced by William Wordsworth, was "the child as swain": The young are wiser than adults in God-given knowledge that can't be taught and often is lost during our education process. "So solemn," Foley says of Markie, "and so wise!" Though Helen Foley is an educator, Markie ironically teaches her how to emerge from repression. "The child," Wordsworth wrote, "is father to the man." Or in this case, mother to the woman. Foley's catharsis is complete as we know from the final shot. After she kills Selden in self-defense, a doctor (Michael Fox) deems her capable of being left alone. Helen Foley is, he senses, on her way to becoming whole.

"The human imagination is often weird," the doctor comments. He, serving as Serling's spokesman, combines ancient theories of Aristotle with modern precepts of Freud. Importantly, he adds: "though sometimes it means salvation." At the end, Helen Foley hears "Twinkle, twinkle little star" from the lobby: the song Markie sang at the midpoint, a verbal reference to the opening credits, pixilated with twinkling bodies of light. Hesitantly but courageously (all self-paralyzing fear now gone), Foley discovers yet another little girl (Susan Capito), entirely real. When she smiles at Foley and Foley smiles back, Foley's healthy smile (as compared to the earlier tense, forced one) signifies that she is on her way to recovery, purged of the dark emotions that forced her to live in a cave of ignorance.

I Wake Up Screaming:

SHADOW PLAY (5/5/61)

Tersely written by Charles Beaumont and darkly directed by John Brahm, this cerebral tale cinches *Zone*'s connection between dreaming and death. Adam Grant (Dennis Weaver) waits in court for a jury to return the guilty verdict he expects, and for the judge to sentence him to death. He can literally mouth their words; for this is part of a recurring dream. He'll be led to a cell that probably looks not at all like one on a real death row. Because Grant knows nothing of the actual thing—only what he's seen in movies—various other people waiting for the electric chair look and act the way characters do in an old Warner Brothers prison film. One convict forlornly plays "Red River Valley" on his harmonica, causing Grant to laugh out loud. He sweats out the minutes to execution, horrified to know that he'll then wake up screaming, as he does every night. When this happens, the entire universe in which the dream took place will cease to be; it only existed in this man's mind while he was dreaming.

Reporter Paul Carson (Wright King), troubled by things Adam said in court, visits District Attorney Henry Ritchie (Harry Townes). Though it sounds preposterous, Carson wonders if perhaps the condemned man may be telling the truth. Would dreamed characters have family and friends, a full history to their world? Visiting Grant, the D.A. is distraught that the prisoner not only expects him, but knows precisely what he will say, having heard it in previous incarnations. Grant calls out to the departing D.A. that he ought to check in the oven and see if the steaks his wife cooked are there; instead a roast now sits in their place. Making a Long-Distance Phone Call (they never quite connect in *Zone*), Ritchie and Carson attempt to reach the governor to call off the execution. But it's too late; Grant sits in the electric chair, the switch is pulled. Total darkness descends as a universe, including the small city where this took place, and ceases to be.

The final sequence is the first we saw, now repeated as Grant dreams his dream again the following night. The players are shuffled: a man we previously saw in prison now serves as jury spokesman; the judge is someone else from the last dream. The tone is effectively Kafkaesque, the entire piece (much like *Eye of the Beholder* and *The Obsolete Man*) set in a surreal version of our own world. The concern here is, as always, fear: When the D.A. wants to know why the execution terrifies Grant, since it's only a dream and he will survive, the reply is that what one experiences in a dream becomes real for the dreamer. Grant doesn't want to go through the pain and horror again. As Carson and Ritchie panic and try to get a stay of execution, Brahm focuses on a clock, reinforcing the Time Element. Carson and Ritchie do so in a suburban house, "the norm" in contrast to a central character who lives on the edge, in a world of endlessly shifting shadows.

The episode reaffirms that all reality exists in the mind, which is cluttered with the ideas and images we picked up from the media. Why is Adam Grant going to walk the last mile at midnight, when that almost never happens? Because that's the way it always occurs in old crime films. Those visual fragments transform into pieces of our dreams. And what are movies but collective daydreams, our modern myth pool? The critic Pauline Kael titled her first collection of essays *I Lost It at the Movies*. So, apparently, did we all!

Till Death Do Us Part:

AN OCCURRENCE AT OWL CREEK BRIDGE (2/28/64)

With thirty-five of the final season's episodes completed, and CBS pressuring Rod Serling and then-producer William Froug about budgets, they picked up a one-time right to air French filmmaker Robert Enrico's award-winning film based on Ambrose Bierce's classic short story. In it, a southern civilian (Roger Jacquet) stands on a high bridge. Captured while interfering with union control of the area, he will be executed. Yankee soldiers slip a noose around his neck, then push him over the edge; he's surprised to discover that the rope has broken. Very much alive, he plunges down into the river. Though the Yanks pursue, firing wildly, he manages to slip away. Finally he runs toward his beloved home where his wife (Anne Cornaly) waits with open arms. As he arrives, though, we experience an abrupt cut to the bridge where he hangs. The escape had been wishful thinking, a daydream in which hours were lived out in the second it takes a dream to unfold.

Coming as it did during the series' final hours, this episode serves as a bookend. The literary cachet of Bierce's name makes clear that

Shakespeare was not the only great writer to whom Serling owed a debt. Enrico's style was appropriate to the emergent French approach, the *Nouvelle Vogue*. This is apparent in the fluid, lyrical camerawork of cinematographer Jean Boffety, replete with details such as a spider completing her web, referencing the seminal American thriller *Night of the Hunter* (1955). Including this short foreign film does not strike us as an arbitrary decision. Had Serling not announced in the opening narration that this marked the first time a piece written, produced, and directed by others would be aired, it's unlikely that anyone would have guessed.

Most significant is the theme itself, the vision of a dream as an alternative reality to the everyday world as no less "true" for the dreamer. There is also the grounding in reality of what will transform into fantasy; here, the Old South during the Civil War is vividly recreated by the Gallic team, right down to the accurate buttons on the uniforms worn by northern soldiers. Though only a few scraps of dialogue (none spoken by the central character) appear, sound plays as important a role as sight. Prior to the hanging, the noise of the Union officer's leather boots crunching on the wooden railroad trestle resounds like loud thunderclaps, allowing us to subjectively experience how aware the condemned man is of all around him. As his life is about to end, what another New Wave filmmaker, Claude Santet once referred to as "the things of life" take on heightened meaning. In particular, he hears the cawing of birds, their hysteria suggesting oncoming death in Hitchcock as on *Zone*. While underwater, he spots the sun above and struggles to reach the surface and its life force. In *Zone*'s context, though, viewers may note that the rays ironically evoke the series' recurrent and all-significant Death Light.

The best *Zones* always carefully prepare us for the final twist and this is no exception. First, the Yankee captain's orders to his men (they are to shoot the escaped prisoner) are distorted. Clearly, this is not how he would objectively sound; rather, that man's voice is frighteningly magnified in the protagonist's mind—which is where this ultimately takes place. Visually, we are cued that this will turn out to be phantasmagoria: Slow-motion sequences, in which the wife steps down from her plantation house, add to the growing sense that we are once again in a parallel universe. This effect is heightened by the repetition of the hero rushing out of the woods, toward home. He appears trapped by time; his pocket watch seized before the execution, demands an extreme close-up, as time-pieces often do throughout the series.

Gentle folk music during the first half is at the midpoint replaced by discordant jazz. Finally, the condemned man encounters his wife and for a brief moment they touch; the dream then ends and the man dies. How fitting that as in many *Zones*, what he most wanted was not life for himself, but to restore the all-important human connection. We can draw considerable meaning from the opening and closing narratives Serling composed and delivered. "A haunting study of the incredible," he insists, delineating the essence of his series. Later, Serling explains that we have witnessed the "occurrence" in "two forms, as it was dreamed and as it was lived . . . and died." The fantasy version is the one that ultimately proves most true, whether it happened or not. Lastly, Serling insists that the tale is drawn from "the thread of imagination," always a primary source of *Zone*'s ongoing appeal.

3

ANGELS IN AMERICA:
Cosmic Capra-Corn

FRANK CAPRA'S *It's a Wonderful Life* (1946) offers a bittersweet if upbeat fable about American-everyman George Bailey (James Stewart) who is persuaded not to commit suicide on Christmas Eve by an unlikely angel (Henry Travers). Even in Capra's less fantastical films—*Mr. Deeds Goes to Town* (1937), *Mr. Smith Goes to Washington* (1944), *Meet John Doe* (1944)—he forwarded a theory of guarded optimism as to our system's durability, despite temporary setbacks. Catching these liberal-minded films helped form young Rod Serling's worldview. The on-screen journey of a Capra hero ("a good Sam who doesn't know that he is a good Sam," as Capra himself put it) has much in common with that of many *Zone* protagonists. Film historian Gerald Mast, writing of Capra, might have been describing Serling's work when he noted that "sentiment, moralizing, and idealization" were basic to the scripts. And how can we not be fascinated to learn that film historians now believe the real-life model for Capra's fictional Bedford Falls may have been Binghamton, Elmira, or Ithaca, the three upstate cites that Rod knew best and the inspiration for Serling's Homewood or Willoughby?

Death of a Salesman:

ONE FOR THE ANGELS (10/9/59)

One for the Angels might be thought of as an inverse to *Wonderful Life*, as this gentle tale is set in summer rather than winter. An ordinary looking fellow (Murray Hamilton) was cast as the angel instead of the hero; Lew Bookman (Ed Wynn) comes off as charmingly cockeyed as Capra's Clarence. Whereas George Bailey considers suicide and is stopped by an angel who reveals how putrid Bailey's corner of the world would be without him, Bookman hopes to hang on to life. In his case, the Angel (here an angel of death) mentors a little man who gradually realizes his need to accept the inevitable. All differences aside, *It's a Wonderful Life* and *One for the Angels* share a central core, each grounded in everyday reality but suggesting a metaphysical element on life's edges.

Both tales proceed as fables, comedic in tone if not impact, honing to the populist ideal of wealth measured by friendship rather than dollars. In Serling's opening, funny-sad Bookman (who, owing to a career of playing the perfect fool, seems a clown even without costume) tries to make a buck. After an unsuccessful day spent hawking ties and toys to passersby on a hot New York street, Bookman heads back to his apartment. Though he hasn't scored a sale, Bookman won't let this bring him down. Entering his humble room, he spots a suited stranger who identifies himself as Mr. Death. This cryptic figure explains that he'll return at midnight to accompany the sixty-nine-year-old to the hereafter. Bookman tries to talk his way out of his fate. He'll learn that in the fifth dimension, free will can stand up to destiny.

An experienced pitch man, Bookman talks Death into allowing him a temporary respite so he can deliver his ultimate sales spiel ("One for the Angels"). Never an unsympathetic figure on *Zone*, Death agrees. Believing that he'll enjoy the last laugh, Bookman gigglingly informs Death that he'll never make a pitch again. Living forever, one of mankind's basic fantasies, recurs in numerous *Zones*. The Capra comparison temporarily set aside, Lew Bookman also recalls Arthur Miller's Willy Loman; more important is the chief distinction between Bookman and Loman. Loman has a family, if a dysfunctional one, and Bookman lives by himself. This might appear to qualify Bookman as one of *Zone's* The Lonely—but that's not the case. To borrow from *Funny Girl*, Bookman is one of those people who need other people. In Serling as in Capra, that qualifies him one of the luckiest people in the world. Bookman may not, like Loman (always lonely), have a biological family, but Bookman is deeply connected to the family of man. What Capra said of his concept for *Wonderful Life* also describes Serling's in *Angels*: "each man's life touches so many other lives. And if he wasn't around, it would leave an awful hole" in the human fabric. Early on, Bookman, like Loman, returns home. Whereas Loman whines in self-pity, taking his frustration out on whoever happens to be near (most often his wife), Bookman warmly embraces whomever he meets. He loves children, a qualifier of "the good" in Serling. Rather than grow forlorn because he has not sold a single Robby the Robot toy, Bookman takes delight in giving those wind-up dolls to poor kids on tenement steps. They await Bookman's return as if he were Santa Claus; each day a magic Christmas in July.

Like so many of Serling's protagonists, Bookman is referred to as a "little man." In this case, that's a compliment. Little people represent the bad only when small indicates not one's physicality, but a diminutive moral stature: an inability to appreciate others. However slight in size, Bookman possesses a huge heart; an immense soul. To him other people do not (as in Sartre) constitute hell on Earth. Bookman appears angelic from the moment he joins the kids. His face beams beatifically; an aged kid himself, Bookman has never allowed "primal sympathy" to slip away. He gleefully plans to join the children for ice cream and storytelling after dinner; as to the latter, that qualifies him as a "book-man." The notion of summer as idea rather than season relates *Angels* to such disparate episodes as *Walking Distance* and *A Stop at Willoughby*. Perhaps we only get one summer, Sloan learns in the former; the tragedy is that he, like most of us, failed to fully appreciate it. Bookman serves as Martin's counterpart, the man who grasps that summer is a state of mind.

Bookman's problem, as compared to that of deeply depressed Sloan (who despises everything about his upscale existence), is how much he loves his life despite the lack of money. Though no physical merry-go-rounds appear here, Bookman has discovered a metaphysical amusement park. For Bookman, life is a carousel, one he rides every day. His gifts and anecdotes allow poor kids a ride each evening. No wonder Serling describes Bookman as "a fixture

of the summer," a living emblem of his best-loved season. Hardly
perfect, Bookman tells Death: "I don't want to go!" He's human and
afraid. "They never do," Death sighs. However remote Death initially
seems, he is humanized, as he will be in the non-Serling script for
Nothing in the Dark. Capable of sincere emotion, Death is touched
when Bookman admits his lack of any worldly triumphs.

Here is our national ethic of success achieved through capitalism,
Horatio Alger's myth for *every* American dreamer. This qualified as
one of Serling's own abiding demons. Serling's life scenario was the
opposite of Bookman's: remarkable critical and commercial success
undercut by a gnawing fear that he had sold himself short by not
pursuing the less lucrative, more esteemed venues: "serious" novels,
the legitimate stage. The idea of expiring without having achieved
one's personal ambition provides significant inner conflicts in many
Zones, including *The Trade-Ins*. "There'll be consequences, you'll see,"
Death firmly insists.

As he can't return empty-handed, Death will claim a child as
Bookman's replacement. So little Maggie (Dana Dillaway) is hit by
a truck. Bookman notices an eerie light pass across her face, suggesting imminent passing. Now the man who initially lived out Dylan
Thomas's dictum—do not go gentle into that good night! —begs to
be taken so Maggie can live. Death explains that this is impossible;
in having made his deal, Bookman altered everything. What at first
appears to be a clever plot device defines Serling's vision of fate in
relationship to free will. Consciously or not, the Serling vision mirrors three sect's of ancient Judaic belief: The Essenes insisted that
fate dictated everything and the Sadducees believed that worldly
events were entirely determined by free will. The Pharisees took a
middle position, arguing that destiny did exist, but could be altered
by an individual's capacity to make choices. That concept underlines
Serling's body of work, as essential to the realistic plays *Patterns* and
Requiem for a Heavyweight as to *Zone*.

The Pharisees also believed (as other sects did not) in the existence
of angels who could visit earth, impacting on the lives of ordinary
people. Such Biblical references may seem pretentious in discussing
a TV series, yet internal evidence proves otherwise. Bookman tells
Death that his great pitch would "make the skies open up," a Biblical

phrase. The little hero of this piece hopes to achieve transcendence from our world to something greater out there. Moses and other Old Testament figures did this via God's helpers; the title of this *Zone* is, after all, *One for the Angels*. Though Serling necessarily avoided direct references to religion so as to survive network censorship and sponsor scrutiny, *Zone* was often an implicitly spiritual show.

Numerous episodes focus on the spiritual side of Serling's heroes or the lack of this quality in his villains. *Zone* (as does the Bible) provides us with role models and cautionary figures, Bookman the first of the former. His last name invokes a comparison with Henry Bemis in *Time Enough at Last*—he a Bookman in the worst sense: dedicated to the written word rather than to his fellow man. Not that reading is condemned; Serling's view is that even such a positive enterprise can turn sour when it replaces human interaction. A living, breathing book who shares his stories with other people, Bookman reveals Serling's faith in mankind. He's the first visitor to the *Zone* who displays the ultimate goodness: a willingness to sacrifice one's own self (not for his country, as with patriotic jingoism, or some abstract, idealistic idea) but for humanity itself. Or for a specific part of humanity, in this case Maggie, her very name grounded in scriptural reference. That fits, for Bookman is something of a savior—the first of many *Zone* martyrs who will if necessary die for the good of others. This, too, recalls Capra's classics, particularly Gary Cooper in *Meet John Doe*.

Following Bookman's brief moment of panic, *Angels* concerns his fervent desire to die. Bookman attempts to figure out a way to reverse the untenable situation his exercise in free will brought about. Once again, Lew Bookman is posited as the inverse of Capra's George Bailey, working his way back to an acceptance of life. Bookman fervently believes that he can achieve by dying what George Bailey could only accomplish by living—to overcome what has been set, seemingly, in cosmic cement. Only through life can Bailey ensure that his younger brother doesn't die; only by death can Bookman be certain that his daughter-figure will remain alive.

Despite what initially appears an intractable fate, Serling insists that Bookman is correct in his belief. Free will can conquer destiny; an individual's brave choice can set aside the grand scheme of things.

Bookman eventually wins by making his "great pitch" to Death, his spiel so enthralling that the grim reaper remains spellbound. Death fails to show up for his midnight appointment, employing *Zone*'s Time Element. At the stroke of twelve, Maggie recovers. Although outwitted by Bookman, Death still can't return alone. Now, Bookman anxiously accompanies him. Serling's vision here is influenced by Shakespeare. Warned of a death trap by friend Horatio, Hamlet quipped:

> *If it be, 'tis not to come.*
> *If it be not to come, it will be now.*

The readiness is all. "I'm ready," Lew Bookman informs Death. Why now, but not before? The obvious answer is that Bookman did get to make that great pitch, his measurement for worldly success. If that were all, this would rate as merely clever: an engagingly superficial tale concluding with a trick. What we encounter is far more profound. Bookman's pitch, grand as it is, rates as his least important earthly accomplishment. Bookman has come to consider death in a philosophical sense, a notion of endgame that dates back to the advent of civilization: not as an interruption of life, but a continuation. And, for those who qualify as "the good," this will be an eternal state that offers relief from life's endless disappointments. The title refers less to Bookman's great pitch than to Bookman himself. Again he hesitates to inquire if he'll be allowed "up there." Death winks, says "Oh, yes," and leads him to his reward. Lew Bookman, more than his sales pitch, truly is one for the angels.

Reflection of a Man:

THE BIG TALL WISH (4/8/60)

Here is the kind of story Capra loved to tell, describing such parables as "fragile, gentle things that 'if you (but) touch them, they vanish.'" Bolie Jackson (Ivan Dixon) is an aging boxer. Though issues of race are never touched on, Jackson and the other central characters are African-American. Serling broke new, important ground by writing and then casting *The Big Tall Wish*, in what would eventually come to be hailed as a color-blind approach, providing TV's first instance of gifted black performers portraying characters not defined by color. While watching, the audience becomes involved with the characters as human beings, hardly aware almost everyone on screen is black—a far more effective way to fight racism through drama than by overtly didactic preaching.

Jackson must enter the ring and face a younger, trimmer fighter. Precisely the situation Mountain faced in *Requiem*, this marks Jackson's final shot at the championship. He faces the equivalent of what Lew Bookman hoped to achieve in sales. For Serling, the second chance represents any man's last great hope. However positive Jackson tries to remain, he's smart enough to sense that the odds are against him. But Jackson has a guardian angel, if an earthbound one. His tenement building (this episode was filmed on the same studio-street employed for *Angels*) also serves as home to little Henry (Steven Perry). The child believes in Jackson in the most profound sense. If this sounds like a sentimental boxing film from the 1930s and 1940s (e.g., *The Champ*), recall the impact of such old movies on *Zone*'s creator.

Yet in this episode, Serling added a metaphysical aspect. We learn from the child's mother (Kim Hamilton) that when Henry wishes, he believes and hopes so intently (he appears to be praying) that his wishes come true. She was desperate for fifteen dollars to pay their bills. Henry wished for it; the money appeared. Henry doesn't wish self-servingly; he only does it for his mother and their survival. A check arrived in the mail. That might have been coincidence. Or, if one perceives life from a different angle, a miracle. Notably, though, the check was for precisely the amount they needed. Whether Henry's faith made this occur may be a matter of perception. "When you wish upon a star," as the theme song to Disney's *Pinocchio* (1940) insists, "your dreams come true." There is only one catch, however; the wish/dream ("a dream is a wish your heart makes," another Disney tune tells us) must be selfless.

Such a dream serves as the secular equivalent of prayer. The star Henry wishes on here is one of those twinkling distant suns that open and close early **Zones**. When he makes such a wish, something Henry does sparingly, they come true . . . temporarily. In Serling as in Capra, Disney, and Spielberg, it's necessary that the gift's receiver be a true believer for the magic to work permanently. Fate does exist in **Zone**'s philosophic stratosphere, as does free will. As the two interact, character proves to be destiny. Sadly, perhaps tragically, Jackson's character has been altered by a harsh life. After Jackson steps into his humble room, he stares at himself in his mirror, experiencing identity crisis at his defining moment of decision. As he's an honest man, Jackson's face serves as an open book. Serling tells us that written on those pages of flesh and blood remain scars from every fight. Once hopeful, he's now defeatist: "Just a tired old man, trying to catch a bus. And the bus is already gone."

Jackson's statement proves apt because he believes it to be; "right you are," according to Pirandello, "if you think you are." But the Jackson who exists in Henry's generous, positive imagination is a winner. When Jackson heads off to the fight he believes he'll lose, Henry throws himself down in front of the TV. The game will be telecast, a self-referential nod to Serling's medium. What Henry wishes for is less for fate to intervene on Jackson's behalf than for Jackson to be positively impacted by Henry's vision, the real Jackson rising to the level of Henry's ideal. That can happen, if Jackson believes with the absoluteness that Henry does. "All is possible," Shakespeare's Henry V tells his outnumbered soldiers at Agincourt, "if our minds are ready!" Perception is reality; the dream that you wish for will come true only if that loving wish is not only sincere for the wisher, but also unconditionally believed by the recipient. Without that yin and yang, even the biggest, tallest wish can't work.

At least not other than briefly. Bolie Jackson enters the ring. When, for a fleeting moment, he surrenders to Henry's faith in him, physical reality and the space-time continuum are violated. Jackson finds himself (via director Ron Winston's use of stop-action photography) no longer defeated on the mat, but hailed as champ. Jackson is, thanks to Henry's power of positive thinking, blessed with the success he hungered for. Yet while Henry's power proved formidable enough to achieve this, the child's belief must be augmented. "Must have been some kind of a dream," Jackson muses. Henry mourns: "If you don't believe, Bolie, it won't be true. That's the way magic *works!*" This exchange takes place after the fight as Jackson approaches Henry on the tenement's rooftop. Jackson (once innocent and open) has been beaten up by the world so often he can't believe what's just happened, not absolutely. Henry weeps, knowing that the slightest lapse in faith will ruin everything. Living out Wordsworth's dictum that the child is father to the man, Henry tries to teach Jackson a truth that years of worldly "education" on mean streets has diminished: the pure vision of life as a pool of endless possibilities.

We can swim in it only if we fully trust we will not sink. "Need to believe," Henry repeats again and again. A hint of primal sympathy surfaces: We note in Jackson's eyes how much he wants to go home again, to a Willoughby of the mind and spirit. His failure to accept the magic on an unconditional level undoes all the good Henry's absolute faith brought about. We are back in the ring, Jackson down, his opponent (Charles Horvath) champ. Bolie Jackson has been defeated less by fate than by lack of faith. If this sounds theological, *Zone's* immediate appeal back then (and its continuing impact for half a century since) derives in large part from Serling's ability to express spiritual issues in a secular fashion. What we encounter is not religion in a sectarian sense (or propaganda for some specific sect), but a universal statement about man's need for ongoing faith in what George Lucas would eventually label The Force. This first appeared when Henry's mother explained: "Bolie, that boy's got you in a shrine," faith necessary even in a scientific/secular society.

Why does Bolie Jackson deserve to have Henry's wish come true? Like Lew Bookman, he's defined as he returns to his tenement and embraces children, that rare adult who through having lost his own childhood innocence, reveres that quality in the young and in adults too, despite their limitations. Jackson smiles at every person he passes on the street, beginning with a drunk on the steps. We note from his sensitive eyes that his greetings are sincere. An uneducated man, Bolie Jackson may not be familiar with the terms "populist" and "humanist." Yet like the writer who created him, Jackson rates as both. Also in his favor, Jackson wants to win more for Henry than for himself. Bolie Jackson signifies the opposite of Henry Bemis in *Time Enough at Last* (see Chapter 6), who is relieved when everyone else dies. Jackson, owing to his humanism, deserves to win. Sadly, a contemporary version of hubris (the Greek concept of false pride in oneself) does him in: "It was me did it, hitting and slugging and winning." When the outcome is reversed, we feel as deeply for him as does Henry.

Still, the ending is hardly pessimistic. We are made aware of a pair of character arcs, both positive. Bolie Jackson and Henry have transformed each other. Momentarily, we fear that Henry's faith may have been destroyed when the child insists that he will wish no more. "I can't believe," he sighs. "I'm too old." Happily, *The Big Tall Wish* doesn't end here. Spiritual victory can emerge from worldly defeat. Henry has *not* been transformed from an optimist to a pessimist or, worse still, to a cynic. "I was proud of you, Bolie," he insists when the prizefighter enters Henry's room to say good night. "Real proud!" For Henry, this provided a rite of passage. If Henry's song of innocence is over, his song of experience has only begun. The child's words show that he'll remain positive. If Henry's faith in magic has been shaken, his belief in man is enhanced. More realistic, less idealistic, Henry remains steadfastly humanistic. Like the writer who created him, Henry now rates as a guarded, rather than a wide-eyed, optimist.

If Henry has grown up, Bolie Jackson has recovered something of his lost youth: a belief in magic which having once been must ever be, and which exists in each of us, if too often dormant. "Maybe there is magic!" he sighs. The sad truth: magic seems gone today because "there's not enough people who believe." Is it all over for Jackson? He can never enter a ring again. Before we accept this as downbeat, we ought to consider a line from *The Good Right Hand*, one of Serling's first published stories. A fight manager tells his downhearted boxer Googy, who has lost a bout from which there can be no recovery: "Just cause you're washed up in the ring ain't no sign you're washed up in everything." Like Googy, Jackson may have blown his second chance at being a champ. That's the bad news. The good news is that each man (much like Mountain at the end of the TV version of *Requiem*) is free to enjoy a second chance at life. Bolie Jackson has not been reduced to rubble; he has been reborn.

Blues In the Night:

A PASSAGE FOR TRUMPET (5/20/60)

The confrontation of a flawed but sympathetic man with an edgy angel takes a different turn in this New York tale directed by Don Medford. Joey Crown (Jack Klugman) appears vulnerable via an opening down-angle shot, implying an internal sense of abject failure. Though the uptight musician grasps a beloved trumpet, Crown (backstage at a club) must anxiously wait while another artist performs. Afterwards, Crown begs club owner Baron (Frank Wolff) to allow him onstage next. Baron treats Crown respectfully, but can't do that. Joey Crown is an alcoholic; this weakness caused him once to ruin an evening at the club. Still, as a humanist, Baron appears likely to allow Crown his second chance until a bottle slips out of the musician's pocket, belying his insistence that he's "clean." Baron slips some money to Crown "for old time's sake!"

The script reveals an impressive psychological probing into the nature of an addictive personality. Serling doesn't just employ alcoholism as a plot device but presents a complex portrait of a person suffering from such demons. We learn more about the workings of an alcoholic's mind here than we do in J. P. Miller's *Days of Wine and Roses*. Though the TV and film versions of that drama portray alcohol's results, Miller's approach provided little understanding of the causes. Here, sad-faced Joey Crown is, we learn, "on a quest for impossible things, like trying to pluck a note of music out of the air and put it under a glass to treasure." Like Lew Bookman as a salesman or Bolie Jackson in the ring, Joey Crown dreams of delivering "one for the angels" in his chosen field. What he most wants from life is magic.

Qualifying each as a Serling hero, however flawed, is a desire to succeed less for his own ego-gratification than as a personal gift to mankind. An idealist, Crown yearns to create perfection; however admirable, this interferes with achieving happiness in the real world. Unless he changes, Crown is doomed by holding himself to absurd standards. He's a fine musician, but fears that he may not be one of the greats; his problem is lack of self-acceptance based on his own worth—a tendency too on the part of the writer who created him. Serling cried all the way to the bank, enjoying a luxurious lifestyle via commercial success, but never did he get around to writing The Great American novel. If Crown's guilt parallels his creator's, his worldly plight is revealed as less pleasing. His "home" consists of a small, dingy room, a fact true of both Lew Bookman and Bolie Jackson; for those men, a small corner of the world proved heavenly owing to their relationships with children. Doubtless, there is a Maggie or Henry in Crown's tenement. But he has created his own hell on earth by not seeking them.

In his sweltering apartment, Crown wallows in self-pity, grabbing the nearest bottle rather than offering the best trumpet performance he can. The other jazz trumpeter, whom Crown observed earlier, had exited Baron's club with a girl. Joey Crown lacks such human companionship, yet the other musician is no more handsome than he. This serves as an effective plant for the eventual resolution. Crown inhabits two universes at the same time: the world of art, jazz his chosen medium, and the everyday world. Crown's failure in one realm connects with his problems in the other. "I can't even talk to people," Crown sighs, "because of this horn." The choice, as he sees it, is between art and life. Crown has yet to realized that a delicate balance must be established between the two.

Crown drinks and then is brilliant; greatness emanates from his horn. Downtrodden, Crown sells (rather than pawns) his trumpet to a shopkeeper (Ned Glass), spends the money at a bar, then steps onto the street, purposefully walking in front of a truck to end it all. He wakes in limbo. People fail to return Crown's greetings, causing him to believe that he's a ghost. In a neat twist (one that would be borrowed and reversed for the 2002 movie *The Others*), Crown grasps that everyone else he passes by is a ghost. Neither dead nor alive,

Crown enters into a twilight zone located somewhere between the two. He can, like Capra's George Bailey, consider his relationship to the world from an objective point of view. Even as Bailey had Clarence, so does Crown proceed with the help of a guardian angel. Crown is (appropriately) named Gabriel (John Anderson), rightly famous for his own abilities with a horn.

As elegantly self-assured as Clarence was sweet but sloppy, Gabe persuades Crown to view his life from a new perspective. Places, Crown discovers, are oblique; judgment of good and bad doesn't exist out there, only in the recesses of a human mind. Though it remains true that fate may burden a person with a difficult scenario, free will allows each of us to make of that situation what we will. "Maybe," Crown muses as he arcs, "I forgot how much there was for me." A dingy room is better than sleeping on the street, precisely what will happen if Crown fails to shape up. Here's the same cautious optimism Serling earlier championed in *Walking Distance*. There, Martin Sloan's father suggests that the fault exists in Sloan, not in his world. Maybe there are merry-go-rounds in the time and place Sloan (and Crown) inhabit. Positivism in the face of a seemingly negative life situation rests at the heart of *A Passage for Trumpet*. "The music I could make on this horn," Crown grasps under Gabriel's guidance, may not be perfect. Why see that as a negative? What Crown creates is his present to humanity, imperfect but hardly worthless.

If Crown's sound brings a little bit of beauty into the life of even one person, he's achieved the essential human connection necessary for living a worthwhile life. We again encounter thinly disguised autobiography. *Zone* (like Joey's performances) may have been far from subtle, so the series was often dismissed by "sophisticated" observers. Serling could (and did) take such criticism hard—as hard as Joey Crown, when facing his limitations. Or, for that matter, Capra. Now considered one of the great Hollywood filmmakers, Capra's films were often panned owing to what critics perceived as sentimentality, precisely the line of attack on Serling. Bosley Crowther of the *New York Times* dismissed *It's a Wonderful Life* as "a figment of Pollyanna platitudes." Writing in a similar vein twenty years later, Richard

Schickel wrote off *The Loner* as "another example of Rod Serling's colossal nerve" (believing that through a TV Western he could "make a difference"). Such attacks sting.

Like Capra, Serling could quote verbatim all his negative reviews. Yet Capra might have been speaking for both when he wrote that *Wonderful Life* "wasn't made for the oh-so-bored critics, or the oh-so-jaded literati. It was my kind of film for my kind of people," intended "to tell the weary, the disheartened . . . the wino . . . that no man is a failure!" If Joey Crown's jazz, like Capra's films and Serling's show, can touch humanity, why not derive joy from that aspect of *The Gift* (a third season episode bears that title) rather than be miserable because other artists (elitist artists) achieve a different sort of acclaim? Accept yourself; work hard; fully understand your own individual identity as an artist and a person; achieve happiness by enjoying the positive impact of the good you can do . . . that was *Zone*'s credo, even as it was Shakespeare's before and Spielberg's later.

"I had friends," Joey Crown sighs, grasping that he's not lonely out of necessity, but because he failed to make the most of his relationships. Again, the Capra connection: Any man who has friends, George Bailey grasped, is rich, no matter how humble his life. Self-pity is a flaw that can only lead to tragedy, though that potential destiny isn't written in the sparkling stars which end each *Zone*. Maybe men are, as the Bard put it, masters of our fates; it is not in our stars but in ourselves that we are underlings. For Serling, tragedy can be averted if an epiphany occurs in time. Here, a grin appears on Joey's face as he's allowed that second chance every inadvertent visitor to *The Zone* hopes (and prays) for. Wisely, Joey Crown uses the money he receives after the accident to buy back his horn, then heads to his building's rooftop and plays as best he can. Forgetting about his limitations, Crown allows his talent—great, mediocre, or modest—to flow naturally through the horn. With a change in attitude comes a change in impact, both for himself and on others. Crown's art, once accepted by him for what it is, liberates rather than imprisons the man. A pretty girl (Mary Webster), newly arrived in the building, hears the sweet sounds from above and takes the stairway to the now heavenly rooftop. There she falls in love with the homely man who produces beautiful music. That her name is Nan cinches the autobiographical element; here's another positive female inspired by Serling's daughter of that name.

Finally at peace with his art and with himself, Joey Crown realizes that whatever he can do, he will do. At that moment Crown achieves the sought-after human connection. The New York that he, like Martin Sloan in *Walking Distance*, condemned suddenly doesn't seem so terrible. "You know, you may like it here," Crown tells Nan. "It's not a bad town." Not, at least, for the Joey Crown who provides an equivalent of enchanting calliope music rather than complaining that it no longer exists. When Nan requests that Crown show her around, his new optimism expresses itself in yet another smile. By this gesture, Joey Crown endows existence with meaning; he a humanist. Crown has "discovered something about life," and Serling sums up "that it can be rich and rewarding and full of beauty" if "a person would only pause to look and listen." Or, as another *Zone* will insist, true beauty exists in the eye of the beholder, and the mind. Best to, like Shakespeare, collapse the two into one another, as so often occurs in *Twilight Zone*: The mind's eye.

Another Miracle on 34th Street:

NIGHT OF THE MEEK (12/23/60)

Frank Capra's favorite holiday in films, from *Meet John Doe* to *A Pocketful of Miracles*, was Christmas. Though Jewish, Rod Serling perceived Christmas as a generalized American holiday; its spirituality remained a part of its appeal. As a child, young Rod nagged his father to buy a Christmas tree; a semi-serious plan was formulated to hide it should Serling's traditionalist grandfather stop by. Carol Serling recalls that even as an adult, Christmas filled her husband with a special joy: "He loved all the trappings of the holiday," as well as its spirit of good will toward men. *Night of the Meek* is, then, Capra-esque not only in ideology but also in tone, style, and manner.

This videotaped episode opens with a department store setting that recalls *Miracle on 34th Street* (1947), often described as "the best example of Capra-corn not written or directed by Capra." While mothers shepherd their children up a walkway to meet Santa in a Macy's-like setting, manager Dundee (John Fiedler) tries to locate their St. Nick. Henry Corwin (Art Carney) has fled the scene, wearing his red-and-white suit, to a nearby bar. Corwin's last name is an homage to Norman Corwin, the radio dramatist Serling revered, recalling from childhood *The Plot to Overthrow Christmas*. As deep in self-pity and alcoholism as Joey Crown is in *A Passage for Trumpet*, Corwin angers the bartender (Val Avery) by trying to swipe a drink. One might believe that Serling watched *Miracle on 34th Street* and, owing to his personal point of view, chose not to write about the "real" Santa Claus (Edmund Gwenn) who, in such a situation, arrives to save the day. This author focused on the foil: that sad store Santa who in the opening of George Seaton's *34th Street* is too drunk to perform, grasping both his present tragic state and his potential for redemption—and so fashioned his central figure from society's dregs.

Henry Corwin truly is the forgotten man. To Serling, he's as capable of being the true Santa as Gwenn's charming codger. Serling's vision comes far closer to the true meaning of Christmas. He finds Henry Corwin worthy because, failings aside, Corwin is at heart a humanist. What most concerns Serling isn't that the man drinks but, as in *Passage*, why he drinks. It's because he can't help the downtrodden, in particular the children who, like Maggie in *One for the Angels* or Henry in *Big Tall Wish*, have nothing to call their own. Also, Corwin feels for old people who wander into a shabby settlement house to get warm, poorer versions of the seniors in George Clayton Johnson's *Kick the Can*.

Corwin's emotions elicit empathy because he doesn't wallow in self-pity, but weeps for others less fortunate even than he. Later, Corwin wanders down an alley, discovering a bag of presents. It's evidently a magic bag, for when he returns to the settlement house and offers the contents to the people gathered there, he pulls out whatever anyone requests, the toys for each child again recalling *Angels*' Lew Bookman celebrating Christmas in July. Conflict occurs when Sister Florence (Meg Wyllie) calls for a neighborhood cop, Flaherty (Robert Lieb). She reports that Corwin likely stole Dundee's stock. But when Flaherty reaches in and draws out stray cats and tin cans, he experiences an epiphany, touched by the meaning (and magic) of Christmas. Flaherty and Dundee then spot Corwin flying high overheard, having morphed into the "real" Santa. This occurs after old Burt (Burt Mustin) asks Corwin why he hasn't pulled out a gift for himself. "I can't think of anything I want!" Corwin concludes that "the biggest gift of all time" would be "to do this every year," to become Santa in spirit and person.

In *Zone*, as in Capra (and Disney), such a non-selfish wish can never be denied. Corwin stumbles back into the alley to discover a child-elf waiting for him, along with a sleigh and eight tiny reindeer. He realizes that his wish has come true. It's worth noting that we do see the slightest glimmer of light pass over Henry Corwin's face before he calls out to "his" reindeer to head skyward. Is it possible that he has died? Like Gart Williams in *A Stop at Willoughby*, this character may have passed away in the snow, then been delivered into a personal heaven. Serling doesn't insist on this by revealing Corwin's frozen body. To do so here would violate the tone of a Christmas show. Whether it's Henry Corwin's soul Dundee and Flaherty see high above or the actual person, there's no question that he has escaped the winter of discontent he knew in New York. Serling appreciates the "magic," a term he employs at the beginning and ending narrations, of this holiday. Henry Corwin wished upon a Disney star and his dream came true. Like Capra's Mr. Smith, Mr. Deeds, John Doe, and George Bailey, he does possess a pocketful of miracles. Miracles occur because, in Serling's words, such a "special power (is) reserved for life's little people." Even Mr. Dundee now gets it. Taking Flaherty home to share the brandy that Dundee received from the bag, he finally smiles, insisting: "Thank God for miracles."

Carol for Another Christmas:

THE CHANGING OF THE GUARD (6/1/62)

Rod Serling may have been unconsciously influenced by a British variation on Capra-corn called *The Holly and the Ivy* (1953), about an aged cleric (Ralph Richardson) who on Christmas Eve reconsiders his life and whether he's made a difference in the world. For this episode, Serling changed the protagonist's profession to teacher to incorporate *Goodbye, Mr. Chips* as well. Ellis Fowler (Donald Pleasence) learns that, after more than a half-century in education, he'll be forced to retire. Sensitivity to the old as well as young characterizes *Zone*'s creator; this is one of the lesser known "delicate" episodes.

Like Capra's George Bailey, Fowler is about to commit suicide when he is interrupted by metaphysical forces, in this case spirits of former students. The beauty of the piece is inherent in Serling's not insisting that they are ghosts. The boys, though deceased, may be figments of Fowler's imagination. That doesn't matter as in *Zone*, reality exists in the mind. What does matter is that each boy reveals what Clarence helped George Bailey to grasp in *Wonderful Life*: They were inspired by him and couldn't have operated in the world with courage and conviction if not for Fowler's influence. He, gratified, returns home to his wife (Philippa Bevans) with a satisfied smile that equals George Bailey's, Lew Bookman's, Joey Crown's, and Henry Corwin's. To paraphrase that line from Serling's early boxing story, just because you're finished in the classroom doesn't mean you're finished in life. If Fowler possessed a flaw, it was that he spent so much time with students that he had not properly connected with his wife. Now they have a second chance to make the most of the years left to them. Retirement, at first a seeming death sentence, turns out to be the greatest gift. It's all in the way you look at things.

Lesson to be learned in *The Twilight Zone*.

4

ME, MYSELF, & I:
An Auteur's Identity Crisis

R OD SERLING WAS fond of recalling an incident that influenced one sort of story he would tell. "I was in an airport in London, sitting there very quietly, with my topcoat in hand and a briefcase at my feet. I looked up and, across the room, there stood a man, five foot six, my identical height, wearing the identical topcoat, with a briefcase of identical cowhide. I kept staring, with this funny ice-cold feeling that if he turns around, and it's me, what will I do?" When the fellow did eventually shift positions, his face looked nothing at all like Rod's own. At the time, Serling breathed a sigh of relief. Afterwards, it haunted him: "This did leave its imprint sufficiently to write a story about it." A *Zone* subgenre concerns individuals who come to terms with the frightening issue of identity under similar circumstances.

The Empty Spot in Space:

AND WHEN THE SKY WAS OPENED (12/11/59)

This early episode, an adaptation of Richard Matheson's short story "Disappearing Act," reveals Serling's ability to add autobiography to preexisting material. In the original, an average guy realizes that people around him are dissolving into nothingness; at the end, he joins them. The most obvious change in Serling's version is the addition of a space-flight. We first see a tarpaulin in an isolated hangar, covering a rocket. Serling's narration reveals that astronauts aboard had lost contact with Earth for the past 24 hours. Director Douglas Heyes then cuts to the hospital where Colonel Clegg Forbes (Rod Taylor), released the previous day, visits a recuperating shipmate, Major William Gart (Jim Hutton). Military men are accurately depicted here, as only a veteran of that branch could provide. Forbes has returned to ask Gart if he recalls a third man, Ed Harrington. Gart has no idea what he's talking about—only they had been together in space, as a newspaper headline asserts.

In a flashback, Forbes recalls fast-fading memories of Harrington (Charles Aidman), a close friend for sixteen years, also having been aboard. Harrington and Forbes bid farewell to Gart a day earlier, then headed out to hit the bars. Once in a saloon, Harrington felt consumed by panic, insisting that he didn't feel as if he belonged here any more. Something had happened when they had passed through an empty spot in space, and if he "let go," Harrington would return there. Moments later, without a trace, Harrington was gone, the beer he dropped no longer on the floor. The bartender (Paul Bryar) and a girl (Gloria Pall) insisted that Forbes had entered alone.

Serling and Heyes convey key concepts with devices already basic to the series. Most notable is the mirror image, employed to visually communicate a character's sense of inner identity. The first occurs in the flashback as Forbes and Harrington stand by the hospital room's wall mirror, Gart (on the far side) contained within the shot thanks to his reflection. Forbes and Harrington exist in a frame of reference all their own; Gart is seen indirectly. A sudden change in camera angle allows us to consider Forbes and Gart, Harrington now denied access to the frame. There are two "sets": Forbes and Harrington (together in the flashback) and Forbes and Gart (the current story). Another mirror stretches wide behind the bar. Serling (to borrow from critic Irwin Panofsky) redeems physical reality by endowing this mirror with meaning derived from the onscreen context.

Harrington's identity crisis begins as he stares at his Mirror Image. He turns to Forbes, insisting, "Maybe we shouldn't have come back from that flight at all. Somebody or something let us slip through, and we shouldn't have." Before he disappears, Harrington heads for a phone booth and places one of *Zone*'s Long-Distance Calls. He's informed by his mother and father that they have no son named Ed. As he staggers out, Harrington sets the stage for Martin Sloan in *Walking Distance*, the inability of a parent to recognize his or her child adding to the truly tragic dimension of his isolation. His journey may have something to do with the space-time continuum, but precisely what isn't easy to say. Still, the recurring idea implied here (a twin Earth, a nearly identical world much like ours existing in a parallel dimension, connected by a black hole) will be fully developed in *The Parallel*. While Serling's fifth dimension partakes of time and space, *Zone* cannot be confined to such easily identifiable ideas. We encounter a geography of the imagination encompassing the inexplicable. That "somebody" or "something" Harrington earlier referred to was God, in the most inclusive sense of that term. So we shouldn't be surprised that, when panicky Cleg Forbes ran into Gart's hospital room, his friend referred to him as a "prodigal," the Biblical reference for a wanderer. The very title of this "scientific" piece is a quote from the Bible.

"You're crazy," Forbes screams at anyone and everyone who doubts that Harrington existed. One aspect of *Zone* is Serling's search for a working definition for insanity during the postwar scientific age. Madness, like everything else in the modernist sensibility, becomes (as Einstein had put it) relative. Forbes was not crazy since, as he made ready to leave the hospital, Gart too saw Harrington. Returning, Forbes hopes that Gart will confirm his perception, certifying that Forbes is not crazy. But Gart no longer believes in Harrington, so he can no longer see him. Yet, Forbes's concern for Harrington isn't entirely due to self-interest. He sincerely cares about his friend, recalls what they did and said. Forbes is then a humanist, worthy of sympathy. "Why doesn't anyone believe me?" Forbes screams after telling a woman (Maxine Cooper) who had known and dated both about what's happened. Her confused reply: "Who's Ed?"

Forbes eventually returns to the scene of the crime, breaking into the now-closed bar. A bird's-eye view of him, in the same phone booth that had swallowed up Harrington, conveys that he's now one of The Lonely—in need of other people, yet denied precisely that. "Somebody up there," he calls out, echoing Harrington's words about a Force above and beyond, one that works in mysterious ways. "Like I don't belong," he tells Gart, as we see yet another mirror image that briefly holds the two in tandem. Serling, the well-liked fellow who inwardly conceived of himself as an outsider, reveals much about his own sense of identity in that line. Then Forbes is gone and Gart can't

convince the nurse (Sue Randall) that he ever existed. Glancing at
the newspaper, Gart notes its headline: only one man returned. In
a striking shot, Gart lies back down; as he does, his face recedes. A
moment later, the nurse informs a doctor that the room which once
housed all three, then two, finally one has been vacant for some time.
No beds are in it now (as each man disappeared, so did his bunk);
the newspaper reveals that all three were lost during the flight.

An abrupt cut back to the hangar reveals the canvas tarp on the
ground: The ship, too, has been drawn back to a celestial doorway.
What does the episode mean? The beauty of the piece derives from
the impossibility of easily answering that. This is an oblique drama
about essence and existence. Solipsism underlines all: If we cease to
believe that we are here, can we long remain? "Got to believe," the
child in *The Big Tall Wish* insisted. The astronauts are "no longer a
part of the memory of man." Cease to believe? Cease to see.

Double Trouble:

MIRROR IMAGE (2/26/60)

At an upstate New York bus depot, director John Brahm brings his
camera down on Millicent Barnes, "age twenty-five, young woman
waiting for a bus on a rainy November night." Barnes is not "imaginative" or "given to undue anxiety or fears," so when seemingly
inexplicable events occur, we recall that this is not some scatterbrain,
but a fitting audience surrogate for any normal (if that term has any
meaning) person. Invoking Hitchcock, Millicent Barnes resembles
Marion Crane in *Psycho*, released just a few months after this episode's
broadcast; each is a career woman who finds herself plunged into
terror. The difference: Hitch ultimately offers a perfectly rational
explanation for the weird happenings; Serling insists that there are
things that can't be fully explained. Both females though are "M"
women. And when Marion Crane (Janet Leigh) is summarily dismissed at *Psycho*'s midpoint, her character is displaced by a look-alike
sister played by Vera Miles, star of this *Zone*.

All the expected elements are here, beginning with time. Barnes looks to the wall clock, then checks her own wristwatch to make sure it's correct while waiting for a bus which has been delayed by a storm. Things grow strange when she asks the grumpy ticket agent (Joe Hamilton) if he knows when the bus to Cortland will arrive and he berates Barnes for bothering him again, though she hasn't spoken before. Then she notices a checked piece of luggage, identical to her own, still sitting beside her bench. This will be the MacGuffin, the inanimate object serving as "the key" via close-ups on what initially might seem insignificant. "You need your eyes" examined, she tells the agent. Perception and reality come into play throughout *Mirror Image* as Barnes realizes that believing is seeing, not the other way around.

As the agent mutters something about Barnes having "nightmares" or possibly being "mad," raising continuing *Zone* concepts, she heads for the ladies' room. There, while making small talk with a good-natured attendant (Naomi Stevens) who likewise comes to doubt Barnes's sanity, she glances into a mirror and spots a double image of herself: Barnes beside a doppelgänger, a dark version of her with a cruel grin. When Barnes returns to the terminal, she doubts her own sanity after her luggage disappears, then reappears. Likely Barnes would have started screaming at the top of her lungs if not for a polite young man, Paul Grinstead (Martin Milner). He steps in out of the rain, realizes that the lady is having a hard time of it, and sits beside her, trying to help.

A regular guy, Grinstead is initially drawn to this demure beauty because of her looks. A decent man, he proves himself a humanist, remaining by the disturbed woman's side, hoping to help her escape from the living nightmare. In a voice-over, Barnes scolds herself for giving in to "delusions," then explains to Grinstead that she suffers from what might be thought of as the opposite of déjà vu, feeling that she hasn't been here before, though every one else insists she has. At one point, Barnes is ready to accept the possibility that they may be right; she is mad. Still, Barnes believes that she'll be okay if she can convince Grinstead to believe in, then see, her evil twin.

Momentarily, it appears that they might make a getaway when the bus arrives. As she's about to board, Barnes glances up and notes the double cryptically peering out a window. She darts back inside, horrified, followed by Grinstead as the bus leaves without them. Grinstead assumes the role of rationalist, calmly insisting: "There's an explanation." Everyone has a double someplace; maybe it's merely that. In her soliloquy, Barnes raises an idea essential to *Zone*: "I'm remembering something I read or heard about, different planes of existence. Two parallel worlds, side by side, and each of us has a counterpart in the other world. Sometimes there's a freak accident, the complement crosses over into our world and in order to survive, has to take over." Grinstead's logical reaction: "That's a little metaphysical for me." Yet this is *Zone*, and things can't be neatly explained. Paul will in time be converted.

Convinced that she's mad, he pretends to phone a friend to drive over and pick both up (one more of those Long-Distance Calls that fails to connect). He actually summons the police, who arrive and carry Barnes away. Serling and Brahm provide a crucifixion scene: Standing outside the doors, her arms spread wide, Barnes appears nailed to a cross owing to a design embossed on the glass. Was Grinstead her Judas? If so, we don't detest him. Clearly, he meant well; for Serling, that's enough to keep him sympathetic. Paul Grinstead will transform into the Bible's Paul, The True Believer, when his suitcase disappears. Glancing to the door, he spots a man who looks like himself running away with it. The moment he's in the vulnerable position of The Lonely, what appeared to be madness on Barnes's part becomes his subjective reality. As an old saying goes, all are mad except me and thee and, sometimes, I wonder about thee! "Obscure metaphysical explanation" is the only way to deal with this. Cognizance of another dimension can "explain away that which cannot be explained."

A Doll's House:

THE AFTER HOURS (6/10/60)

Marsha White (Anne Francis), yet another of Serling's attractive, Hitchcock-like "M" women, enters a typical big-city department store, searching for a gold thimble she'd like to give her mother. Other customers enter a crowded elevator; off to one side, another appears reserved for her. The operator (John Conwell) brings White up to the ninth floor. After stepping out, she realizes that it's empty. Then a strange, vampish woman (Elizabeth Allen) joins White and sells her the very item she was looking for. Incredibly, it's the only item for sale on the floor. Riding back down, White realizes that the thimble is scratched and complains to a fussy sales manager, Mr. Armbruster (James Millholin). He won't make an exchange, insisting that there is no ninth floor, and that the saleswoman White claims to have spoken to doesn't exist. Then White spots the saleswoman—but she turns out to be a lifelike mannequin. White faints and is carried off to the office of the owner, Mr. Sloan (Patrick Whyte).

Director Douglas Heyes, effective at realizing Serling's eeriest tales, here visualizes *Zone*'s fear of the unknown, the one fear "you cannot share with others," causing a hero to become The Lonely. Both Armbruster and Sloan assume that White is mad since she experiences a reality they cannot share. Her status in the episode's second half, when White awakens in the office after hours, having accidentally been left behind when the staff left, takes that elemental fear to the extreme. Before that can occur, Serling and Heyes convey in dialogue and imagery *Zone*'s recurring motifs. When the saleswoman appeared to White, she emerged from out of shadows, recalling such classics as *The Eye of the Beholder* and *Shadow Play*. The saleswoman knew White's name, suggesting either a sixth sense or an alternate dimension—the elevator in this case a doorway, the ninth floor a parallel world. As White wakes from a troubled sleep, she stops to study a Mirror Image of herself. Finding oneself locked in a small area will be explored in *The Obsolete Man* and *The Howling Man*, claustrophobia as essential to Serling's vision as Hitchcock's. Like Nan in *The Hitch-Hiker*, White at her most desperate tries to phone her mother, one more Long-Distance Call that will not be completed.

When White again arrives on the ninth floor, she hears voices emanating from the mannequins, though their mouths do not move. In time, she comes to believe that they are real; when she does, their lips move. White slips out of denial and grasps what happened: She is a mannequin. One of their ilk slips out of the store to walk among real people each month. Liking what she saw, repressing the truth of her identity, White had to be manipulated into returning. White muses: "When you're on the outside, everything seems so normal. As if we were like the others—the outsiders—the (real) people." One possible interpretation is that like the pod people in Jack Finney's *The Body Snatchers*, *After Hours* serves as an allegory for modern society: All of us living in the atomic age have lost something of our humanity. Serling refers to Marsha White as "a wooden lady with painted face." Who among us hasn't been confused, drifting past a shop window, when what we'd taken to be a mannequin moved? Or what we thought was a saleslady turned out to be one of the life-sized dolls that take on "characteristics of someone as normal and as flesh and blood as you and I?" Serling then takes what we've seen to another level. "But it makes you wonder, doesn't it? Just how normal we are? Just who are the people we nod our hellos to as we pass on the street?" We will find no obvious moral here. Instead of an easy message, Serling offers a complex meaning. More often than not, *Zone* raises questions for the audience rather than provide viewers with clear-cut answers.

Where's Charley?

MINIATURE (2/21/63)

A fourth-season Charles Beaumont classic also tackled the twin themes of insanity and identity crisis. This time, it isn't the manne-quin who becomes confused, but an adoring male. Charley Parkes (Robert Duvall) wants to be a face in the crowd, but people won't let him. He remains after hours in the office where he's employed to complete his work, then is ostracized by co-workers ("little goodie two-shoes!") and fired by his boss (Barney Phillips), who believes that Parkes's uniqueness renders other employees dysfunctional. Worse, at home, his well-intentioned but dominating mother (Pert Kelton) offers misguided advice. Though he promises to get a new job, Parkes spends time at a museum, where a Victorian dollhouse becomes an object of interest, then an obsession. Inside, a female doll (Claire Griswold), dressed in fin-de-siecle clothing, sits by a toy piano. As Parkes stares in, he hears her play. A delicate one-way love develops as the doll never acknowledges Parkes watching.

Director Walter E. Grauman's camera angles were chosen to make Parkes, peering in the window, appear to be watching TV. One reading of *Miniature* is as an allegory for TV as escapism. Parkes loses all touch with his outer reality; like an addict of daytime soap operas who believes that they are not actors playing characters, but real people, this strange antihero handles the emptiness of his everyday life by immersing himself in vicarious living: He believes a black-suited doll (Richard Angalora) who arrives at the house to be a villain, ready to carry the innocent virgin off to a fate worse than death—unless, of course, Parkes wills himself into the situation and saves her, leading to the inevitable ending.

Many **Zone** themes are present here. A friendly museum guard (John McLiam) serves as Parkes's foil. Representing the norm as compared to an "exception to the moral order," the guard neither sees the doll move nor hears music. Reality, like beauty, exists in the eye (or ear) of the beholder. Dr. Wallman (William Windom), Parkes's psychiatrist, explains: "No one is saying you don't see these things," only that "you see them in your mind." Believing is seeing for "sometimes, the brain sees," then transports its "message to the eye." We also sense in Parkes a desire to escape, like Gart Williams, into an idealized past. We feel less for Parkes than for Williams, though, because he fails to qualify as a humanist. "Do you like your fellow workers?" Parkes's boss asked. "I never really thought about it that way," Parkes replies.

Still, there's a capacity for emotion to Parkes that we do not note in, say, *Time Enough*'s Henry Bemis, who is incapable of feeling. "I love you," Parkes whispers to the doll. No wonder, then, that when the guard spots Parkes in the dollhouse beside her, there's a smile on Parkes's face. He is no longer one of The Lonely, even as Henry Bemis slips into that state. For Parkes loved; loved absolutely and unconditionally.

The Road to Hell:

MUTE (1/31/63)

Serling's opening narration sets one of the series' least fantastic stories in a self-consciously theatrical context. We watch four married couples meet in Dusseldorf, Germany, in 1953. Though the sequence is realistically played, our host insists that we're watching "the curtain raiser" of a play to be performed "almost entirely offstage," the "final scenes" taking place 10 years later performed by a "different *cast*." In them, the "main character" will be a child named Ilse. While the prologue unfolds, she, age two, sleeps in her crib, unaware a "singular drama" will evolve. Why so much theatre-talk for a *Zone* intro? The answer won't be clear until the end, when we grasp that not only fantasy and reality but also life and theatre are interchangeable.

The agreement these eight people enter into ("a pact" honoring "the commencement of a project") combines elements of atavistic superstition and evolving science. An eerie tone, inherent in Richard Matheson's screenplay (from his short story) and strikingly visualized by director Stuart Rosenberg, surfeits the piece. Prior to the inception of language, these great minds have decided, man communicated by telekinetic means. With the development of words, this primal power was lost. Now, when it's obvious that language fails us more than it helps us communicate, the far-reaching thing is to reconnect to that once universal ability, a primal sympathy forgotten—if far from gone. The experiment involves raising their children isolated from other humans, without teaching them to speak, encouraging mental telepathy.

One lady expresses concern as to whether "we have the right to impose this on our children." The others, certain that such a power will provide a "gift," convince the one doubter that it's their responsibility to proceed, heightening their own children's brilliance while paving the way for a futuristic form of humanity. They mean well. But as an old adage insists, the road to hell is paved with good intentions.

Never are such idealistic plans as open to question as when they involve innocent children, devoid of any power to choose for themselves. We recall the Biblical pronouncement that, in the beginning, "there was The Word." As this cult rejects that, they can be perceived as defying God's will. Each rates as a reverse Prometheus, not hoping to steal some celestial secret and deliver it to mankind, but to return us to an earlier state of innocence (i.e., ignorance.) The Bible states that, after the fall, we must live to the east of Eden. That is, we can't go home again. On another level *Mute* can be perceived as a social allegory. 1953 was the year in which Dr. Spock's theories of child-rearing entered the mainstream. Suburban parents rejected traditional methods and raised their offspring in a "progressive" manner. Some observers insisted that the Spock approach led (when the children became teenagers) to the rebellious 1960s youth movement. That syndrome is predicted here. A decade later, the terrible consequences of an adult decision brings terror to Ilse (Ann Jillian). The 12-year-old has been raised in rural Pennsylvania by Frau (Claudia Breyer) and Holger (Robert Boon) Nielsen, the American-born (though of German descent) cult members. A sudden fire at their farm sends Sheriff Harry Wheeler (Frank Overton) and firefighters to a place where such neighbors have not been made welcome. The Nielsens are killed in the blaze, but rescuers discover Ilse, who has inexplicably escaped. Ilse is embraced by Cora (Barbara Baxley), the sheriff's wife and one of The Lonely. Cora never recovered from the drowning of their little girl, Sally. When it becomes obvious that this child hasn't been taught to speak, and there are no relatives nearby, Cora institutes adoption proceedings. She will watch this child closely—something she failed to do with her own baby. Cora has been given that greatest of all gifts in the *Zone*: a Second Chance.

Little Sally's former bedroom appears a nice, normal spot—one in which this clearly abnormal child may, in time, come around. On closer examination, we notice macabre elements. Sally's doll remains in its old place on the pillow. Cora can't appreciate Ilse as an individual, but instead tries to mold her into a new Sally, something this little person can't be. On the far wall, a framed picture drips with death: A tree, seemingly a willow, bears branches hanging downward. "She's beautiful," Cora weeps. "She looks just like Sally . . . doesn't she?" Harry's eyes reveal that this girl looks nothing like

Sally. He sees objective reality; Cora lives in a world within her mind. However kindly she may be, Cora is about to commit *Zone*'s worst sin: to deny the uniqueness of a human being. She can't help but enact more harm than good.

This becomes clear when Harry writes letters to the people in Germany, asking whether they wish to claim the child. Cora burns their replies. Ilse's telepathy allows her to sense this. Joy at the thought that "they will come for me now and put me with the other children like me" implodes. "They'll never find me," she fears, sensing Cora dispose of evidence. In a devastating sequence, the frightened child runs from the house. In many *Zones*, a "normal" character darts in horror through some surreal funhouse. Here, the opposite occurs: an abnormal child finds herself caught in a land-scape that to us looks like one more lovely Main Street, U.S.A. The greatest fear is of the unknown working on you, however normal it appears to others.

We hear people's voices as Ilse experiences them: hollow and loud, garbled, threatening. As Ilse is the same age as many teenage viewers, they encounter a small-screen drama which allows them to associate with this girl, who embodies every teen's inner fear that communication with the adult world may be impossible. For most such kids, the only thing more frightening than well-meaning but misguided parents is some teacher who had the child's best interests in mind, yet managed to do remarkable damage. So Miss Frank (Irene Dailey) is introduced. Her dark clothing and menacing manner recall Margaret Hamilton in *The Wizard of Oz* (1939). Yet her sweet, sincere voice recalls Anne Bancroft as Annie Sullivan in *The Miracle Worker* (1962). Taking Theodore Roosevelt's advice, she speaks softly but carries a big stick: a ruler, which she employs to whack children (Ilse included) when they fail to conform to her standards.

Marc Scott Zicree damns *Mute* as "crushingly pro-conformity," as if the filmmakers were on Frank's side. What the team (Herbert Hirschman having replaced Buck Houghton as producer) deftly achieved was a condemnation of Miss Frank's methods without attacking the woman herself. We learn that she, in her own youth, was kept mute by parents who wanted her to become a medium.

Frank sincerely fears that the same has been done to Ilse, whom she wants to rescue. If wrong in her deduction, Frank believes that by forcing Ilse to conform (that is, to speak) she'll do the child a service. To a degree, she's right. If Ilse never speaks, she'll be treated as a freak. In *Zone*, those with good intentions but weak impact find themselves in a purgatory of their own making; unlike those without concern for others (however misguided), they aren't headed for hell. Miss Frank's methods (verbal and physical abuse, emotional intimidation) are horrific. Still, such terms describe the manner in which our hero Annie Sullivan forces Helen Keller (Patty Duke) to connect with the concept of The Word in William Gibson's fact-based drama.

Serling insisted that *Zone* question whether the end justifies the means. If the teacher we meet here were to be interviewed about what she does, Frank would as staunchly defend her methods as would Sullivan. We do not have to accept her approach as right to grasp how deeply she believes (that key *Zone* concept) in what she's doing. Like Helen Keller, Ilse does eventually speak, allowing her to at least approach "normal" life. Ilse's scream of her name, Zicree complains, "is treated as a happy ending." It most certainly is not, rather an ambiguous one. On the positive side, Ilse has been rescued, like Keller, from a solipsistic existence. On the other, her unique gift—mental telepathy—has been taken away. Then again, that ability was nurtured by Ilse's biological parents, who were as wrong in wanting to make the girl entirely unique as Miss Frank was in hoping to turn Ilse into a total conformist.

Though written by Matheson, *Mute* also expresses Serling's own hatred of absolutes and his firm belief in the Greek Golden Mean: Each of us must combine uniqueness and individuality within a sense of the greater human community. Only then do we avoid equally dangerous poles of chaos and conformity. "The welfare of a child is everyone's business," a wise adult character states. This is undisputed, certainly, though we can endlessly argue as to how best we might achieve that. That the script has an ironic edge is made clear by a subtle touch in the classroom sequence. As Miss Frank angrily insists that Ilse speak her name, the close observer will note that on the blackboard, a semi-erased word requests: SILENCE! If *Mute* refuses to offer a simple telegraphed message, that only allows its meaning to exist on the level of the legitimate stage. Hence, the theatrical allusions in Serling's opening.

Fear and death are present here, as are two positive motifs that override those terrible ones: love and humanism. When Professor Karl Werner (Oscar Beregi) and wife Maria (Eva Soreny) arrive in America to reclaim Ilse, they realize that she is truly loved by these fallible people. The Werners come to see that that unconditional love is more important than any scientific experiment. "Perfect love casteth out fear," Serling quotes from the Bible. The love we witness here was notably imperfect. At the very least, good people do the best they can. In the imperfect world we inhabit, that may be all we (like Rod Serling and Richard Matheson) dare hope for.

"I'm leavin' on a jet plane!":

A WORLD OF DIFFERENCE (03/11/60)

This memorable first season episode displays Matheson adapting the Serling vision to his own unique narrative form, allowing for creative collaboration that nonetheless proves that Serling was indeed the series' auteur. In comparison to *Mute*, *World* rates as a fantastical episode in which early middle-aged businessman Arthur Curtis (Howard Duff) is shocked to realize that he's not a person but a character in a movie being filmed on a Hollywood sound stage. His actual name is Gerry Reagan. He's so unhappy with his life and wife Nora (Eileen Ryan) that he's slipped into a state of happy dementia in which the miserable Reagan no longer exists; he is, instead, the well-adjusted (and happily married) Curtis. Instead of calling "Where is everybody?" as Earl Holliman's character did in the first *Zone*, Reagan shouts out the inverse aspect of loneliness: "Where am I?" In tune with the tenor of the show itself, Reagan's wife is a beautiful, money-crazed blonde while Mrs. Marion Curtis

(Susan Dorn) is a quietly appealing brunette. The former only wants to take her ex-husband for all he's worth; the latter hopes to help him in any way she can. Both an old-fashioned "stand by your man" type and simultaneously a modern woman with a mind all her own, Marion is a prototype of *Zone*'s "good women/good wives" providing traditionalism and progressive thinking.

In what the opening refers to as a "tableau of reality," Serling and Matheson set the pace for such *Zone* influenced films as *The Truman Show* when their wounded hero gazes out of what he believes to be his office and sees the motion picture crew staring at him, all of the technicians stunned that he appears amazed they are there. When a person's fantasy life becomes more real to them than reality, who's to say what is real and what is not? Like so many of Serling's own focal characters, Reagan has a history of drinking that has impeded his career and relationships. He tries to make contact with what he desperately wants to believe is "the real world" through a series of phone calls, all of them supposedly local. But, in their endless disconnects, each turns out to be symbolically Long-Distance. Postwar American car-culture is evident as he tries to drive to the home and beloved daughter (another recurring motif) he needs to believe await him; this is the only sequence in which we share, via a point-of-view shot, Reagan's dilemma rather than merely watch it. We are all, the stylistic device tells us, now a nation of commuters. "I'm going home!" Reagan regularly shouts, relating him to so many other first-season heroes; again, home is a dream, not an actuality. The entire concept deconstructs the fact that we are watching a film about the filming of a film; Reagan is not alone among *Zone* protagonists in looking for an "escape clause" which occurs when that eerie Death Light shines on his face and, continuing the theme of technological flight as a kind of modern miracle, he leaves on a jet plane to paradise: One of those essentially decent types who finds his own heaven even if that renders him dead to the world. As always, Serling sums it all up to suggest his modernist outlook on subjectivity as the essence of existence: "How thin a line separates that which we assume to be with that manufactured inside a mind."

Doppelganger:

THE DUMMY (5/4/62)

The Dummy displays Serling's ability to take a story told many times before and adapt it to his own vision. Here is one more variation on the theme of a ventriloquist who gradually falls under the spell of his dummy. That concept has been employed often, including a memorable sequence in the 1945 film *Dead of Night* with Michael Redgrave as the man controlled by his wooden companion. In Rod's version Jerry Etherson (Cliff Robertson), while performing in a second-rate club, insists nasty "Willie" bit him as they hurried backstage. We see the nick in Jerry's hand, though this may have accidentally occurred when Jerry stopped to flirt with pretty chorus girls. No sooner are Etherson and Willy back in the dressing room than Etherson pauses to confront his looking glass. Here is the most complex of *Zone*'s Mirror Images. First, we see Etherson confront himself (or, more correctly, his semblance). Director Abner Biberman cuts to a close shot on Willie as the doll considers his owner. The angle changes again so we see all three—Etherson, his semblance, and Willie—though now it's difficult to see Willie clearly, suggesting that his personality already is stronger than Etherson's. As agent Frank (Frank Sutton) stops by, our point-of-view shifts again so as to include (for the first time on *Zone*) a mirror within the mirror, signifying all of Serling's stories within stories, dreams within dreams. Now, a small circular mirror on the right hand side of Etherson's desk creates a doubling of the doubling: We view him both in the large rectangular mirror and the small round one. Willy, meanwhile, glares at the fragmentation. Everything that will subsequently happen in the drama has been visually set up.

As with *A Passage For Trumpet*, *The Dummy* reveals itself to be a meditation on alcoholism and the more specific issue of an artistic alcoholic personality. Like Joey Crown, Jerry Etherson drinks because he fears that his gifts, however considerable, are not great enough to qualify him as one of the best in his field. Like the club owner in *Passage*, agent Frank provides the voice of reason, compassion, and humanism, trying to help Etherson grasp that all an artistic person need do is the best he can. The popular art form portrayed in each—jazz, ventriloquism—serves as a metaphor for the art of TV writing, the main character an alter-ego for Serling. Etherson proves a far more fitting substitute for Serling, earning a paycheck and delighting the crowd, even if he cannot enjoy the rewards because he believes that he should stretch himself further. The club might be a representation of *Zone* in comparison to the "loftier" *U.S. Steel Hour* and *Playhouse 90*. When Etherson pauses to light a cigarette, we can't help but notice the resemblance between him and Serling. "I thought I had a talented article here," Frank sighs, "who was eventually going to crawl out from under a bottle and hit it big!" Though Joey Crown never hit the big time in his profession, he succeeds when he comes to grips with his considerable, if limited, talent and accepts himself, finally winning a girl. *The Dummy* allows us to witness what could have happened to Crown had the angel Gabriel not appeared and revealed the path to his salvation. After failing to free himself from Willy, we watch Willy (George Murdock) perform as the ventriloquist, now totally in control, as Etherson, now reduced to the dummy, spouts whatever words Willy commands.

Why was Joey Crown spared such a terrible fate? He deserved to be saved by divine intervention because he was one of those people who need (and love) people. His alcoholism came about because he feared that he might not provide his audiences with high-quality music. Such humanism is missing from Jerry Etherson as revealed in his relationships with women. Early-on, he bumps into a bevy of showgirls. Each clearly would like a relationship with him. Etherson flirts with them but does not acknowledge any of the women as human beings. He winks at each, touches the girls, but they are all (to relate this to other *Zones*) mannequins. Seeing them only as sex objects, Etherson cannot make the human connection with any. Later Etherson, terrified after deserting Willy, stands shivering on a street corner at night. One of the women, Noreen (Sandra Warner), happens by. He, now one of The Lonely, sees this as an opportunity to relieve his tension because Willy would not haunt him when a normal person is around. So Etherson rushes to Noreen, who is initially happy. It would be easy for him to get Noreen to go someplace with him. When he lies, claiming that he's been waiting for her, Noreen's eyes brighten; this is what she's been hoping for. Within a minute and a half, Etherson blows the potential relationship by pawing Noreen. All Etherson had to do is tell Noreen what he was scared of, and the nice lady would have helped. Instead he demands that she stay with him, leaving her with no other option but to run away. Joey Crown is what Rod Serling tried to be and believed, at his best, he was; Jerry Etherson posits Serling's nightmare image of himself, the manner in which he could behave on his worst days. Either way, Serling understands that the key to hanging on to one's true identity is, ironically, being able to accept and appreciate the unique identities of others—as well as the human core that ties us all together.

All Quiet on the Eastern Front:

A QUALITY OF MERCY (12/29/61)

In *The Dummy*, Jerry Etherson's tragedy derives less from personal limitations than from an inability to learn and grow. His perfect opposite is Lieutenant Katell (Dean Stockwell), protagonist in one of Serling's WWII tales (from an idea by Sal Rolfe) that rings with the authenticity only a veteran could bring to such a piece. During the final days of combat in the South Pacific, this 90-day wonder who has never seen action struts into the remains of an infantry platoon stationed near a rock formation held by twenty starving Japanese. Rugged Sergeant Causarano (Albert Salmi) and his battle-scarred men, aware that the war will likely end soon, hope to wait this situation out. They're less than thrilled when Katell, with his naive, romantic view of war, orders them to attack. Though these seasoned vets are devastated, they (like the soldiers in Tennyson's "The Charge of the Light Brigade") know that theirs is not to reason why; theirs is but to do and die.

A Quality of Mercy reveals how Serling, in the process of developing a single key concept (identity), also includes other themes. The title, from *The Merchant of Venice*, reveals his ongoing fascination with Shakespeare: The quality of mercy is not strained; it blesseth him that gives and him that takes. "Bless" implies the religious aspect of a Serling script. In the opening, Serling insists that the American infantrymen are waiting for a "miracle" to save them, if one of a realistic order: word that the war is over. The story ends with the dropping of an atomic bomb on Japan, an event that initiated the nightmare scenario of postwar existence at the heart of *Zone*'s anti-nuke vision. The cave itself is modeled on the one that appeared in the first season's opening as symbol for the pit of man's fears. "Weight of command" is here placed on the tender shoulders of Katell, who at first does not understand (as do seasoned officers in Serling-scripted *Zones*) the responsibility to others inherent in his status. Death, so basic to the show, haunts the men on both sides.

Perhaps the greatest of all *Zone*'s recurring concepts is the complex relationship of (physical) sight to (true) insight. Here, Serling implies this via a set of binoculars. In the opening, one of the Americans employs the binoculars on the most realistic level to study the enemy's position. When Katell arrives, he takes the set and attempts to "see" what's out there. When Katell accidentally drops them and a soldier picks the binoculars up, everything changes. The soldier is Japanese; Katell has morphed into Lieutenant Yamuri. They have been ordered to attack the Americans, who are in the cave. Is this reversal one more daydream, occurring only in Katell's mind? Or does he actually violate the time-space continuum? The answer, here or in any *Zone*: It doesn't matter! We can view this as time travel (now it's Corregador at the war's beginning), or only a hallucination. It matters not whether this is "true" in any objective sense; all that matters is that Katell believes it (and is changed by it). It's undeniably true for him. The doubling theme is revived, as Katell becomes the Japanese Mirror Image of his American self. "They're Japs," Katell earlier told the Sarge, offering his rationale for an attack. "They're men," Causarano countered. At this point, Katell can't grasp that; after walking a long mile in the "enemy's" shoes, he matures into a humanist. This happens precisely as the binoculars break. As in Greek drama, when sight disappears, insight occurs. A man comes to understand his self, his place in society, and his relationship to the larger world (and cosmos) in a way he never did before. With insight, sight is no longer necessary. Katell's binoculars smash, as do the glasses of Henry Bemis in *Time Enough at Last*. But whereas Bemis was lost forever, Katell is saved. He comes to comprehend his responsibility not only to the American soldiers but the Japanese as well. As to the metaphysical theme, it's crystallized when Causarano wonders if perhaps this "war to end all wars" will likely be soon followed by yet another. "God," the reinvented Katell sighs, "I hope not!" And, by implication, prays not.

5

FUTURE IMPERFECT:
The Shape of Things to Come

STEPHEN KING BEGINS *Danse Macabre* (1981) with that moment when he first understood the nature of fear. On Saturday, October 4, 1957, King attended a matinee of *Earth vs. the Flying Saucers*. Suddenly, the projector snapped off and the theatre manager shuffled out. "I have to tell you," he began, "that the Russians have put a space satellite into orbit around the Earth." At that moment, actuality caught up with fantasy; from then on, it would be ever more difficult to tell the two apart. For the future best-selling author, this led to a personal definition of terror: "a pervasive sense" that "things are in the unmaking." The rock-solid existence we previously believed that we inhabited gave way to a future at once horrifying and exciting. Beginning on that autumn day, what had long been relegated to space fantasy (*Buck Rogers*, *Flash Gordon*) transformed into science fiction, the realm of glorious escapism giving way to a more serious-minded consideration of the history of events yet to happen. This was true of novels and movies. Our oncoming penetration of space would play a key role in *Zone*.

Hi Robot:

THE LONELY (11/13/59)

This episode opens with the camera's descent from sky to mountains overlooking a barren land. The exteriors were shot in Death Valley, setting the pace for many future *Zones* in which that American desert substitutes for some distant asteroid. Here we encounter (to borrow from Conrad) nature's heart of darkness. In this desolate (some might say God-abandoned) terrain, we meet James A. Corby (Jack Warden), framed with this stark world behind his muscular body. Corby lovingly tinkers with a touring car, an antique suggesting the theme of a golden age that has sadly passed. This, though, is not Earth, but a distant rock. A condemned killer, Corby has been banished to a place in space where infinity remains maddeningly visible in every direction.

Director Jack Smight establishes that, to survive with his sanity intact, Corby has ceased looking up and out. Serling mentions both Corby's "mind and body," the yin and yang aspects of human existence so significant to this series. Serling then opts for a double narration, allowing us to enter the man's mind. Corby keeps a journal, now in its fourth year; we learn that his only contact with other humans occurs when a supply ship lands every four months. The parts required for him to assemble his precious car were so delivered. Corby was happy that the automobile did not arrive pre-assembled, as the work gave him something to focus on for a year. So the roadster contains Corby's creative spirit, a machine-age work of art he's come to love and the first such man-to-machine relationship in *Zone*. The automobile, shortly to be forgotten, has yet another dramatic function: By suggesting how intensely a forgotten man can relate to a machine, Serling perfectly sets up everything that will follow.

However offensive we may find Corby's earthly criminal activities, we empathize because he, like other *Zone* antiheroes (and unlike the show's villains) needs people. Corby would have long since gone mad if not for the quarterly appearance of Allenby (John Dehner), who arrives with food and water. How starved Corby is for companionship becomes clear when Allenby reveals that on this trip he can remain but fifteen minutes. This doesn't allow time enough (that Time Element again) for a quick chess game. Allenby does mention that on Earth, liberal forces are loudly denouncing such isolation as extreme and cruel punishment. "Who knows what the years may bring?" Allenby has brought Corby a gift: a large boxed item. "Give my regards to Broadway," Corby sarcastically quips as Allenby takes off. He opens the box to find another machine, this one preassembled: a robot created in the image of an attractive young woman. "My name's Alisha," the lifelike cyborg (Jean Marsh) says, "What's yours?"

"Get out of here," Corby snarls when she attempts to serve him a glass of water. "I don't need a machine." In truth, another machine is precisely what he needs. Alisha is the car all over again, if in far more attractive form. A scientific wonder, it can perform virtually any act a human might. Though the sexual aspect of his relationship with the shapely cyborg is never directly addressed, when eleven months pass (during the commercial break), the two have clearly grown close. Earlier, his words were full of resonance: "Why did they build you to look like a woman?" he cried. "Why'd they turn you into a lie?" Still, he gradually relates to Alisha when, causing it to cry, Corby is amazed to learn that the cyborg is capable of emotions: "I can feel!" In the *Zone*, feelings are more significant even than thoughts.

Time was Corby's great enemy; it's not now. During their strange interlude, Corby inadvertently programs Alisha's blank grid to think and feel precisely like himself. By instructing it on daily activities, Corby lives out the Pygmalion-Galatea myth, inventing the perfect woman as hell transforms into heaven. Yet Serling implies a criticism of the universal male fantasy Corby lives out. In loving Alisha, Corby admits, he adores the projection of his own self onto female form. "The things that she has learned to love are the things that I love," Corby admits. Numero uno among them is himself. If one accepts that technology can be considered mass-produced/functional art, Alisha is precisely that. Such a mythic dimension is further accentuated when our Pygmalion and Galatea lovingly gaze up at the stars. Corby picks out constellations for Alisha, noticing Hercules: God's beauty. How happy the two appear! Nothing, as Shakespeare insisted, is good or bad; thinking makes it so.

Then Allenby returns with "good news." Corby has been pardoned, so it's time to return to Earth. At first, this sounds great. But there's a catch: Alisha must be left behind because of weight restrictions. Here is the twist ending that provides entertainment. Yet here, too, is an ideological issue that transforms the script into art. Corby won't leave without Alisha. He knows, on a rational level, that Alisha is a robot. But his feelings insist otherwise and override intellect. Sharing his life with a perfect "female" allowed Corby to briefly experience an ideal. But perfection cannot exist in the real world, which is where he must go. Realizing that Corby is paralyzed, Allenby puts a bullet through Alisha's "head." Glancing down, Corby sees not flesh and blood but metal and plastic. "All you are leaving behind is loneliness," Allenby insists. Corby dutifully agrees to remember that as they prepare for the take-off.

Serling then reminds us what, on a deeper level, *The Lonely* was all about: "made in his image (the title of an upcoming episode), kept alive by love." That was Alisha, whose ruined frame was left behind like the antique car that once held meaning for the loneliest of men. As in so many **Zones** involving a looking glass, Rod insists that we ought not confuse the companionship of other people with the act of embracing a mirror image of oneself. To love a person makes one more human. The other? Nothing but destructive self-worship.

Ray Bradbury Presents:

I SING THE BODY ELECTRIC (5/18/62)

Ray Bradbury's sole contribution to **Zone** serves as a companion piece and counterpoint to *The Lonely*. *I Sing the Body Electric* (the title references a Walt Whitman poem) concerns another female robot who helps dispel a lost soul's lingering loneliness, here in a small town of the type Serling and Bradbury each grew up in. "Grandma" (Josephine Hutchinson) was synthetically created from interchangeable parts (hair, eyes, torso, arms, etc.). Three orphaned kids picked out each element so their harried businessman (and widowed) father (David White) can be certain they'll be happy. At first, Anne (Veronica Cartwright) refuses to warm up to the sweet (if mechanical) lady; it appears too much like the mother Anne loved and lost. Afraid of the unknown in general, and death in particular,

Anne would rather remain one of The Lonely than take the chance of loving (and perhaps losing) again.

Here we encounter a rare positive portrayal of future technology, suggesting the differing sensibilities of the author who wrote *The Lonely* and the one who penned this TV adaptation. The point of the former was that the central human character must reject his robot companion; to fail and do so would lead to madness and a wasted life. *Body Electric* tells us the opposite: Only by coming to see that a robot is superior to a human can Anne save herself. The two writers concern themselves with the same issues (death, the cyborg revolution, psychology of loneliness), but reach opposing conclusions. No wonder Serling's narration is notably atypical: he interrupts the drama two-thirds of the way through to comment on the action. Serling does not close the episode with the expected reference to *The Twilight Zone*. This makes sense. In a show dedicated to revealing the nightmarish implications of science, Ray Bradbury presents such stuff as a dream come true: i.e., Future Perfect!

"Our Planet is Dying!":

THIRD FROM THE SUN (1/8/60)

Older *Zone* fans, who caught the series during its initial run, remember this installment warmly. New converts tend to find it disappointing. The problem does not exist in Richard Matheson's original short story, the teleplay Serling fashioned from it, or the effective direction of Richard L. Bare. All were sound, beginning with the concept itself: Two families, knowing that an all-out nuclear war will erupt in hours, fly away in a stolen test rocket. We assume that they are modern Americans and the cold war is about to get hot. One fellow explains to his friend that they're headed for a distant star, where they will beam down on the third planet from the sun: "It's called . . . (pregnant pause) . . . Earth!" That line can elicit a guffaw today from naive viewers who wonder: How did they dare use that old ploy?

The answer? Such a turnabout had never before appeared in any filmed or televised fantasy. During the next decade, a dozen TV shows and films shamelessly ripped off a denouement that could work only once. Two B-budget movies, *Voyage to the Prehistoric Planet* and *Voyage to the Planet of Prehistoric Women*, offered variations. The final straw came in the late 1970s when ABC-TV based a series, *Battlestar: Gallactica*, on this notion. None of this takes away from its originality when we consider how innovative the idea was back then.

A fairer approach is to analyze *Third from the Sun* as a time capsule as it combined three pressing issues of the day into a single story. First, there was the ever more potent possibility of manned space probes, a concept that by the onset of the sixties had been posited (by JFK in his New Frontier speech) as an oncoming event. Second, UFO sightings mushroomed in the postwar years when, one night in 1947, a pilot flying over Washington state spotted saucer-shaped flying crafts moving at over a thousand miles an hour. Third, apocalypse haunted the fifties, as everything from Hollywood movies to educational films like *Duck and Cover!* reveal. In between *On the Beach* (1959) and *Dr. Strangelove* (1963), such stories were most likely to be found on *Zone*.

What's impressive is how Bare made the twist work. We assume from the opening shots that this must be Earth. The planet where William Sturka (Fritz Weaver) works looks like a government-operated piece of property, with security guards and barbed wire fences. When darkly handsome Sturka, wearing jacket and tie, stops for a cigarette, he appears to be one more of Serling's autobiographical figures. Carling (Edward Andrews), a nosy coworker, shuffles near to engage Sturka about dark rumors. Thick glasses make him appear myopic (fitting since Carling is emotionally blind). "Time for supper now," Serling narrarates, and for "a cool drink on a porch." A sweet image of a Homewood-like neighborhood anchors us in the everyday. While this is a "summer night," Matheson warns us, that doesn't mean a winter's frost can't descend. We have no reason to believe we're anywhere but in our own backyards when narrator, Serling, inimicably speaking Matheson's words, solemnly states that "a horror without words" is imminent, this being "the eve of the end."

If this realistic approach continued, a viewer might finally feel "had." Step by step, Bare deconstructs this "normal," "Earthly" realm. As a concerned Sturka enters his home, we note a huge, strangely shaped telephone. It might be a futuristic one on a near-future Earth. If that were the case, why isn't anything else futuristic? This can't be the future America, then. Paintings on the wall behind Eve Sturka (Lori March) and daughter Jody (Denise Alexander) are not of this Earth, implying that this is another world. Eve's name, besides bringing the series' Biblical sensibility into play, suggests something subtextual. Shortly, the last woman in this world becomes the first on our planet, a setup not only for this show's ending but also the third season's opener, *Two*.

The Biblical element is augmented later when Sturka, discussing possibilities for escape with pilot Jerry Riden (Joe Maross), who will navigate, assesses what they need for a safe launch: "A little bit of luck . . . a couple of breaks . . . and God!" Other recurring *Zone* themes appear: the Time Element (Sturka and Riden constantly glance at a ticking clock) and Mirror Image (we realize Sturka is split down the middle when he studies himself in a looking glass). A highly welcome proto-feminist (and pro-youth) moment has daughter Jody disarming Mr. Carling (who attempts to ruin their plans) when the men are caught unawares. Important too was the decision to reverse the typical directorial pattern set in place early on. According to the rules of *Zone's* game, most episodes begin with a realistic camera observing things from eye level, the style then growing ever more oblique and edgy to convey the character's intensifying descent into abnormal existence. Here, our heroes are headed to Earth (i.e., normalcy), so that wouldn't work. From the opening shot and throughout the first half, every image is disconcerting, visually informing us that this is not a prelude to entering the fifth dimension, but the fifth dimension itself! Once the characters are onboard, bizarre camera angles give way to a simpler shooting style. Even before Sturka reveals the name of the target planet, we receive one last hint that they are from another world. When we finally see the ship whiz by a backdrop of stars, it resembles not an American rocket but a flying saucer, courtesy of a brief clip from *Forbidden Planet*.

Definitely typical of *Zone* and its creator, though, are Serling's final words on the subject. However horrible the loss of a planet may be, his optimism (guarded as ever) allows for a positive summation. For these two families, at least, "it's the eve of the beginning."

2001: A Space Oddity:

I SHOT AN ARROW INTO THE AIR (1/15/60)

Serling's teleplay (from an idea by Madelon Champion) concerns the first manned space flight. *I Shot an Arrow* opens at night, rendering the descent from that legendary starry opening a less striking contrast than in the *Zones* that begin in daylight. Here, one set of stars (animated) gives way to another (actual) as the people behind "Arrow 1" prepare to make history. Documentary footage of rockets in the testing process is included. Director Stuart Rosenberg cuts back and forth from the craft (a realistic one) tearing off into the sky and members of a ground team attempting to keep "Arrow 1" on target. As the control commander discusses the intensifying problem with fellow scientists and military personnel, we learn that they've lost contact, a device employed in numerous future *Zones*. Worse, the crew of the spacecraft, despite state-of-the-art equipment, cannot determine in which direction they veered. We are drawn away from their concrete cave to the awesome infinity of space as the chief of ground operations stares at far-flung stars and mutters: "It landed, I know not where," adding: "Wherever you are? *God* help you!" (emphasis mine).

This is, after all, *Twilight Zone*, where progressive science and traditional religious forms are never posited as being in conflict. Rather, they coexist as differing language systems by which man might better comprehend unknown aspects of his cosmos. The moment the scene shifts to crew members of the lost rocket, this notion of God (and the importance of mankind acknowledging the metaphysical) returns. *Arrow* plays as a philosophical meditation on earthly morality coming to grips with imminent mortality (the death theme). It questions whether our (by implication, Judeo-Christian) values can (or should) be carried by man beyond his humble sphere, into a larger world . . . as well as another dimension.

Only then do we at last meet the survivors on what Colonel Donlon (Edward Binns) informs us "appears to be an uncharted asteroid." It might be the same floating globe of cruel rock the antihero of *The Lonely* would, at some future point, be forced to inhabit, shot in the same Death Valley locations. Already, Corey (Dewey Martin) has regressed to an animal state, clear when he seizes Donlon's journal and angrily insists that their commander do something to help them survive (on a bestial level) rather than worry about a record for the future. Corey is the rugged individualist, the embodiment of Herbert Spenser's theory of social Darwinism. If man is, as evolution teaches us, an extension of the animal kingdom, why shouldn't survival of the fittest serve as our basic rationale? Corey berates crew member Pierson (Ted Otis) for offering a drink of the precious water supply to a dying crew member. "Why waste it?" Corey scoffs. After all, aren't they back in time as well as far out in space, on some ugly chunk of unrewarding rock that never reached the Paleolithic age? If so, aren't they now a trio of would-be Adams?

For Donlon, the opposing liberal-humanist, the answer is decidedly "no!" He insists "we're still a crew," Serling positing Donlon as spokesman for the democratic group, a community that will prevail through cooperation. Important to their subsequent actions is what Donlon refers to as "The Book." He directly refers to the military manual, its code of conduct and theory of discipline basic to his career, but he infers the Bible, civilization's so-called "good book." The metaphysical has already appeared: "See if there's anything in this God-forsaken place," Donlon tells his crew, "that can keep us alive." God (and the morality that stems from belief) has entered into not only their discourse, but their destiny as well. The question has been raised: Is survival, in the immediate physical sense, worthwhile if achieved by forsaking the soul and conscience? Or does such behavior belie all that's best in man's 5,000-year climb out of "the pit of our primitive superstitions" while on a trek toward "the peak of our intelligence"?

Donlon's moral doppelgänger, a dark oppositional force to the colonel's values, would answer: Yes! Survival is the ultimate. Me, myself, and I must exist or the hell with the world. In time, Corey murders Pierson, stealing his water supply so Corey can go on living. Later, he plans to do the same to Donlon. "Two men can last maybe five days" on what they have left, Corey mutters; one man, perhaps ten, Corey grunts before pulling the trigger on the colonel. Then Corey climbs the canyon's rim and discovers his fate, which he's attempted to rewrite through free will. For in *Zone*, one may change the future but cannot alter the past. They are on Earth. Many viewers have guessed that; ample oxygen seems unlikely for a faraway asteroid. Even that doesn't diminish *Arrow*'s impact. Our collective cognition of what likely will be revealed helps transform what could have been a clever mystery into a more profound work of suspense. We wait for these characters to learn what we likely know, for here is the logical explanation as to why the scientific crew on earth detected no trace of "Arrow 1" when they tried to track its position "up there." The scientists were looking in the wrong direction; "Arrow 1" returned to where it came from, living out one of those cyclical patterns at the heart of *Zone*. "This," Donlon tells fellow survivors just before the midpoint, "is home now, gentlemen." How many characters, including Martin Sloan in *Walking Distance*, long to return to the spot where their life's adventure began? Donlon could not possibly have grasped how (ironically) correct he was.

As in Einstein's theories (particularly E=mc²), *Zone*'s protagonists are motored by galactic or, if one chooses religious idiom over scientific terminology, God. Like the space traveler in Stanley Kubrick's *Zone*-influenced *2001: A Space Odyssey* (1967), they realize that they will end their journeys where they began. Serling also has an opportunity here to play with an ending he would perfect in his screenplay for *Planet of the Apes* (1968), adapted from Pierre Boulle's novel. Donlon discovers Pierce, left for dead. The doomed man manages to draw a crude sign in the sand, revealing what he spotted on the ridge's far side. The sketch appears to be of a cross. After Corey kills Donlon and climbs up to the top, he peers down, realizing too late that what Corey had attempted to convey was a telephone pole. Now Corey notices such poles lining a highway, leading to Reno in one direction, Vegas in the other. The realization that they are back on Earth (the poles will be replaced by the Statue of Liberty in *Planet of the Apes*) is by this point enough to break Corey's thin hold on his sanity.

So he laughs out loud at the absurdity. And perhaps flashes back to what he hissed at Donlon's body seconds after killing the man: "You brought the book to the wrong place." In truth, it was the right place. Even if they were on some remote asteroid, that would be the right place. "The Book" may be a set of military rules or the spiritual/legal foundation of civilization. Or it may be any verbal text; Corey's first action was an attempt to rip up the writing Donlon (the civilized man, identified as such by his grasp of the importance of words to people) composed. A throwback to the Beast attempted to destroy an advanced man's desire to transform the chaos of life into an understandable order via what separates us from animal brutality: the written word.

Likewise, those telephone poles are indistinguishable from a line of crosses on a Spanish mission. The dichotomy between religion (at its least divisive) and science (at its most humanistic) doesn't exist for Serling. Civilization, at its best, contains crosses and telephone poles. The same holds true for secular books and sacred texts. In the alternative world of the fifth dimension, Serling says, as in the real world, without a strong sense of how individualism ought to be countered by loyalty to the human community, there is nothing. Only jungles, composed of vegetation or asphalt.

"Bring 'Em Back Alive!":

PEOPLE ARE ALIKE ALL OVER (3/25/60)

What would have happened to Corey and Donlon had they realized that the heavenly body they'd crashed down on was not earth but some island in the sky? Mars, perhaps. We might also consider the great unanswered question left open at *Third from the Sun*'s finale: What kind of treatment would people from the stars receive when they at last beamed down, hoping to be accepted with open arms? Such questions are answered here. Freely adapting the Paul Fairman short story "Brothers Beyond the Void" (*Fantastic Adventures*; March 1952), Serling opens his version with a shot of two men, bookish scientist Sam Conrad (Roddy McDowall) and astronaut Warren Marcusson (Paul Comi), gazing at the rocket that will, the following day, spirit them off to the skies. Director Mitchell Leisen (closely following instructions in Serling's script) shoots them from behind a wire fence. They look, for all the world, like animals in a cage. That's precisely what, in the concluding shot, Conrad (Marcusson does not long survive the landing) will become. The attractive and highly intelligent men and women of Mars rescue the scientist only to place him on display in their intergalactic zoo; a sign on Conrad's cage (resembling a suburban house) reads: "Earth Creature in his Native Habitat." If we are watching closely enough from the moment the show begins, this was carefully prepared for.

That was not the case with Fairman's story, explaining why this final irony did not seem as sharp as it does in Serling's superior version. The Bard of Video, Serling employs this story not only for entertainment but to communicate his vision. In the opening, Serling more or less divides himself in two, like an amoeba, as the brave astronaut attempts to comfort the scared scientist.

> **CONRAD:** I'm frightened of what we'll find up there.
> **MARCUSSON:** The unknown? Sure. The one thing you shouldn't be frightened of is people.

As Serling's own words on the subject indicate, fear is an essential element of mankind's existence. And there is no greater fear than fear of the unknown. In its own way, each and every **Zone**, whether personally written by Serling or by one of his colleagues, employs this idea as its point of departure. Every bit as basic to Serling's attitude is a double vision of the human race. He includes an ongoing condemnation of man's inhumanity to man, whether it be the Nazi holocaust of Jews (and other minorities) in Germany or institutionalized racial prejudice against blacks at home. Still, this concern is counter-balanced by a hopeful belief there is indeed goodness in man, however dormant at our worst moments, that will in time win out over evil. This allowed Serling to go on insisting that progress can be made, resulting in a cautious optimism that justifies his humanism.

This quality is what keeps **Zone**'s creator from falling into the modern abyss of nihilism. Marcusson tries to convince his co-voyager (a chain-smoker like Serling, a point driven home by the fact that this episode's only close-up is of a cigarette in Conrad's hand) that the milk of human kindness will flow even on Mars: "I've got a philosophy about people: They're the same all over." Then Serling slips in a single reference to the ongoing Biblical theme: "I'm sure when God made human beings, he developed them from a fixed formula." God as the ultimate scientist: a fusing of the two schools of thought that tragically would be lost early during the twenty-first century. Marcusson represents that side of Rod Serling that wants to go on believing in the goodness of man; Conrad, the other half. For he has seen firsthand, or read about, so many examples of man's dark side that his belief in human goodness has been tested.

The Time Element is introduced, as is a recurring focus on death. Marcusson, mortally wounded, begs Conrad to open the ship's door so he can peer out at this brave new world: "I don't want to die in here. I want to see what I'm dying for!" Importantly, his line indicates an ongoing belief in the meaning of life; even as he faces death, the man wants to witness what he accomplished, like Moses looking on the Promised Land he will not enter. Conrad, still terrified of what may be out there (an unknown race of beings or some variation on humans) tries to shush his friend, gasping: "There's plenty of time!" But there isn't. Marcusson expires without being granted his final wish. No sooner is he gone than Conrad becomes one of The Lonely: "Don't leave me alone," he begs of the corpse. A moment later, the ship's door slides open. In shadows, we notice silhouettes of the Martians. Like Conrad, we expect them to be as ugly as those in the second season's *Eye of the Beholder*, where people we expect to find attractive turn out to be monstrous.

That turnabout works in the opposite manner here. As the Martians step forward into the light, they appear gorgeous; particularly

Teenya (Susan Oliver), the woman surrounded by stately Martian men (Byron Morrow, Vic Perrin, and Vernon Gray). Looks, however, can be deceiving, in life as on *Zone*. Before this episode ends, we will grasp (as Serling often warns us) how inwardly ugly the most attractive specimens can be. We receive an advance hint of that title to come: beauty is not objective but subjective, existing only in the eye of the beholder. The Martians wear variations on Greco-Roman costuming. This effectively hints that we are to take them as advanced beings who cling to the tenets of western civilization as developed in Athens. They are intelligent, intellectual even, fans of truth, beauty, and (as Socrates emphasized) knowledge. One sticky problem in space travel tales (how will Earthlings and Martians communicate?) is solved in a single sentence: These beings have developed transference of thought so language is rendered irrelevant.

Setting the pace for a memorable ending, Serling's writing and Leisen's direction provide hints that all is not as it seems. Though the Martian men assure Conrad that he will not be harmed (clearly, they are sincere), a certain remoteness their manner creates audience anxiety. We may be surprised (on first viewing) by the final revelation (our hero in a gilded cage), but not shocked to learn that something cryptic was about to happen. In Fairman's short story, readers received no preparation for a similar conclusion. With Serling, we come full cycle: "You were right," Conrad screams out to his deceased partner, "people are the same everywhere!" We members of the human race have great potential for good but an equal propensity toward evil. The point is, we are not fated for one or the other, Serling suggests, but must choose between the two (again, our capacity for free will). The advanced intellect of the Martians does not free them from a Frank Buck ("bring 'em back alive!") mentality. They entrap animals of inferior intelligence, then put them behind bars for casual perusal. They won't viciously kill what they consider dumb beasts just as we resist slaying gorillas. That hardly stops mankind from capturing them for zoos even though evolution suggests that these are our closest relatives.

This is precisely how the Martians view Conrad, the height of animal evolution on Earth, if a giant step below these smarter creatures.

Here is where "Brothers Beyond the Void" concludes, ending on a negative note. Serling then adds his distinct signature. No matter how insensitive the male Martians appear, Teenya is conscience-stricken. Fairman's story ended with a group of Martians gawking at the captive. Serling adds an important bit: In the middle of the crowd, Teenya breaks into tears, turns, and rushes away. If we were to chart this character's path after the episode is over, she might become a radical protester. That certainly occurred on Earth, when a minority demanded the end of bars and cages. However scoffed at when this movement began in the mid-sixties, such thinking gradually spread; the old notion of caged zoos disappeared from the American scene. Perhaps Teenya will be back the next day with a sign attacking such unfair cruelty to dumb animals (Earthlings). In the *Zone*, things may be as bad as in real life. Yet Serling reminds us they can be changed for the better, in life as on *Zone*.

"Honey? I'm home!"

THE PARALLEL (3/14/63)

Serling here takes a concept already employed for *And When the Sky Was Opened* and further develops its themes, notably Identity Crisis. One "reading" of *The Parallel* is as a semi-prequel to *And When*. That show opened after three astronauts returned from a mission during which they lost contact with Earth; here we witness such a mission from the beginning. In the earlier story, Clegg Forbes (Rod Taylor) was *the lonely* once he grasped that the others were disappearing. Here Major Robert Gaines is lonely from the start, taking off on a one-man mission. *The Parallel* opens on a shot of his wife Helen (Jacqueling Scott) and daughter Maggie (Shari Lee Bernath), she one of many Magdalenes who inhabit the *Zone*.

When we do get to see Gaines (Steve Forrest), he's told by Colonel Connacher (Frank Aletter) that the superior officer called Helen to let her know the take-off is "on." Gaines response: "Bless you!" We shouldn't ignore the implications of Gaines' little joke: "Any messages for the angels?" He also offers to bring back one of their "gossamer wings." He might just be one more for the angels. Gaines will undergo an experience in space that resembles the way death appears to *Zone* visitors. First, though, we're introduced to the setting and supporting characters. The opening is one more "normal" suburban neighborhood. The buildings look vaguely familiar; it comes as no surprise to learn that director Alan Crosland, Jr. shot this on the same street used for earlier suburban-set *Zones*. The first dramatic event is one more recurring phone call, which may or may not in this case be Long Distance (Helen receiving Connacher's message). When she and Maggie head into their kitchen, we notice everything is typical, normal, average for the early 1960s.

This, despite Gaines being a famous astronaut. Again Serling collapses the unique and exceptional into the everyday and ordinary. Every bit as telling, Helen and Maggie watch the lift-off on TV, just like everyone else. One more *Zone* that qualifies as a television show about watching TV, the sequence ends with a jolt: Fearful for her husband, Helen snaps off the set as the countdown reaches zero. If Helen doesn't see the event, we do. Serling chose not to reuse that recurring flying saucer shot from *Forbidden Planet*. Everything here is grounded in reality. NASA footage of a rocket launching leaves no doubt that this is one of those rare cases when Serling did leave the realm of imaginative fiction behind to create full-blooded science fiction.

There will be no bug-eyed monsters here, no beautiful female aliens. *The Parallel* serves less as another universal parable than an accurate case study of what in 1963 seemed likely to occur during a manned flight of a type less than six years off. That qualifies this episode a predecessor of Stanley Kubrick's *2001: A Space Odyssey* (1967). The degree to which that filmmaker drew, consciously or otherwise, from memories of Serling is clear from his forever-famous shot, a close angle on astronaut Keir Dullea's face as he's shocked by a sudden burst of light. Gaines is struck by the light that often signifies death in *Zone*. Likely, he has not died, but undergone a near-death experience, justifying the image of him passing out midway through his experience.

We next see Gaines on a hospital bed, attended to by doctors and nurses. Crosland's lighting choice is effective. The hospital sequence opens in darkness, providing a perfect contrast to the blinding light with which the previous shot concluded. Most of what then takes place occurs in shadows, making it impossible to see the faces of the medical people. Unlike *Eye of the Beholder*, here the effect is abandoned after a minute. Still, the impact has been achieved: We sense that while all seems well, something strange has transpired.

If we've observed closely, we'll note a difference between the house we saw and the one Gaines returns to: There's a now white picket fence around it which he can't recall. In the next 24 hours, Gaines comes to realize other things are also different. He's a colonel, not a major. He tells his daughter not to put sugar in his coffee though he has always requested a teaspoon before.

Helen knows that this is not the man she married the moment that she kisses him. The implication, toned down for TV in that era, is that she discovered this when they made love. This is hinted at in what today seems mild but was daring at the time: an image of Gaines and his wife lying close together on their bed. All the while, officers at the base attempt to grasp how Gaines could have been out of contact for six hours, yet landed his craft without damage. "There's an explanation for everything," a man insists. We will hear one before long, though hardly the here-and-now rationale this realistically minded fellow hopes for, justifying the documentary approach at the beginning. What happened turns out to be so fantastical that, if this episode were not visually grounded in realism, it would be too weird to watch. But an anchor in actuality was there, so it works.

The hero becomes aware of his Identity Crisis while considering his Mirror Image. "I'm all right," he insists. "It's you people I'm worried about." Happily, he's one more humanist who cares more about others than himself. Viewers tend to accept Gaines's assessment (the crazy man is the sane one here) when he insists that John Kennedy is president, though no one else has ever heard that name. The romantic theme is also present. "Daddy, you're different," Maggie shouts out tearfully. From the mouths of babes . . . a young sage who cannot, like adults, remain silent about the truth. Finally, Gaines puts two and two together: "It's as if there were another world, parallel to ours. As if this world were a twin, except for some minor differences. Two

Earths; two sets of people" with the same names and similar identities. Even as Major Gaines took off from Earth I, so did Colonel
Gaines from Earth II. When that light appeared, things got mixed
up. The similar men from different Earths hit an invisible gateway
up there and traded places. A terrific concept, one "borrowed" for
countless sci-fi films to come (e.g. *Journey to the Far Side of the Sun*,
1969). Now Gaines must fix that.

All's well, in Serling as in Shakespeare, that ends well. "Do me
a favor, honey," Gaines says to Helen after re-arriving at his house
and finding no picket fence there, "tell me who I am?" The nostalgia theme is present. For once, the hero learns that he can go back
again. Gaines's last words as he, Helen, and Maggie step in to their
suburban American Dream home, is simple, optimistic, reassuring:
"It's good to be home!"

6

IT'S ABOUT TIME!:
Had We But World Enough . . .

ONE OF ROD'S scripts for Cincinnati's *The Storm* was called *Time Element*. A decade later, he rewrote that story as an hour-long drama. Though CBS brass considered it far too intellectual, producers Desi Arnaz and Bert Granet filmed the piece for *Westinghouse Playhouse*. The plot concerned psychiatrist Dr. Gillespie (Martin Balsam) analyzing patient Pete Jenson (William Bendix). Title aside, time travel was one of many future **Zone** themes introduced here. Recurring nightmares appear: Jenson dreams that he's transported back in time to Pearl Harbor on the eve of the bombing. Gillespie is intrigued that Jenson knows more about Honolulu in 1941 than any ordinary man would in 1958. Still on the couch, Jensen falls asleep, and dreams the dream once more. But it's Gillespie who wakes with a start, realizing that his "patient" only existed in his dream. When the doctor heads for a bar to buy a much-needed drink, he spots a framed photograph of Jenson on the wall. Inquiring, he's informed that the former bartender died at Pearl Harbor. Dreams, death, and a relationship between the two would soon serve as **Zone**'s essence. The glue that holds them together is time travel.

Apocalypse Now?

TIME ENOUGH AT LAST (11/20/59)

Time Enough may be read as *Where Is Everybody?* turned upside-down and backwards. The first **Zone** opened with Mike Ferris posited as entirely alone, ending with him rejoining the human community to his great relief. Here Henry Bemis (Burgess Meredith) is introduced as a man who exists within society, yet not of it. At the conclusion, he finds himself isolated, facing the infinity of solitude Ferris escaped from. Each protagonist's key line cinches the parallel as both installments reach their mid points: "Where is everybody?" Ferris shouts; "is someone there?" Bemis calls.

Bemis works as teller in a bank. To the chagrin of Mr. Carsville (Vaughn Taylor), Bemis is an avid reader who slips down to the vault during lunch hour. There, he forgets about food while consuming beloved literary works, Charles Dickens foremost among them. At home, Bemis's wife Helen (Jacqueline de Wit) also complains about his devotion to reading, not only great books but newspapers, and magazines, as well. The next day, directly defying his boss's orders, Bemis again sneaks down to the vault. As he reads a news headline about H-bombs destroying the world, a blast goes off. Shaken, Bemis crawls up and from the vault where, below the earth, the thick walls protected him. On the surface, the owl-eyed fellow discovers he's the last man on Earth. This references the title of a paperback Mike Ferris spotted on the drug store's metal rack.

Ferris's worst nightmare occurs, though Bemis perceives the situation as a dream come true. The little man in thick glasses takes delight in discovering the library intact. Myriad books, if scattered about, remain readable. He now has, as Serling put it, time enough at last or in the words of poet Andrew Marvell, world enough and time. Joyfully, Bemis sits down to read without interruption. His eyeglasses slip off, fall, smash on the concrete. "That's not fair," he whines. "Not fair!" At first glance, he seems correct. Bemis is one of those offbeat guys Serling ordinarily adores: the individualists, eccentrics, eggheads who made the Eisenhower era's conformists feel uncomfortable. Why then does the author suggest we ought to take pleasure in Henry Bemis's fate?

Toward the first season's end, Serling would recreate Henry Bemis in *Mr. Bevis* (6/3/60), a pilot for a possible series not picked up by CBS. The opening narration, written and recited by Serling, posits the character in a positive light: "In the parlance of the twentieth century, this is an oddball." Bevis's taste in literature connects him to Bemis, as we're told that Dickens rates high. Like Bemis, Bevis is "accident prone" and "a little vague." Yet we are meant to love Bevis; since he and Bemis have so much in common, why shouldn't we feel the same about Bemis? It's not fair! Actually, it is, once we determine what this moral fable is about. Serling conceived Henry Bemis not as an edgy protagonist, to be admired, but a cautionary figure whose attitudes must be avoided if the viewer is to learn from this episode.

Bemis and Bevis are not identical. Bevis incarnates the bumbling nerd-hero, a man we root for while he attempts to survive among the suburban crowd. Bemis is the opposite, a "little fellow" not only in size, but in spirit: mean, cold, selfish. He's a villain, not the protagonist, although he's an offbeat, appealing one. The key distinction is made clear by Serling's description of Bevis: however out of synch with everyday reality, "without him, without his warmth, his kindness, the world would be a considerably poorer place, albeit perhaps a little saner." Bemis's only "passion" is "the printed page." He cares not a whit for what Serling informs us is most important: humanity and a commitment to others. Eccentricity is not necessarily admirable, nor should it be disparaged. The ultimate test of one's worth is: humanism.

And Man Must Have His Mate:

TWO (9/15/61)

Written and directed by Montgomery Pittman, *Two* encapsulates virtually all *Zone* themes. As in the final moments of *Time Enough*, we view a world ruined by atomic war; as with *Third from the Sun*, we encounter a handful of survivors. If *The Lonely* could be considered a two-character drama, *Two* is precisely that. As there, the viewer meets a man and a woman (this female is flesh and blood) who come to need each other. *I Shot an Arrow* pondered whether civilized human community would give way to rugged individualism on the lowest level, as does *Two*. Finally, we recall *People Are the Same All Over*, acknowledging that while humans share instincts, emotions, and ideas, we each possess free will to make important choices as to how we will behave. Similar to *Third from the Sun*, *Two* begins darkly only to conclude with oncoming brightness; while the script is by another author, *Two* also expresses Serling's own ongoing guarded optimism.

"The time; perhaps a hundred years from now, or this may have, already happened two million years ago." As George Lucas would state at the beginning of *Star Wars*: "Long, long ago, in a galaxy far, far away." A fable can be set in both the future and the past. First, a young woman (Elizabeth Montgomery) in military garb reaches a devastated metropolis. This tale involving two people focuses on she before he, allowing for a proto-feminist aspect. A rugged fellow (Charles Bronson) happens upon her. She instinctually struggles, he knocks her down . . . only to offer her the food he's found as they, following several setbacks, set aside old enmities, which now seem absurd. Together they attempt to recreate something akin to civilization. The man (ape-like Bronson embodies the Missing Link) speaks English, while the woman utters only one word in Russian. We watch a mostly silent drama, concentrating on facial gestures and body language to grasp what they think or feel. There's an anti-cliché playing of the incidents: the simian man turns out to be gentle; the lovely woman, barbaric. Pittman defies all gender clichés.

Each character must choose between rah-rah jingoism and an inward sense of right and wrong. If fate throws them together, free will determines whether they'll kill or kiss. Though their lips never meet (more an admirable subtlety than a dramatic omission), he and she manage sweet smiles. "This has been a love story," Serling insists in his briefest wrap-up, "about two people who found each other in *The Twilight Zone*." They walk away, a new Adam and Eve (or possibly the originals). No longer The Lonely, they will try to survive—together. Their chances are good. They have, if with difficulty, made the all-important human connection.

The Time Tunnel:

BACK THERE (1/13/61)

Traditionally, science fiction writers have assumed one of two approaches to time travel: No matter what a visitor may do while back there, all will inevitably turn out the same as before as this is where events necessarily led; the intrusion of a traveler into the past automatically alters everything, so the accidental transforms the future into a totally different world. The former theory is fatalistic, while the latter leaves a doorway open for free will's impact. As always, Serling offers his own approach, an intriguing compromise between those extremes.

On April 14, 1961, a number of solid Washingtonians gather at their gentleman's club. "Nothing could prevent (a time traveler) from altering the course of history," one insists. Others challenge him, claiming that such an intrusion could radically change the present. The group's youngest member, engineer Peter Corrigan (Russell Johnson), leaves for home, bidding good night to William (Bartlett Robinson), an elderly attendant. Director David Orrick McDearmon blurs the image; Corrigan, we sense, has slipped into the *Zone*, the date now April 14, 1865. Peter wanders postwar Washington just hours before Lincoln's assassination. Can he prevent it? Peter, our audience surrogate, rushes to Ford's theatre, bangs on the stage door, screams for those within to do something. Assuming that he's a lunatic, they call the police. Corrigan is handed over to a benefactor (John Lasell) who calls himself "Wellington." But this is John Wilkes Booth, who heard of Corrigan's wild ramblings, and hopes to muzzle a man who might upset the plans.

Before Corrigan can guess his host's identity, Booth serves him a drugged drink. Back at the police station a serious-minded officer (James Gavin) refuses to follow orders when his Sergeant (Paul Hartman) insists that Corrigan should not be taken seriously. Tracking him down, the officer comes upon the awakening Corrigan. They are ready to try to prevent the tragedy when crying on the streets alerts them to the fact that they're too late. Is the future then set in cement?

The episode does not end there, or with Corrigan realizing that he's returned to the present. Re-entering the club, Corrigan notices that William isn't in his usual place by the door. He's surprised to now find William seated among the wealthy.

The one policeman who had tried to help was considered such a hero that he became police chief. That put his offspring in a loftier position, so William—descended from him—did not become an attendant, but a club member. Serling sums it all up: "a journey into time with highly questionable results." For "on the one hand" Corrigan proved that "the threads of history are woven tightly and the skein of events cannot be undone." This is but the first half of Serling's thesis. For "there are small fragments of tapestry that can be altered." Serling resolves the poles of fate and free will; life (like this story) combines the two. Serling also includes a "ticket" at the end. Trying to decide if he's been dreaming or has gone mad (two key *Zone* themes), Corrigan reaches into his pocket and finds a handkerchief with the initials J.W.B. embossed on it. How could this have been a delusion when he has "ocular proof"?

Tomorrow and Tomorrow and Tomorrow:

NO TIME LIKE THE PAST (3/7/63)

This 60-minute fourth-season episode rates not only as a valid final statement on the subject of time travel, but a necessary one in terms of all that had appeared before it. The tone of its bittersweet conclusion, ably realized by director Justin Addiss, reassesses Serling's earlier ideology. Paul Driscoll (Dana Andrews) prepares to journey back in time on a humanistic mission. As with Greek tragedy, the ill-fated idealist hero has a rational companion who will challenge his impossible dream. Driscoll converses with friend Harvey (Robert F. Simon), who warns him against returning to the past—even to try to accomplish great things, as what's already happened is inviolable. Yet Driscoll insists on trying and Harvey expresses compassion for this good man who "does not care for the twentieth century." As if

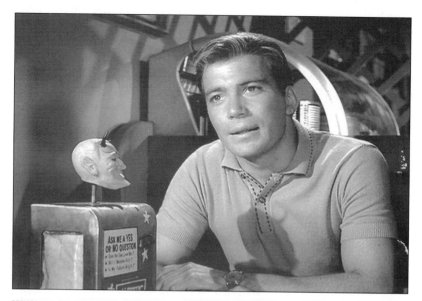

William Shatner, future star of TV's "other" legendary imaginative fantasy/sci-fi series, *Star Trek*, received his introduction to this genre in a pair of classic **Zones**: *Nightmare at 20,000 Feet* and *Nick of Time*.

What the poet Wordsworth would have called the "primal sympathy" of a modern suburbanite (Gig Young) is stirred as he witnesses his own former self (Michael Montgomery) during a summer-long Song of Innocence in *Walking Distance*.

Broken glass will mirror the emotional state of many *Zone* visitors including Robert Cummings as a lost (in every sense of that term) air force pilot in *King Nine Will Not Return.*

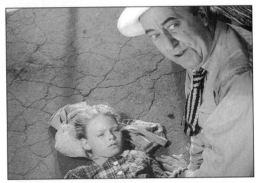

One of life's lovable losers (Ed Wynn) proves himself worthy of heaven by caring more about the life of a child (Dana Dillaway) than he does his own in *One For the Angels.*

Once again, the concept of watching TV to escape from real-life is suggested as Robert Duvall dreams of entering a highly romanticized notion of the past that's enshrined within a doll house's screen in *Miniature.*

Dean Stockwell plays both the American and Japanese WWII officers in *The Quality of Mercy*.

Throughout *The Lonely*, we are never certain if Jack Warden's title character has a night-time fantasy that a spaceship is headed his way, or if his dream of such an event is actually about to occur.

Always at the heart of **Zone** is the man-woman relationship, a need to make that conventional arrangement work no matter how difficult the circumstances: In *Two*, former enemies (Charles Bronson and Elizabeth Montgomery) set aside their former differences to become a couple in the post-apocalyptic world.

The concept of film noir—a cinema of darkness in which lone wolves walk the mean streets of some asphalt jungle—dominated Hollywood films during the postwar era. In *The Four Of Us Are Dying*, **Zone** brought that vision to the small screen; Harry Townes as one of the four.

A student of Freud, Serling and director Richard L. Bare employed the physical concept of a broken mirror to visually portray the shattering of his hero's (William Reynolds) psyche in *The Purple Testament.*

Zone provided a modernist equivalent to the work of Lewis Carroll; a small, seedy loser (Joe Mantell) discovers there's something beyond that odd wall-mirror in *Nervous Man in a Four Dollar Room.*

Once again, a mirror image outwardly displays the way in which the central character feels inside: Mickey Rooney in *Last Night of a Jockey*.

The last remains of the title character are about to be scattered by the wind, even as he passes from the memory of man, in *Long Live Walter Jameson*.

At the same time that she incarnated "Catwoman" on the *Batman* TV series, Julie Newmar sported horns for her role as a deliciously duplicitous temptress in *Of Late I Think of Cliffordville* with Albert Salmi.

An old-time gunfighter (Dan Duryea) falls prey to alcoholism in *Mr. Denton on Doomsday*; Rod employed the episode to de-romanticize TV's cowboy heroes.

A seemingly all-powerful alien invader finds himself vulnerable to the sound of music in *Hocus Pocus and Frisby.*

Dennis Hopper as a bush-league would-be American Führer in *He's Alive.*

The ugliest girl in the world (Maxine Stuart) nervously awaits an operation that may make her look presentable in *Eye of the Beholder*.

Man (William Shatner) meets monster (Nick Cravat) in *Nightmare at 20,000 Feet*—or does the gremlin exist only in the disturbed hero's mind?

For a spiritual sensibility to survive in the scientific age, the secular humanist finds evidence of God in the good that humanity is capable of achieving; *Zone*'s recurring image of warmly held hands (here from *Nothing in the Dark*) would, a generation later, inspire the logo for Steven Spielberg's most acclaimed film, *Schindler's List*.

granted three wishes by a genie (after all, what is science-fiction but a modern re-imagination of ancient mythic fantasy?), Driscoll visits three catastrophes he'd like to help mankind avoid.

First comes the bombing of Hiroshima. Driscoll approaches a Japanese police captain (James Yagi), trying to convince the man to evacuate his city. Believing Driscoll to be crazy or an American spy, the captain does not act; the bomb falls even as it would have without Driscoll's arrival. Most striking here is Serling's humanism. Driscoll could have (like the hero of *The Time Element*) tried to save American lives, but it's Asian lives the decent American, untroubled by ethnicity, hopes to protect. The captain turns out to be surprisingly sympathetic, asking the American to "remember that the voice of the enemy is not without compassion." When the bomb hits, the image cuts to a framed photograph of the captain's wife and child. This tugs on an audience's heartstrings, racial issues set aside.

The second mission involves an even more complex moral issue, as Driscoll ponders saving many lives by ending one. In Nuremberg at the time of Hitler's mid-1930s Nazi rally, Driscoll rents a hotel room with plans of assassinating the Fuehrer before his evil regime can emerge. Serling does not didacticize about whether it's moral to kill under such circumstances. Instead he provides what might be called a mimetic approach: Rod makes his statement through the drama that provides a complex meaning rather than simple message. When Driscoll assembles his rifle and pulls the trigger, the gun fails to fire. Zicree misreads this as a "test run," complaining: "No assassin in his right mind would get his intended victim centered in the cross hairs (of his sights) without intending to fire." He errs in assuming that Driscoll purposefully slipped in a dead slug. The look on Driscoll's face makes clear that he's in shock. This was a real bullet that turned out to be dud. Here, our hero's mental transformation begins: Perhaps the gun failed because some higher power deemed that, in the greater scheme of things, it was not supposed to fire. History has to happen as it did, however much we resent evil events. The metaphysical theme has already been raised. When the Japanese captain inquired if Driscoll's plea constituted a request, he answered: "More in the nature of a prayer."

A third, equally unsuccessful attempt to change the course of history (warning the Lusitania before a German sub can sink it in 1907) also fails. Driscoll segues home, convinced that Harvey was right: "I believe (now) that it is impossible to alter the past." He serves as the author's spokesman, illuminating Serling's vision. At that point, what we have experienced is essentially one more half-hour time travel show.

Following a commercial break we segue into a *Willoughby* scenario, only with a world-wise hero. Driscoll now heads for Homeville, Indiana. "I'm going back in time," he decides, to 1881, "not to change anything" but to become "a part of it," to live out his life on Main Street, a preferable alternative to modern times, which Driscoll (again the author's spokesman) considers "bedlam," a "cesspool." Like Martin Sloan or Gart Williams, Paul longs for band concerts, fourth of July parades and picnics, a calliope softly playing, and an icy glass of lemonade on a front porch some sultry summer night. Again the voice of reason, Harvey fears that this will fare no better. "Everything is cause and effect," Harvey vainly warns in his best scientific voice. When that doesn't work, Harvey grows spiritual: "Heaven help you, Paul!"

No sooner has Driscoll entered the town than his promise to not alter things is tested, for this is the day before the assassination of President James Garfield. "It begins," Driscoll gasps. "Right away, it begins!" Echoing Macbeth, he repeats three times: "It's tomorrow, *tomorrow*, tomorrow!" Wanting to help but knowing from experience that this can't work he (barely) controls himself. At a pleasant boarding house, Driscoll meets Abigail (Patricia Breslin), a pretty, intelligent, sensitive school teacher. She senses something otherworldly about the deep-thinking stranger, guessing him to be some religious figure rather than a time/space traveler. Perhaps the two are one and the same, recalling Robert Wise's *The Day the Earth Stood Still* (1951), with its gentle carpenter (Michael Rennie) arriving on Earth, his journey a Second Coming. Here, though, is where Driscoll's unsentimental education begins, for Serling's latest alter-ego realizes that the good ol' days weren't so good after all. Fourth-season characters, like the man who created them, achieve greater maturity than than their predecessors.

At dinner, Driscoll listens to the insufferable tirades of a banker named Hanford (Robert Cornthwaithe). An opinionated fool, he rants about the need for American imperialism in what *Time*'s Henry Luce in real life hailed as "The American Century," forcing Driscoll to grasp that everything wrong with his world derived from forces already at work in what only seemed a kinder, gentler era. Abigail is the exception. Serling's anti-war (though not anti-military) position becomes clear when Driscoll rails at Harford and other "armchair warriors" who send young men out to fight and die for questionable goals. When Driscoll realizes that he doesn't fit in here any more than in his own century, Abigail tags him as standing "on the outside, looking in." That well describes the author's self-image.

But Driscoll's final test is yet to come. Before arriving, he read that a fire in the schoolhouse will leave twelve children seriously burned. The incident will begin when a runaway horse and wagon sends a kerosene lamp flying into the building. Driscoll now feels pushed to the limit. We know from previous time travel episodes that major events can't be altered. Yet things insignificant in the grand scheme were changed in *Back There*. Garfield, like Lincoln, can't be saved; that, in a Biblical sense, is "written." But what about the lives of those kids? Though Driscoll initially plans to let fate take its course, he loves humanity (particularly children) so much that he can't hold back. Hurrying to the schoolhouse, Driscoll notices a wagon with a kerosene lamp. Grasping that this likely will cause the fire, he desperately pleads with the owner (Malcolm Atterbury) to detach the horses. When the man refuses, Driscoll tries to do so, causing the animals to panic and run loose. The lantern hits the building and the fire begins. Attempting to prevent a tragedy, Driscoll causes it.

Again we note the similarity to Greek mythology in general, Oedipus in particular. Upon hearing a terrible prediction (Oedipus will kill his father and marry his mother), the man named for his swollen feet ran away from home to avoid this, inadvertently bringing it about. Man, Oedipus learned too late, is not the measure of all things. The road to hell can be lined with good intentions, for Driscoll as well. Apparently, Serling didn't believe this when his series premiered.

Early on he insisted that one's personal future could change due to free will if major historical events remain inviolate. Four years later, Rod's vision has altered. Little things can't be changed, not even when the motivation is purely humanistic. This paradigm is more profound, less naive than Serling's earlier one.

"I shouldn't have come here," Driscoll tells Abigail as they kiss goodbye. "I know about too many tomorrows." He heads back to the twentieth century, like Serling realizing that his earlier position represented hubris. Humbled, Driscoll not only understands but accepts that a Force in the universe makes all such decisions. If its choices strike us as questionable, that's because we mere mortals can't envision their full scope. Driscoll returns to the place "where I belong." Here is the only place a traveler through the *Zone* can go home again to, the one he never should have left. If that ending sounds dark, that's not the case. Driscoll, when we leave him, hasn't become embittered to the point of stasis. One more guarded optimist, he's inspired to again try to enact "good," if in a more constructive way. Though Paul Driscoll will never again try to alter yesterday, he will dutifully work to better our common tomorrow.

That Magnificent Man in His Flying Machine:

THE LAST FLIGHT (2/5/60)

The Last Flight was the first non-Serling script to go into production. However much guidance Serling gave Richard Matheson during the writing process, or whether he performed a final tweaking of the script before director William Claxton began to shoot, may never be known. What we sense while watching is that even if Serling didn't write this one, it would be easy to believe he did. Creator-producer-writer Rod Serling rates as the original television auteur because, though a team effort, *Zone* consistently expresses his point of view.

Our opening image is of an American air base in France. The time is "the present," when the episode was shot (1959). Jets are everywhere. Then from the sky a WWI Nieuport, circa 1916, descends. To the amazement of military personnel, out hops Flight Leutenant. Decker (Kenneth Haigh). A cocky young man, Decker strikes everyone as an imposter or a freak. But he wins over Major Wilson (Simon Scott), particularly after Decker breaks down upon learning that his one-time squadron mate Mackaye, now (in 1959) an elderly air marshal, will arrive. That can't be, Decker insists. Why? Wilson asks. "Because he's dead," Decker sobs. Like other *Zone* heroes, Decker is "hopelessly lost" in space and time. He qualifies as one of The Lonely even after re-joining the human community.

The idea of flight in general ("the miracle of flight," and the air force in particular) evoke Serling's deepest interests. Decker's earlier disappearance into a strange cloud recalls numerous *Zones* in which black holes and invisible doorways allow for entrances of aliens and exits by Earthlings. Then again, the piece also connects to Matheson's own great gifts and ongoing vision. The cloud looks precisely like the one that passes over Grant Williams in *The Incredible Shrinking Man*. His dialogue rings with psychology:

WILSON: Why are you so afraid of meeting Mackaye?
DECKER: I'm not afraid—not afraid of anything!

Precisely the opposite proves true; Decker's unconvincing words convey denial. For that matter, he's afraid of everything. In a confessional tone, Decker admits to Wilson that he and Mackaye, as young men, flew side by side while German planes attacked. Decker panicked and tore off, leaving Mackaye to likely die. A moment later, Decker passed through a strange cloud and "couldn't hear" anymore, his sight (that recurring theme) also blocked out. As Decker makes that statement, director Claxton captures this man peering through Venetian blinds, out the window at midday. The image allows for the strange light so often associated with death to appear on Decker's face, although in this instance it's difficult to tell whether it's the metaphysical light of doom or a realistic ray of sunlight. Either way, Decker wants someone—anyone!—to believe him when he admits that he deserted the friend he once nicknamed "Old Leadbottom" and then somehow found himself here:

WILSON: Such a thing doesn't happen every day.
DECKER: Well, it happened today!

Wilson notes that Mackaye not only survived, but went on to become an even greater hero during the second World War. Thanks to his courage thousands of Brits survived the Blitz. Guilt-stricken, Decker admits, "I'm a coward!" Though he joined the air force to be a hero, Decker buckled. Again we encounter a theme from numerous Serling scripts about war, including realistic dramas (see Introduction). Wilson tells Decker that "it isn't a crime to be afraid," the theme of *The Sergeant*. As to Mackaye's living through it all:

WILSON: Maybe he got help somehow.
DECKER: (eyes lighting up with understanding) Maybe it wasn't an accident that I landed here. Maybe I was sent here for a *reason*.

Time, he realizes, has given him *Zone*'s second chance. This allows Decker to overcome all his fears. He runs back to his plane, takes off, disappears into that cloud . . . shortly, elderly Mackaye (Robert Warwick) arrives. When questioned about the bygone incident, Mackaye recalls that he did indeed believe Decker deserted him when that flyer rushed off. Then Decker came roaring down out of a cloud, firing away, taking down three enemy planes before they got him.

As Serling sensed after analyzing *Where Is Everybody?*, there must be a "ticket" for the final punch. The best *Zones* contain two tickets (Serling's equivalent of a double MacGuffin in Hitchcock), which is the case here. Wilson and General Harper (Alexander Scourby) show a stunned Mackaye Decker's personal belongings, seized after he landed. That, Mackaye notes, explains why the Germans didn't return these to the British as usual during World War I. Also, Wilson knows that Decker's nickname for Mack was "Old Leadbottom," though that was a private joke between the two friends.

The scenario jells with *Zones* early notion of time travel. Can a single man's free will change the past? Yes and no. Decker does go back and save Mack. But that occurs because Mack was fated to be saved; "a power greater than we can comprehend" (*Romeo and Juliet*) took matters into his hands, proving that cowards and heroes are not different types of people, but the same man at alternate moments. Serling quotes Hamlet and repeats the Bard's words for emphasis: "There are more things in heaven and earth . . . than are dreamt of in your philosophy."

You Can't Go Home Again:

THE ODYSSEY OF FLIGHT 33 (2/24/61)

Though Rod Serling is listed in the credits as the sole author, this episode was a family affair. Older brother Robert, professional writer on the subject of aviation for UPI Washington, traveled west for a visit. At about the same time he arrived, so did an offer from American Airlines to rent a mock-up of a 707 passenger cabin to any studio. So Rod seized on the idea for this episode and asked Bob (credited as Executive Producer) to supply accurate "cockpit dialogue." This struck Bob as ridiculous, since the plot (while flying from London to New York, a plane picks up a weird tail wind and hurtles back in time) struck him as impossible. Still, he consulted a friend who worked for TWA; their contributions, incorporated into Rod's scenario, made for a classic. The reason why the great revelation just before the midpoint (a brontosaurus where midtown Manhattan ought to be) works is because the episode is grounded in details of specific reality.

As John Anderson (the episode's lead actor) would recall, years later a pilot from United recognized him and admitted: "Sometimes up there during a long flight, you do get crazy thoughts like what happened" on that show. Within this straightforward story's narrative, Rod slips in several ongoing themes. "I felt something," Captain Farver (Anderson) announces to his crew when the plane picks up a freak air stream and passes through time. He repeats this, lending the phrase extra emphasis, implying meaning beyond the obvious. Several crew members echo his words, as does one passenger. When all grasp what's happened, the captain insists,"nothing in logic can explain it." Throughout *Zone*, Rod presented scientifically minded characters thrust into situations that can't be comprehended in rational terms. We must return to a more primitive form of understanding as emotions override ideas and heart overwhelms head if we are to accept, if never completely grasp, each such strange event.

No wonder then that while the first half of *Odyssey* is dominated by highly realistic technical jargon, such talk disappears after they spot the brontosaurus. Now the characters revert to an earlier form of speech, in which spirituality proves more significant to survival. They may all be dead, for that bizarre light appears. That's debatable. Other aspects are not, including their chosen words. "What," Farver exclaims, "in the name of everything holy is going on?" He attempts to return to the present by reentering the air pocket. When they descend once more, the New York skyline becomes apparent below. But exaltation is short-lived; the airport has never heard of a "jet." What occurs is the opposite of what we witnessed in *The Last Flight*: Farver considers landing in 1939, where the World's Fair (which opened the gates to our modern scientific age) is in full swing.

"We came back," Farver informs the passengers, but "dear God, not far enough!" Unlike Lieutenant Decker, Farver decides not to land. He brings his plane, low on fuel, up once more, willing to risk all on the gamble that perhaps this time they'll "go home" again. Now all logic/science must be cast to the wind. Following Farver's act of free will, those aboard surrender their fates to a higher power and hope it proves benign. Farver's final words to his flock are "Remain calm . . . and pray!" Is there a reason why this happened? They (and we) don't know. We do sense that they will succeed or fail, live or die in accordance with some master plan. The good Lord works in mysterious ways, the old saying goes. As does the Force that controls the *Zone*. For the crew and passengers, ideas are rendered as worthless as emotions. They must rely on the most basic of human ideologies: faith.

Chasing History:

THE 7ᵀᴴ IS MADE UP OF PHANTOMS

Serling returned to the Western with this time travel tale about three contemporary members of the National Guard (Ron Foster, Warren Oates, and Randy Boone) assigned to engage in war games on June 24 and 25. The event is scheduled for rural Montana, near the fork where the Big Horn river runs into the Little Big Horn. The episode doesn't open on them, however. On June 24, 1876, two of General Custer's troopers along with a civilian scout happen across a teepee and then skirmish with Native Americans. Those modern guardsmen, just beyond the next hill, hear shots and wander over, confused. They, too, notice the remains of a small Sioux encampment, although no one is in sight. Gradually, the guardsmen realize that by following the precise trail the 7th Cavalry took on its route to attack Sitting Bull's camp, they have become linked with history. Then, step by step, they are drawn back in time to that bloody Sunday. At first they resist. In time, the three accept their fate, guns blazing.

Later, their initially dubious captain (Robert Bray) discovers that three of his men have disappeared. He grimaces, accepts what has happened as an incomprehensible truth, and wishes they'd taken a tank along: "It would have helped!" Then he notices that, on the Memorial's list of the dead, his missing guardsmen's names are included: The final irony, twist, and (in *Zone*'s vernacular) "ticket."

Numerous elements, as envisioned by Serling and realized by director Alan Crosland, Jr., qualify *The 7th* as a legitimate and unique time travel piece. One aspect of its success is that we never see the Sioux, not even in the prologue. This allows us to decide for ourselves whether (in this case) the Native Americans are there or if the guardsmen have succumbed to shared hysteria and, having convinced one another that the battle along the Rosebud rages forever on these two days in June, surrendered to a fantasy so strong that, for them, it must be considered real. Whenever the guardsmen hear war cries, such sounds are preceded by the wind, allowing individual viewers to decide if, in the recesses of their minds, the men transform natural contemporary noises into evidence of the ghosts of the Sioux. Sight also works in this manner. The only thing the guardsmen ever see is a riderless horse hurrying by. Is it a runaway, its owner killed by one the guardsmen who, panicky, fired in that direction? Or is it one of the wild horses that still roam here? That is left open. As in episodes as different from this as *The Parallel*, the men lose walkie-talkie contact with headquarters: One more Long Distance Call that does not connect, as modern machinery fails and people are left to their own devices. That this is a 1963 (rather than 1959) episode becomes clear when we note that a lieutenant (Greg Morris) at the base is African American. The civil rights movement, initiated shortly before *Zone* began, has (finally!) made itself felt on network TV, thanks to Serling.

A modern person's relationship to history is given a characteristic Serling spin as the guardsmen realize that over the next hill, they will enter into the massacre:

> **CPL. LANGSFORD:** You going to stop it?
> **SGT. CONNERS:** Or join it.

Free will allows them to enter the fray; fate decides the outcome. "It's like chasing history," Conners notes, "and trying to change it." Yet as previous *Zones* have made clear, try as we might we cannot achieve the latter. Even if they had, as the captain muses, taken the tank along, it couldn't have altered Custer's battle. The unanswered question posed by discovery of their names on the marker is essential to Serling's way. Did they arbitrarily find themselves at the wrong place at the wrong time? Or were they drawn back, their names added to that marker by some divine force at work in the universe? Or might this have been their destiny? If the latter were the case, their names had existed on the list since 1876: Their arrival constituted the only way the Force could draw them back to where they were always supposed to have been.

Zicree condescendingly points out that Serling "takes for granted that Custer's men are on the side of the good." This reduces the piece to one more example of the old "Cavalry vs. 'Injuns' mentality." The fallacy in such reasoning derives from the flaw of holding singular artists to the dictates of what has come to be called politically correct thinking. Nowhere does Serling suggest the 7th is "good" or right, Indians bad or wrong. Rod had long since become a pacifist, hating and despising all war, the one depicted here included. As a veteran, however, he never challenged the integrity of a soldier on either side. He fashioned this *Zone* as a tribute to the fighting men he knew firsthand, the universal soldier. Admiring those who make the ultimate sacrifice is not akin to admiring the conflict itself. Or even to take their side. In *The Quality of Mercy*, Serling humanized the Japanese he had himself fought. That hardly implies that he believed their cause was right.

Sentimental Value:

A SHORT DRINK FROM A CERTAIN FOUNTAIN (12/13/63)

Poetic justice of a sardonic sort visits an insincere wife in *A Short Drink*. Flora Gordon (Ruta Lee) is a gorgeous former chorus girl plucked out of the line by a love-struck older man, her now-husband Harmon (Patrick O'Neal). She berates him for not keeping up with her crazy lifestyle owing to oncoming infirmity. Harmon begs his scientist brother Raymond (Walter Brooke) for a youth serum no human has yet taken. Shortly Harmon looks as fit and handsome as he did at thirty. Unfortunately, the potion doesn't stop there—Harmon is soon little more than a baby. Flighty Flora, if she's to retain her husband's money, must now become a more serious person, giving up her walks on the wild side to attend to this needy child.

Many *Zone* elements are present, including topicality. When the first episodes aired in 1959, young people were seen dancing the lindy hop, considered radical then. Now they twist and, in so doing, render that previous dance old-fashioned. Significant too is unconditional love. We can sympathize with Harmon because he takes the potion not out of a selfish desire to be young again, but sincere love for Flora. The only reason his brother (who bears a strong resemblance, in physicality and psychology, to Serling's brother Robert) allows Harmon to sip from that "certain fountain" is because if he is denied, Harmon plans to kill himself. As Harmon stares down at the cement below from Raymond's penthouse, we can almost hear him whisper "To be or not to be . . ."

Harmon is a typical Serling hero. His wife (who recalls sarcastic Mrs. Sloan in *Willoughby*) laughs at her "boring" husband's desire to "go to a band concert in the park." Harmon tells his brother that Flora, flaws aside, is "the only thing on God's earth I care about." No wonder Raymond puts his trust (and faith) in something out there, hoping for a "miracle." Ray's biggest concern is how the serum will impact on Harmon's mind. Mirror Images abound; Harmon tries to grasp his inner identity by studying what he looks like. As to mythology, the last image of Flora director Bernard Girard offers has her headed for the bedroom, where she will attempt to love a man who is now husband and son to her: Oedipus Redux.

A Certain Fountain also allows Rod to answer critics who found him, like other popular artists from Walt Disney to Steven Spielberg, too "sentimental." The charge isn't fair in any of those cases; Serling speaks for them all as he dismisses the claim. Flora drops and breaks a small item on the table. The piece has no financial value, but means a great deal to Harmon as it was his mother's. "Sentimental value," he sighs, before castigating Flora—"a word you may not understand"—which momentarily posits her as one of Serling's critics. Harmon/Serling explain what the word actually means: the capacity to love. That, or a lack of it, is the source of judgment for every character who entered the *Zone*.

Properly understood, sentiment signifies something altogether different from sentimentality. A writer can be charged with lapsing into sentimentality if in his work he tries too hard and yet fails to achieve the desired emotions. In such cases, the receiver laughs at those very points when the writer wants him to cry. The beauty of Serling's work (as well as those other aforementioned artists): we do experience what Spielberg refers to as an "up-cry," allowing us to smile (but never laugh) through our tears. The multitudes react precisely as those artists hoped they would, qualifying their work as successful. Sentimentality might best be defined as an (awkward) excess of feeling; sentiment implies the (perfect) presence of it. Serling's stories do indeed include sentiment. That hardly means that the effect of his (or Disney's, or Spielberg's) work in any way degenarates into sentimental.

7

THE UNDISCOVERED COUNTRY:
Death in the Fifth Dimension

ROD SERLING'S ATTITUDE on death might be thought of as the opposite of Dylan Thomas's. That Welsh bard's advice on the subject: "Do not go gentle into that good night. Cling to life at all costs." Serling's approach more resembles that of Sir James Barrie, whose Peter Pan grows melancholy while considering the setting sun in Never-never-land, that Victorian bard's equivalent of the fifth dimension. Everyone around Pan wishes they could, like him, remain forever young, as another Dylan might phrase it. Pan knows better, sensing that life is but a prelude to Shakespeare's undiscovered country, which he alone will never explore. So Peter sighs wistfully: "What a great adventure it would be to die!" *Zone* characters begin their stories feeling much the same as Dylan Thomas. By the end, each accepts death as a release from life's travails.

The Hollywood Hallucination:

THE SIXTEEN-MILLIMETER SHRINE (10/23/59)

The Sixteen-Millimeter Shrine offers an abbreviated version of *Sunset Boulevard* (1950). Norma Desmond (Gloria Swanson) in Billy Wilder's classic gives way to Barbara Jean Trenton (Ida Lupino), yet another self-imprisoned hermit in a fading Hollywood mansion. Like Norma, Trenton endlessly watches her old films, dreaming about the past. She visits the studio in hope of convincing a producer, Marty Sall (Ted de Corsia), to let her play ingénues again. At the finale, Trenton even parades down her staircase, dressed to the hilt, for one final bow. Serling allows for imaginative fiction in his version by having Trenton achieve what earthbound Norma could only dream of: Serling's faded star dissolves into a silver screen.

When Trenton literally slips into her alternative (and preferable) world, she leaves behind a handkerchief for her loyal agent Danny Weiss (Martin Balsam). Here we encounter another example of the ticket Rod failed to include in *Where Is Everybody?* In Barbara Trenton, we meet a character who, like Lew Bookman in *One for the Angels*, grasps that death should not to be feared. Alcohol is as problematic an escape for her as for the leads in *A Passage for Trumpet* and *The Dummy.* Trenton longs for a bygone world she believes to have been better than the one emerging in the 1950s with its rock 'n' roll, impolite actors in torn T-shirts, sweat instead of sentiment at the movies, and glamour giving way to grit.

Trenton misses the way things were in 1930s Hollywood as much as Martin Sloan in *Walking Distance* yearns for the charm of his old small town. A predecessor to Gart Williams in *Willoughby*, she is the first **Zone** visitor who's too far gone to crawl back to reality with a wiser view. Despite warnings from her agent who insists that memories are "nostalgic, nice—but *not true*," and despite Trenton's face-off with her once-handsome leading man, Jerry Hearndan (Jerome Cowan), now a grocery store owner (shades of Serling's father), Trenton can't handle reality. Like Williams, though, she dies with a smile on her face. Life had become for her a living death; death allows an escape into a wonderful alternative.

The first shot of Barbara Trenton features "the image of a woman looking at a picture." *Looking*, as **Zone**'s consistent focus on observing eyes makes clear, is what the series is about, essential to episodes as diverse as *The Eye of the Beholder* and *The Masks.* We note Serling's Disney-like belief that "when you wish upon a star, your dreams come true!" "If I wish hard enough," Trenton sighs, closing her eyes, "it will all go away." Her projector pours out old movie images; not the past as it was but a lovely idealization. "I wish I could be up there with them. Oh, how I wish!" For Serling as for Disney, a dream is a wish your heart makes. Trenton then glances out from the screen at a stunned Marty Sall; she smiles, waves. Though it takes him a while,

Sall manages a return smile. The lesson to be learned: We need not fear death. If the individual proves deserving, one's necessary journey to the undiscovered country will lead to a better place.

One for the Devils:

THE FOUR OF US ARE DYING (1/1/60)

"The Death of Another Salesman" describes this follow-up to *One for the Angels*. Serling again focuses on a little man who never achieved the big score. All similarity between Lew Bookman and Arch Hammer ends there. At thirty-six, Hammer appears close to realizing his life's ambition. But *Zone*'s villains always receive their comeuppance, as will Hammer, whom Serling informs us is a "cheap nickel-and-dime man." A populist, Serling would never condemn anyone on the basis of low status. A liberal, he'd be more likely to try and find something good in a member of the underclass (see Chapter 11). In truth, though, any moral judgment on a *Zone* character is based on his or her actions as an individual. Bookman's heart and soul resembled the legendary "diamond as big as the Ritz" F. Scott Fitzgerald (in a rare excursion into imaginative fantasy) envisioned back in the mid-1920s. Hammer is possessed of a spirit of "cheapness that goes past suit and the shirt; a cheapness of mind"; he callously uses people. This categorizes him as an anti-humanist.

Death comes to all men. That much is fate. For Serling, there is also free will. In choosing to do the right thing Bookman ensured that his earthly end marked the beginning of a splendid eternity. Manipulating other people for immediate gratification, Hammer so completely sets himself up for "the other place" that the episode *A Nice Place to Visit* might be thought of as a sequel. One thing separates Hammer from that episode's Rocky Valentine: Hammer's unique gift at changing his face to look precisely like anyone he wishes to resemble. The concept derived from an unpublished story by George Clayton Johnson. Serling purchased the piece, fashioning his own script so that the Serling philosophy would emerges.

Johnson's character had a face that altered on its own, appearing to anyone he met as whomever that person wanted to see. His death occurs when he bumps into a bitter man who plans to kill an old enemy whom the bittered soul believes he's accidentally stumbled on. The character's death play as arbitrary, in no way related to his cruel actions. Serling's spin allowed Hammer more control over his destiny. The man can transform into anyone he chooses. As Foster (Ross Martin), Hammer impersonates a deceased jazz artist (referencing *Passage For Trumpet*) to seduce the man's girlfriend (Beverly Garland). As Sterig (Philip Pine), Hammer berates a gangster (Bernard Fein) and grabs money from a heist; next he assumes the face of prize-fighter Marshak (Don Gordon). Here, Hammer's luck runs out. He runs into Pop Marshak (Peter Brocco). A newsstand owner, Pop never forgave his son for all the pain he'd caused, and shoots down the person before him. At that moment the four guises dissolve into one another.

Having Hammer killed by a father who mistakes this man for his son (this act done by a complete stranger in Johnson's story) adds an element of myth. This can be read as Biblical, Greek, or a collapsing of cultures into one another. The concept also underlines modern horror, notably the Claude Rains/Lon Chaney, Jr. relationship in *The Wolf Man* (1941). Serling's conclusion offers a variation on James Cain's *The Postman Always Rings Twice*: Though Hammer gets away with his crimes, he's finally (and fittingly) punished for one he did not commit. Still, we should note that Pop shot his "son" owing to Arch Hammer's lack of commitment to the human community and those flawed individuals who compose it. The problem is not that Hammer wanted nice things for himself (who doesn't?), but that his "master plan" was "to destroy some lives," and take pleasure in doing so. Hammer deserves precisely what he gets.

Autobiographical bits abound. The name 'Sterig' plays as a reference for Serling. Virgil Sterig is one more of the physically small men who stand up to the big boys in his world, even as Serling did to the CBS brass. Hammer is initially seen contemplating his Mirror Image. The girlfriend references both the Bible and Alfred Hitchcock, whose films are full of "M" women. Homages to "serious" literature abound:

HAMMER/FOSTER: Mourning becomes you.
MAGGIE: Me and Electra.

Serling also humorously references his own medium, television. When Sterig slips into the gang lord's living room, Penell sits watching TV, sipping a beer. Frightened, he turns so fast that his bottle smashes against the screen, exploding the tube. Only harsh reality can pull us away from our favorite escapist show, destroying the set in the process. This self-reference would eventually be cross-referenced by Spielberg in the final shot of *Poltergeist* (1984). At this episode's heart, though, is death. "Death," John Donne wrote, "thou shalt die," referring to those who achieve positive things in life and reap eternal rewards. Lew Bookman was such a man. Not Arch Hammer. Death does not die; he does. All four of him.

Do Go Gentle!:

THE HITCH-HIKER (1/22/60)

Like the first half of *Psycho*, released half a year after this *Zone* appeared, *The Hitch-Hiker* focuses on a beautiful blonde driving cross-country. Even the Bernard Herrmann music that accompanies the doomed odyssey of Nan Adams (Inger Stevens) sounds similar. Like Hitchcock's heroine Marion Crane (Janet Leigh), Adams unknowingly drives toward her death. The key difference: In Hitch's film we experience a sense of arbitrariness as to the outcome of the shower sequence. This is how death comes in Hitchcock: His female victims, like his wrong-man heroes, happen to be in the wrong place at the wrong time. This is hardly the case with Serling's leads. Adams comes to realize that her death was destined.

An autobiographical note: Serling lived in Los Angeles, where Marion is headed, when he wrote this episode. The author wondered if, in moving, he had sold out to commerciality. Serling left behind the New York City he loved and the fast-disappearing era of East Coast live TV. Though *Zone* rates as one of the finest filmed dramatic shows, Serling questioned whether his own journey represented a spiritual and artistic death. Already, he'd explored that issue in a realistic play, *The Velvet Alley*. In *The Hitch-Hiker*, he addresses this in imaginative fantasy terms.

We first encounter Adams by the side of a highway. A well-meaning mechanic (Lew Gallo) services her automobile, which suffered a blow-out while Adams was speeding. Amazed that Adams survived, he says that in most cases "somebody would have called for a hearse!" Serling has set up the inevitability of the denouement. A strange, grim man (Leonard Strong) tries to hitch a ride. Repulsed at the sight, Adams drives on. He reappears and, at the mechanic's garage, attempts to enter Adams's car. Although Adams is concerned that this cryptic figure (he looks like a combination of some contemporary tramp and Biblical prophet) could arrive there before she, the mechanic, who never sees the figure, shrugs it off as coincidence—the fellow got a ride with someone in a faster car. But there is more in heaven and earth, for Serling as in Shakespeare, than dreamt of in such a realist's philosophy.

Though Serling based his teleplay on an earlier radio drama by Lucille Fletcher, he made the material his own, revealing an under-standing of TV as a visual as well as aural medium. Director Alvin Gunzer's realization allows us to initially spot the hitch-hiker over Adams's shoulder. We grasp her set of reality while maintaining our separate identity. The next time he appears, we share the frightening image via a point-of-view shot. Now, we're not merely with Adams, but we are her. *The Hitch-Hiker* features an effective double narration as Serling transforms the audience from objective viewers to subjective receivers. Adams might otherwise seem a strange bird, someone we watch from afar. Hearing her thoughts, we are rendered complicit, and so accept Adams as our alter-ego.

At this point, Adams becomes something of an Everywoman. Her own commentary, original writing by Serling rather than a holdover from Fletcher, induces us to share her terror. "Not menacing," Adams informs us while describing the hitch-hiker, avoiding any stereotype of danger. Neither evil nor ugly, rather "drab," even "mousy," he is a "scarecrow man." Adams's sojourn is interrupted by strange interludes that include a daylight diner stop, a late night moment of panic at a closed gas station, and her desperate attempt to relieve what she describes as "anxiety" more than "fear" by picking up another hitchhiker (Adam Williams). He's an ordinary fellow, a plump sailor on his way to San Diego's Navy Yards. Adams tries to run the "other" hitchhiker down when she spots him by the side of the road, causing the sailor to abandon ship. He rushes into the night when Adams, after explaining that the hitchhiker seemed to be "beckoning me," offers the sailor sex if he'll only remain. Like the mechanic at the beginning, or the owner of the gas station (George Mitchell) who peeks out at Adams but slams the door, the sailor is one more agent of the norm. Though this female is stunning, he senses that destruction is waiting somewhere up the road.

Now, Adams is not only alone (physically speaking) but one of The Lonely. "Her fear is no longer vague," if fear is the correct term. More likely, it is anxiety. She finally stops at a phone booth to place one of *Zone*'s Long-Distance Calls. Connecting with her home, Adams hears a strange voice. Her mother has been hospitalized following a total breakdown after learning that her daughter has died in a highway accident. The mechanic's dimly remembered words take on significance. A more conventional approach here would have Adams scream out in fear. Serling instead communicates his philosophy. "The fear has left me now," Adams sighs. It was logical for her to worry that the stranger might rob or rape her. But as Serling would further develop in episodes yet to come, there is no sense whatsoever in fearing death.

The knowledge that she's dead frees Adams from fear. She no longer avoids the hitch-hiker. "Somewhere, I'll find out who he is" and "what he wants," she thinks. An acceptant smile appears on Adams's face as she slips back in the driver's seat and spots the hitch-hiker in her rear-view mirror. "I believe you're going my way?" he whispers in a voice less cryptic than eerily seductive. Nan's body relaxes. Death does not come for her, as it will for Hitch's Marion Crane, as an interruption of a life that has not been allowed to play itself out. Serling's heroine is relieved from any unexplained emptiness that caused her to take a holiday alone, a female equivalent to Martin Sloan in *Walking Distance*, who also roared away from New

York in hopes of finding himself, and to Gart Williams in *Willoughby* who finds himself, and solace, in death.

War Is Hell:

THE PURPLE TESTAMENT (2/12/60)

Whereas *The Hitch-Hiker* dramatizes death in the most mundane setting, the *Purple Testament* takes place during the latter days of WWII as American troops retake Manila. Serving as a paratrooper in the 511th's demolition platoon Serling was in close proximity with death. In a studio-recreated encampment in the shadows of the Mahonags, the names of four men killed during that day's actions are reported to the commanding officer. The last is "Levy." An incident that would forever haunt Serling from the two-week bloodbath on Leyte occurred when a soldier standing beside him, one Melvin Levy, was without warning decapitated by a food crate that parachuted down. The absurd abruptness of death, even when no enemy soldiers were nearby, will be addressed here. *Purple Testament* poses the question that fascinated Serling throughout his own brief life: Are such happenings predestined, an act of fate?

The title, Serling will explain, derives from Shakespeare (*Richard III*): "He has come to open the purple testament of bleeding war." As with everything else, Serling found himself conflicted as to his feelings on combat. One close friend, Norman Miller, always insisted that Serling chose the paratroopers because it "had the highest mortality rate." Yet Serling's flag-waving naiveté shattered when he experienced the harsh distinction between the grim, terrible thing war is and how romantically battles had been portrayed in old movies. Any man who who proved fortunate enough to crawl away alive understood war to be dehumanizing, a terrible concept for a humanist who had earlier waxed jingoistic. Wiser for his experiences, Serling (still a patriot, if a more cautious one now) praised the courage of fighting men, but lambasted the institution of war in early pre-*Zone* scripts as he set out to analyze the impact of WWII on ordinary people.

Lieutenant Fitzgerald (William Reynolds) admits to Captain Riker (Dick York) that he notices a strange light around the faces of those who will not return. Suddenly, Fitz spots that light over the captain. Riker could try to save his own life by reassigning command of an upcoming attack to someone else, but he stoically heads off to face his fate—leaving behind his wedding ring and picture of his wife and kids. The question is, would Riker have fared better if he had remained behind? Perhaps the commander of that mission would have returned alive while Riker, like Serling's companion Melvin Levy, might have been killed by accident at the camp.

Further tying this episode to *Zone* is one man's willingness to assume personal responsibility as a true test of character. Are you ready to stand up and say, Harry Truman-like, the buck stops here? As to death, the difference between hero (Lew Bookman in *One for the Angels*) and villain (*The Four of Us Are Dying*) is that the former can, like Hamlet, claim that the precise moment of death is irrelevant: If it be not now it is yet to come; if it is not to come, it will be now; "the *readiness* is all!" Good men do their best in the world. While they may not welcome endgame, neither do they fear it. The same holds true for Fitz. Ordered back to Division Headquarters for R&R, he glances into a makeshift mirror and spots the death-light surrounding his face. Quickly, Fitz recovers, and accepts this as his lot in life and beyond. Captain Gunther (Barney Phillips) tells the driver (Warren Oates) to be careful because the enemy may have mined the roads; this allows Fitz a vision of precisely how he will die. He could complain of a sudden sickness, remaining in his tent. Then again, he could be decapitated by a free-falling package. Fitz smiles wryly. We have seen that smile before, on the face of Nan Adams when she glances into her rearview mirror and spots the hitch-hiker.

The Bad Old Days:

DEATHS-HEAD REVISITED (11/10/61)

No such smile appears on the face of Captain Lutze (Oscar Beregi) in *Deaths-Head Revisited* at episode's end. Nor does this man die. Here,

Serling works in a Greek mode; in tragedy, the central figure cannot die, for that would allow him a relief from the horrors of life. In the final shot, Lutze rolls on the ground, a madman, as a doctor (Ben Wright) attempts to grasp how a seemingly sane person could go crazy after spending two hours in a deserted camp. We know more than he does. This is Dachau. Lutze was the commandant who tortured, maimed and killed inmates here. "He walked the earth without a heart," Serling informs us. Lutze is a man unable to make a human connection, as his mercilessness makes painfully clear.

Serling refuses to supply a simple reason why Lutze returns to the scene of his crimes. How easy it would have been to let us know that the man who calls himself "Herr Schmidt" happened to be passing on a train and hopped off for a quick look. That would have ruined the piece. The unanswerable mystery is why any criminal feels the necessity to return to the scene of any crime. However casual Lutze may seem, he's haunted by guilt. He returns because he has to. Becker (Joseph Schildkraut), one of Lutze's many victims, appears. Lutze may only imagine Becker as a waking dream, or ghosts may truly haunt him. For Serling, it doesn't matter. Believe a dream and it is true. For you.

A window provides the Mirror Image that reveals Schmidt and Lutze together onscreen, implying the duality of man. Insanity explodes when the two collide, which happens as Lutze believes himself on trial by men he formerly sat in judgment of. *Deaths-Head* derives from Serling's identity as a Jew. As always, though, Serling makes clear that in his assessment of things he is a human being first, a Jew second; he is less a Jewish man than he is a man who happens to be Jewish. The term "Jew" is never mentioned; this is Serling's choice, not the whim of some censor. When a starved inmate reminds Lutze of the number of people who died in camps, he shouts: "Ten million!" The number of Jews who died by Nazi hands is roughly six million. Add other minorities and the total number reaches ten. Here was a horrible crime not just against the Jews but against humanity.

Though a villain, Lutz resembles hero Martin Sloane heading back to Homewood or Gart Williams and mythical Willoughby. Lutze admits that "one grows nostalgic for the good old days." The goodness of those characters was clear in their yearning for quaint carousels on summer afternoons; Lutze's wickedness has him longing for torture without restriction. Though nostalgia is common to good and bad, what we miss defines us. As this story closes, ghosts of past victims find their peace after revisiting on Lutze the horrors he forced on them. No doubt Lutze would gladly go gently into that good night, but he doesn't deserve quietude. The ultimate punishment is to live on in pain. That the metaphysical is at work is clear from Serling's finale. Why do the Dachaus remain standing? Those who cannot learn from history are doomed to repeat it. Without constant reminders, that might be our destiny. This must be avoided, as Rod at last says, "wherever men walk God's Earth." Serling never involves the term "God" lightly.

Soul Survivor:

THE THIRTY-FATHOM GRAVE (1/10/63)

Like Lutze, Chief Bell (Mike Kellin) cannot escape the ghosts of WWII. Bell, however, is a moral man. Like *Purple Testament*'s Fitzgerald, he's allowed a last smile while diving into the ocean for a final reckoning in 1963. Captain Beecham (Simon Oakland) senses that this troubled soul who's been hearing strange noises will enjoy the rest he has hoped for since a haunting wartime incident. Bell was sole survivor of a submarine that sank; he's since suffered survivor guilt. When the modern destroyer on which he serves passes over that sub's remains a hundred miles off Guadalcanal (fate or accident?), Bell, who has repressed his feelings for 20 years, hears a clanking below—his crewmates are summoning him.

Establishing absolute authenticity, in large part due to Serling's knowledge of the military mentality, the *Zone* team literally thrust all viewers, veterans or not, into the situation. Recalled here is Serling's realistic wartime drama *The Sergeant* (see Introduction). Captain Beecham tells Bell: "One case of sudden fear does not add up to a coward." A sudden resurgence of guilt from reconnection with the repressed memory relates this to *King Nine Will Not Return*, as does Bell's humanistic concern for others. Seeing ghosts, even as Captain Embry (Bob Cummings) did, Bell echoes Embry's words: "I should be with them!" He feels responsibility for their deaths though there is no reason to.

This unique concern relates to Serling's weight of command theme. In such fantastical presentations, he could objectify his own survivor guilt for having lived and later prospered, as others, like Levy, did not. Had Serling been spared for a purpose? Was it to write about survivor guilt so other vets could better understand what they suffered, and so the rest of the public could appreciate that syndrome? In *Zone*, however random it may seem, everything has its purpose and means something. An anti-war attitude emerges as, in his closing, Serling points out that what's "worst about war" is "not what it does to the body" but "what it does to the mind." The theme of that human organ and its dazzling powers is evidenced as all of this destroyer's crew members hear the ghosts after Bell's mental construction becomes so real to him that it affects everyone around him. Perception plays a role, as the ghosts appear to Bell after he convinces himself they are calling to him; once again, believing is seeing.

There's even a "ticket" at the end. After telling Bell that he's delusional, and that there are no ghosts aboard, Doc (David Sheiner) is stunned to see seaweed at precisely that point in the corridor where Bell believes former crewmen appeared. And the metaphysical theme: After Bell dives into the ocean and rejoins his old mates (his dog tags will be found inside the sub, suggesting that he managed to go home again), Beecham raises his eyes heavenward, convinced that God will at last have mercy on Bell's soul. In Serling's vision, the road to hell is not lined with good intentions. Any man who harbors the best desires, however much he failed, is deemed worthy.

Variations on a Theme:

A NICE PLACE TO VISIT (4/15/60)

NOTHING IN THE DARK (1/5/62)

DEATH SHIP (2/7/63)

In Charles Beaumont's *A Nice Place to Visit*, Rocky Valentine (Larry Blyden), a petty criminal, is shot by policemen. When his head clears, Valentine encounters Mr. Pip (Sebastian Cabot), a natty figure from beyond. When Pip provides Valentine with wine, women, and song, the nasty fellow assumes that he made it to heaven, though he can't imagine why. Valentine soon becomes bored with easy access to luxuries, and tells Pip that he doesn't deserve this, and would probably be better off in "the other place." Pip grins devilishly, informing Valentine: "This is the other place!" As in Jean-Paul Sartre's vision of hell, there is "no exit." Valentine carried his hell around inside him.

In *Nothing in the Dark*, writer George Clayton Johnson added a fitting epilogue to *The Hitch-Hiker*. Instead of the open road, there's an underground enclosure. A sad older lady, Wanda Dunn's (Gladys Cooper) last name suggests her present state. If Nan Adams initially had no thoughts of death, Dunn thinks about nothing else. She has locked herself away in a self-made prison. When Mr. Death does appear it's not as a scraggly old bum, but a good-looking youth (Robert Redford) with as relaxing an effect on Dunn as the hitch-hiker had been upsetting to Adams. The episode ends similarly. Death isn't something to be afraid of, but a release from life's darker side. If the young man's identity had been withheld from us, the piece would play as dishonest. But Johnson and director Lamont Johnson (no relation) insist from the outset that it's not a gruff old man (R. G. Armstrong) but the sweet youth who embodies Death.

"I know who you are," Dunn tells him, not one time but three. When she later describes seeing death on a bus years earlier, the figure she describes is the one sitting before her. Dunn has been, Rod informs us, "living a nightmare": her isolated existence, devoid of important human connection, is death in life. Death's deliverance of her from this sad state marks her transport to a better place. Why, she asks, didn't he take her at once? "I had to make you understand," he compassionately explains. It wasn't death she feared, but the unknown. He articulates the title: "There's nothing in the dark that wasn't there when the lights were on." A snowstorm raging outside gives way to a warm summer's day. The weather reflects inner attitude: we all have our season in the sun. Dunn discovers hers, as Death whispers, "What you feared was the end is only the beginning!"

Like *Judgment Night*, Richard Matheson's *Death Ship*, based on his 1953 short story, tackles the Flying Dutchman motif. We encounter three sympathetic people, so our realization of the endless ritual they must forever replay results in a darker vision than in *Deaths-Head Revisted.* Captain Paul Ross (Jack Klugman), Lieutenant Ted Mason (Ross Martin), and Lieutenant Mike Carter (Fredrick Beir) beam down on "the thirteenth planet." Stepping out of the saucer-like ship, they notice a crashed spacecraft, similar to theirs. In fact, it is theirs; inside they discover dead semblances of themselves. Did they pass through a time-warp and witness what might happen if they try and take off? Or are there invisible aliens here, hoping to make the astronauts so afraid of an ascent that they will remain, never telling Earth that this planet has oxygen? Finally, they ascend again. When the captain insists on landing once more, all are shocked to see the crashed craft again, realizing the truth. They have already crashed, and are dead. This is their frustrated dream of escape . . . which they will ritualistically run through again . . . and again.

Even as the astronauts land we see a strange light pass over them; the veteran *Zone* viewer can guess that they are already dead. Rather than destroy a neat mystery, this adds suspense as we wait for the trio to learn what we already guess. The dead bodies provide their Mirror Image, while the captain carries that all-important weight of command. The meaning of perception reappears: "You may see it," Ross says to his shipmates of their doomed double, "but that doesn't prove it's there." Proof can only be achieved by an ascent, that thin red line between courage and cowardice once again explored.

Sorry, Wrong Number:

LONG DISTANCE CALL (3/3/61)

Telephones appear in so many *Zones* that this object becomes an ongoing motif. One memorable episode proved effective in tying the phone-as-symbol to the death theme.

Long Distance Call began with an idea by William Idelson, restructured by Richard Matheson, further refined by Charles Beaumont, finished by Serling. The process allows for a sense of collaboration, as well as a realization that finally what went on the air came down to one man. "This is a house hovered over by Mr. Death," we're informed, though what we initially see in the Bayles home appears "so very full of life." The Serling view: that precise moment we feel most alive is when Death likely arrives. Average parents Charles (Philip Abbott) and Sylvia (Patricia Smith) shower son Billy (Billy Mumy) with presents for his fifth birthday. He loves best a plastic phone from his elderly grandmother (Lili Darvas). Even when she's not around, the old woman insists, Billy can keep in contact. When Grandma dies of natural causes, Billy engages in "imagined" conversations.

Initially, his concerned parents worry that Billy has become what we today refer to as "autistic." Things grow more serious when the child believes that his grandmother wants him to die, to join her and relieve her loneliness. *Long Distance Call* passes from tidy thriller to profound fiction. Here is an ordinary (in appearance) suburban home constructed over a dark cellar, symbolic of every "normal" family. However happy they seem, these people are miserable: Grandma believes that her son has been stolen away by a willful woman, though Mrs. Bayles strikes us as a fine person. Grandma's paranoia is explained: Before Chris, she had two children and lost them both. This revelation allows her to emerge as a wounded, rather than evil, old lady. Chris finds himself caught between the two women he loves.

A slew of *Zone* themes recur: Grandma calls little Billy her "angel," connecting this episode to so many of the Capra-influenced stories. Chris describes Grandma's unhealthy intimacy to Billy as an attempt to "go back again" (the nostalgia theme) to what they once had. Like other visitors to the fifth dimension, Grandma wants a "second chance." Moments before her death, she whispers to Billy that she fears becoming The Lonely once she's passed.

If we accept *Long Distance Call* on a fantastical level, Grandma is on the other end of the line. Alternately, we can take this realistically: Grandma now exists only in Billy's imagination. Even when his mother interrupts a conversation and hears her voice it doesn't necessarily mean the old woman is there. It's possible that Billy's belief is so strong he can pass it on. Mother has, after all, just risen from a troubled sleep in which she dreamt this; perhaps she, like Billy, now imagines Grandma's voice. Then again, if both believe that

Grandma is there, she is there. For them. Billy throws himself into a goldfish pond, hoping to drown. Some firemen struggle to revive the boy. When his father picks up the phone and begs Grandma to return Billy, her voice is not heard. *Long Distance Call* does not insist on one interpretation or the other. When Chris hangs up, a fireman (Bob McCord) announces that Billy will be all right; we must conclude that it was the father's "act of faith"—his willingness to believe in something greater than the here and now—that saved Billy. Either way, Grandma "let go," realizing that unconditional love has to do with caring more for the object of one's affections than one's own self.

Good Night and Good Luck:

IN PRAISE OF PIP (11/15/63)

The fifth season's opener begins in Vietnam, where Private Pip (Bob Diamond) is carried into a medical center. An army surgeon (Stuart Nesbit), realizing that the wounds are far too severe for him to handle, insists the youth be sent to a hospital. Glancing down sadly, he offers a wisp of guarded optimism: "Well, Private Pip, I wish you a long life!" Serling's narrative then cuts to a dilapidated hotel room as director Joseph M. Newman creates a vivid example of the shadow play we witnessed in the script of that name. Max Phillips (Jack Klugman) wakes in horror from an all-too-real nightmare: His son, "somewhere in southeast Asia," has been killed.

Dreaming and death once again interlock. On the humble table beside this lowlife's rumpled bed we notice a new variation on the doubling theme: Two photographs of that beloved son, one at age nine, and one as he looks now. This transforms into a Mirror Image as Phillips staggers to his looking glass, hoping to reconcile what he's become with everything he once wanted to be. Phillips reaches for a bottle, searching for a cigarette, combining two of *Zone*'s most significant human weaknesses. A moment later, we learn that Phillips's "profession" concerns the third: He's a gambler. Max

Phillips emerges not only as a typical Serling "little man," but the as apotheosis of them all.

However sleazy Phillips appears, he proves worthy of our sympathy since he's a humanist. Though word on the street has it that "Phillips never gave nothing away," contradicting that is his obvious concern for others. A young gambling addict, George (Russell Horton), about to be executed by a mobster (John Launer) for a $300 debt, is twice saved by Phillips. His good deeds may be a direct result of his dream in which his son died in combat, absurdly enough in "a place where there isn't even supposed to be a war going on." Phillips can't be sure Pip was wounded (we aren't positive whether what we saw in the opening was a reality or visualization of Phillips's nightmare), yet the thought that this may have occurred (it did, but did he dream it because it happened or did it happen because he dreamed it?) sparks Phillips's guilt. He wasn't a good father, he promised to take Pip to an amusement pier only to get involved with business, forgetting to show up.

Different as Phillips is from successful Rod Serling, this emerges as the last great confessional piece. Then comes one of those Long-Distance Calls: Landlady Mrs. Feeney (Connie Gilchrist) phones to say that the army just called. Pip is on the verge of death. A skirmish with gangsters leaves Phillips hurt, perhaps dying. Drawn by some Force beyond his control, Phillips staggers to the amusement pier. Whether this place will prove as horrifying for him as for Edward Hall (Richard Conte) in *Perchance to Dream* or as sweet as for Martin Sloan in *Walking Distance* remains to be seen. Similar to Sloan, Phillips meets a child (Billy Mumy) on the midway—it's the beloved son he always meant to bring here. Is it possible that Serling knew he should put his work aside to take daughter Nan to such a place?

"Hey, Pip," Phillips sighs. "You're my best buddy."

Magically, the lights switch on, a cotton candy machine churns out sweets, and the rides all work with no one to operate them. If only in his mind, Phillips goes home again. Not to his ugly reality but an alternative: a finer, better version of the past. Phillips now lives out the way things should have been. But even his imagination can't summon up Pip. That can only be achieved by divine intervention. "Oh, God! If I could just talk to him, see him!" Phillips cries, likely not realizing that he's praying. Uttering that request, Phillips gazes upward: When you wish upon a star, your dream comes true. But as with Bolie Jackson (Ivan Dixon) in *The Big Tall Wish*, the wonderful experience can't last unless the adult absolutely surrenders to it. Got to believe! Pip does appear: as always, believing is seeing. Though Phillips revels in the moment, he, like Jackson, is too jaded to commit, so Pip grows distant and hurries away. When Phillips pursues the boy into a hall of mirrors, the man smashes into his own image, providing *Zone*'s final broken mirror.

"No one ever loved a boy like I did you," Phillips cries out to his vanished son. The problem in the past was not that Phillips failed to love, only that he failed to love his boy unconditionally. As a humanist, the flawed man deserves and receives a Second Chance. Phillips invokes the metaphysical: "Hey, God?" the wounded (in every sense) man calls out. "I'll make a deal with you." He isn't the first *Zone* protagonist to proffer such an offer though he will be the last. "Take me, take me!" Phillips begs. His words echo Lew Bookman (Ed Wynn) in *One For the Angels* five years earlier—and perhaps coincidentally, perhaps not, Phillips is a book-maker.

In the epilogue, Private Pip visits the park, recalling that his father was found dead at the same time Pip "miraculously" rose from the dead in Vietnam (this the first TV drama to openly address that war). Now, it's Pip's turn to imagine that his father is here with him, enjoying the games and rides. Pip can recall the fantasy we saw Phillips live out, if only in his mind. Forgivingly (extending unconditional love to Phillips as he did at last to Pip), Pip accepts this fantasy as reality. If this is not the way they were, it's how things should have been: Their grand illusion. "Hey, Pop," Pip sighs. "You're my best buddy." With eyes tearing up, he adds: "You always were." At least in the mind's eye.

8

DEALS WITH THE DEVIL:
Dr. Faustus in the Fifth Dimension

IN HIS FINAL years, Rod Serling often quoted da Vinci's dying words, "May God forgive me for not having used my talents," Serling here referred to some routine movie scripts and commercials for beer. The possibility that he'd sold out "concerned him all the time," according to friend Del Reisman. "Don't pay too high a price for the status of popularity," Serling warned a young would-be writer in 1966. Where did such guilt come from? It was a result of childhood trauma. During the Depression the family grocery store went under. Serling came to believe that no matter how well one did in life, it could all be taken away. "How could I turn down those offers?" he asked a reporter as to his hawking cigarettes on TV. Yet those words go against the grain of what he'd insisted in *The Velvet Alley*: Don't sell your soul for money, no matter how large the amount. Were then the man and his message at odds? Serling apparently thought so, at least during his darkest hours. Still, he then did what the best artists do under such pressure: He wrote about it in some of *Zone*'s most poignant scripts.

No Exit?:

ESCAPE CLAUSE (11/6/59)

In his recurring Faustian fables, Serling personalized the ancient concept of a person who sells his soul to achieve his heart's desire, only to long for a way out. *Escape Clause* was *Zone*'s first comedy, and the results were so strong that *Variety* singled it out as ranking "with the best that has ever been accomplished in half-hour filmed television."

Walter Bedeker (David Wayne), a hypochondriac, rarely rolls out of bed. He insists that his long-suffering wife Ethel (Virginia Christine) wait on him. The Doctor (Raymond Bailey) tries to explain that there's nothing wrong; Bedecker might rate as yet another charming eccentric except that he berates Ethel, and so is not a humanist. Bedecker strikes a deal with Mr. Cadwallader (Thomas Gomez) after this devil appears in Walter Bedeker's bedroom.

As the pact is struck, Serling seizes the opportunity to put his own spin on this age-old device. Ordinarily, a man who enters into such a bargain desires, like Oscar Wilde's Dorian Gray, youth, wealth, or beautiful women. None, though, are present here. The narrative illustrates this author's moral vision. Gruesome things that usually upset a hypochondriac (disease, germs, and so on) are secondary to Bedecker, who hates people. He does not long for earthly luxuries, but deeply fears death. Bedecker is concerned about sickness only because he's terrified that it might bring about his end. Despite contempt for others, Bedecker wonders how, when he does die, "will people survive without" him. We can understand that his specific deal with the devil (he must surrender his mortal soul) includes not youth, but "indestructibility."

The devil assures Bedecker that "nothing can hurt you!" Afterwards, Bedecker makes no attempt to do all the things a man might be expected to with his new power. On the rare occasions when he ventures outs, he jumps in front of subway trains or oncoming buses. Surviving, Bedecker collects checks from firms desperate to avoid lawsuits. Even here, though, Bedecker proves atypical, settling for small amounts. He might continue this for time infinitum except for one problem: there's no thrill any more. Bedecker longs for the excitement he experienced lying in bed, fearing death—he is yet another *Zone* visitor who gets what he wants only to grasp too late that the reality can't live up to one's dream. Like Rocky Valentine in *A Nice Place to Visit*, Bedecker is bored. Unlike Rocky, Walter has never done a single act that could be considered evil, and his punishment must uniquely fit the crime. There's an escape clause in his contract: Bedecker can at any time choose to give up his immortality. He does so after Ethel accidentally falls to her death from their apartment house.

Bedecker misses Ethel terribly. Who can he emotionally torture now? With no desire to continue, Bedecker confesses to a killing he didn't commit, assuming that he'll be convicted of first-degree murder. He didn't count on his gifted lawyer talking the judge into converting the sentence to life, condemning Bedecker to live forever in his cell, where risk is nonexistent. Serling's unique twist conveys his meaning. As a life sentence is here portrayed as worse than execution, the episode might be read as anti–capital punishment. We can empathize (if not sympathize) with this lonely little man. Cadwallader shows up and grants Bedecker the mercy of a heart attack, ending an eternity of dullness. Bedecker did, in his own peculiar way, love his long-suffering wife. Even Henry Bemis in *Time Enough at Last* only had to suffer a lifetime of boredom, not an eternity of it!

"The Devil with People!":

THE FEVER (1/29/60)

Serling's opening remarks (gambling described as "a deadly, life-shattering affliction") suggest that this episode is not only about gambling but all addiction: What any "fever" can do to a person. Franklin (Everett Sloane) and Flora (Vivi Janiss) Gibbs from Homewood-like Elgin, Kansas, arrive in Vegas. Director Robert Florey opens with a dissolve-montage of the famed Strip; again, Serling portrays a modern city with potential to corrupt even such stern heartland types. An autobiographical element is established as we learn that this trip came to them owing to her "knack with a phrase;" Flora won a jingle contest. Her writing brought them to an even more jaded Tinseltown than Hollywood, where Serling's own way with words opened the door for him.

It is the moralist Franklin Gibbs, however, who will become an unlikely victim. This relates to the writer's own life; discussions of both *Zone* and Serling's realistic scripts center on the degree to which he was "a moralist." The irony of his own life situation, apparently, was not lost on Serling who here incorporates it in this tale of a serious fellow who scoffs at gambling ("not moral!") yet falls under the spell. Florey cuts to close-ups of freshly minted silver dollars inside a devilish machine before Gibbs is seduced by the sound. To heighten its irresistible pull, Florey and Serling decided that the machine's seductive "voice" (which only Franklin hears) must tinkle like money falling from a slot. So they recorded dropping coins, then blended them with a human voice whispering: "Franklin!"

To make clear that this powerful indictment of gambling is not limited to that addiction, the team allowed the camera to drift from the central issue on several occasions. We constantly see pretty girls (Carole Kent prominent among them) delivering free drinks to high rollers. These cocktail waitresses sport revealingly short skirts, legs masked in silk stockings. "The fever" refers not only to gambling, though that is central. Visually, we are informed that the entire scene seduces Gibbs, and others. This is *la dolce vita*, as Fellini would put it: The sweet life, its superficial appeal threatening to steal away the soul of one who exerted self-control all his life. If Franklin Gibbs can become a victim, so can any of us—including the man writing this play. What happens to Gibbs will lead to his death, set up when a blinding light is projected onto him by the slot.

"The Gibbs's know the value of money," Franklin insists when Flora first slips a coin into a machine. After a drunk (Art Lewis) offers Franklin Gibbs a coin and, to his surprise, he wins, Gibbs can't sleep that night. Close-ups of money on a table help provide a case study in addictive behavior. At first in denial, Gibbs tells Flora that he wants to toss the "tainted" money back in the slot. Hours later, when he fails to return, she slips down to the casino. He's already cashed several checks and is gambling away their savings, obsessed with winning the $10,000 grand prize, yet throwing away much more. "It teases you," he whines, "lets you win a little, then takes it back. It's *inhuman*!" (an irony, since it's obvious to all but he that this is a machine he's talking about). Watching from the sidelines, a floor manager (Lee Sands) sighs to the cashier (Marc Towers), "When they get hooked, they *really* get hooked!" Momentarily a Greek chorus, the two men make clear that this is a modern tragedy: While we pity him, we also fear for ourselves as Gibbs passes from one stage of addiction to the next—intrigued, obsessed, desperate, methodical, crazed, forlorn.

Yet Gibbs never considers quitting, despite Flora's pleadings. A reversal of luck "is bound to turn up sooner or later," he howls. "You've just got to stick with her long enough!" The use of the feminine adds to the notion that he's seduced. Florey follows the pattern established in previous *Zones* during the second half by employing ever more oblique angles, relying on fast editing between shots to convey the surreal nightmare Gibb's life becomes. "It's got to pay off, "he cries, "got to!"; these are the forlorn words of every addict who ever lived.

When the slot breaks down after Gibbs slips in his last coin, he explodes, attacking the machine. Dragged to his room, he considers his own pathetic self in another variation on the Mirror Image. The slot now appears at their door, calling out "Franklin!" with that tinkling voice. It's clear that Flora doesn't see this "entity." We're free to believe that the sound and sight exist only in Gibbs's mind; he has projected his inner demons onto an amoral object that, in his subjective vision, symbolizes evil. If the episode ended with Gibbs in the grip of mania, falling out a window to his death, *The Fever* would lack a metaphysical theme. But after people drift away from Gibbs's corpse, we see that last silver dollar roll toward his hand in a left-moving pan to reveal the devil machine observing Gibbs. We can't write this off as "subjective," since Franklin, now deceased, couldn't be imagining it. If this monster thing is subjective, it is in our minds now. And if not, it did exist as an evil entity beyond a compendium of nuts and bolts. Each viewer must decide. Perception, in the *Zone*, is reality.

Two For the Road:

NICK OF TIME (11/18/60)

A young, attractive couple pause on their journey in *Nick of Time*. The direction is reversed from *The Fever*: they drive through a small-town (Ridgeview, Ohio) on their way to New York. Don (William

Shatner) and Pat (Patricia Breslin) Carter pause on their honeymoon when their convertible needs repairs. To kill time they wander through a hamlet untouched by changes in postwar society. In an ancient diner Carter grows fascinated with a table-top fortune telling machine. Insert a penny and the devil-faced contraption spits out a card with an ambiguous destiny. At first amused, then concerned, finally devastated, Pat watches as her husband becomes an addict. Richard Matheson wrote the play, yet certain aspects appear to echo Serling's life. Shatner resembles Serling: short, darkly handsome, conventional—but with an edge. More notable is the resemblance between Patricia Breslin and photographs of Carol Kramer Serling from the late 1940s. The beautiful brunette with a probing intelligence and firm moral (though not simplistically moralistic) stance suggests that this couple stands in for the Serlings, who did journey from heartland Ohio to Manhattan after Rod's early success.

The machine "predicts" that Carter will receive a promotion. When Carter learns via another Long Distance Call that he did get that raise, he becomes convinced that the machine is all-knowing. Thanks to Pat's insistence, Don Carter manages to make the break: "We'll drive out of this town and go where we want—anytime we please!" Carter sums up the courage to counter his addiction thanks to a wife who is his equal, as compared to what an earlier generation might have considered a mere appendage. This metaphor extends beyond the Serlings: Don and Pat Carter escape because they represent new Americans: young people redefining marriage as a true team. They serve as contrasts for the old paradigm of marriage (the Gibbs's)—the woman subservient to the man.

Why does Don Carter deserve to be "saved" when Franklin Gibbs did not? Youth and attractiveness aside, Carter displays the warmth of a humanist. Before the problem begins he and Pat hold hands, suggesting not only sensuousness, but a true affection for one another. He's also warm when speaking to others, including the diner's counter-man (Guy Wilkerson). Gibbs, on the other hand, sealed his fate when, in response to Florence's request that he stop yelling because others were noticing, he shouted "(To) the devil with people! I'm not concerned with people, (only) this devil of a machine!"

Here we also encounter a final capper, if a realistic one: No sooner have Don and Pat Carter left than another (notably older) couple (Walter Reed and Dee Carroll) enter. He feeds the machine pennies; she weeps as the Satan-headed fortune teller regurgitates cards that, in the man's mind, imply they are its slaves. The actors are dead ringers for Everett Sloan and Vivi Janis in *The Fever*. By implication, the older generation accepts its fate and so remains a prisoner of it, while the new breed of partners in life exert free will and escape. For them, then, there is hope for the future.

Shooting in a Telephone Booth:

NERVOUS MAN IN A FOUR DOLLAR ROOM (10/14/60)

LAST NIGHT OF A JOCKEY (10/25/63)

Serling sensed that *Zone*'s appeal did not require the elaborate special effects of theatrical science fiction (*War of the Worlds*, *This Island Earth*), but an eerie intimacy. His script for *Nervous Man* offers just this: Jackie Rhoades (Joe Mantell) is one more little loser, whining that the world never allowed a runt like himself a chance. Rhoades's devil-in-the-flesh is George (William D. Gordon), a gangster for whom Jackie has performed nasty jobs. One night, during one of those *Zone* phone calls that deliver only bad news, Rhoades receives his latest assignment: Kill an old bartender who won't pay protection money. Robberies, however sordid, were one thing, but if even a hint of the humanist Rhoades once was remains, he won't go through with a murder. His guardian angel turns out to be none other than himself, a Mirror Image of the man he might have been: strong and decent, if no taller. Jackie Rhoades realizes that the world did not deal him a lousy hand. Rather, he has made a weak man's choices.

Director Douglas Heyes features more bird's-eye-view shots in this episode than appear in any other *Zone*. Jackie Rhoades emerges as a typical Serling antihero in numerous respects: fearing that he's a coward (so long as he believes himself to be one, he is, though there's room for change), chain-smoking throughout. At one point, Rhoades stares at his strong alter-ego in the mirror and asks: "You talkin' to me?" Here we may have encountered the inspiration for Travis Bickle in Martin Scorsese's *Taxi Driver* (1976). "You could have gone either way," the mirror-Rhoades insists. In personal matters, free will takes precedence over fate. Given a Second Chance, Rhoades goes for "guts and goodness," redeeming himself. He doesn't murder the bartender, but beats up George when he returns. Having embraced the better side of himself, Jackie Rhoades can now return to what Serling calls "the company of men."

Three years later, Serling scripted *Last Night of a Jockey*. In yet another cheap rented room, another cheap little man is discovered lying in bed desperate about what he's done with his life. Grady (Mickey Rooney) is banned from racing for life because he had been doping the horses. Like Jackie Rhoades, Grady engages in a pathetic phone call that fails to connect him with anything good. He then confronts his image in a mirror, referring to himself with the nasty epithet used by Rhoades: "You runt!" Not surprisingly, he grabs for a bottle. Then, Grady also spots a stronger image of himself in the mirror: "I am what you call the alter-ego," this version of him insists. Here *Last Night* veers from *Nervous Man*; whereas that redemption saga allowed us to watch a forlorn fellow overcome past failings when allowed a second chance owing to his humanism, we witness now a cautionary fable about a man who cares for no one and so can't find redemption.

There is no outside force to corrupt him; the devil is within Grady. However bad he may be, the mirror image is worse still! Unlike Jackie Rhoades, Grady feels no remorse for what he's done to people or animals, so he's offered a single (self-serving) wish. Easy enough: he wants to be big. When he wakes from a troubled nap, he's ten feet tall. Then a call comes from the racetrack: they have decided to give Grady a Second Chance, allowing him back in the game. Now, however, he's too tall. As Serling notes at the end: "Unfortunately for Mr. Grady, he learned too late that you don't measure size with a ruler, you don't figure height with a yardstick, and you never judge a man by how tall he looks in a mirror. The giant is as he does." Lesson to be learned . . .

Dust Be My Destiny:

LONG LIVE WALTER JAMESON (3/19/60)

This Charles Beaumont contribution concerns a college history professor (Kevin McCarthy) whose lectures come to life in the classroom. This creates a gnawing problem for elderly Professor Samuel Kittridge (Edgar Stehli). Each day he feels closer to death, while Jameson looks no older than when they first met. Kittridge listens in as Jameson reads from Major Skelton's Civil War journals to a spellbound class. Later, Kittridge looks up Skelton (a variation on "skeleton," which Jameson will shortly become) in a book of Matthew Brady photographs. Standing next to General Sherman, Skelton is a precise double (Mirror Image) for Jameson, right down to a facial mole. Jameson finally confesses: 2,500 years ago, he paid an alchemist for eternal life.

Serling puts his own spin on Beaumont's script by informing us that Jameson's eternal youth hails from "a book on black magic." Jameson got what he wanted, only to grow bitter once the dream proved unpleasant. His situation forced a wedge between Jameson and other people, qualifying him as one of The Lonely. Jameson cannot warrant audience sympathy, for he plans to use Kittridge's daughter (Dody Heath) as he did previous women, temporarily marrying her only to desert once she grows old. He fails to display a humanist's concern for others. But poetic justice catches up with him. An elderly woman and one-time lover (Estelle Winwood) shoots Jameson. Professor Kittridge discovers Jameson in his death throes, watching in horror as a 3.5-millennia old man disintegrates.

Serling closes with his take on what this means: "Yet another human being returns to the vast nothingness that is the beginning, and the dust that is always the end." If that sounds nihilistic, *Walter*

Jameson includes enough spiritual references to offset it. Faith in something greater than ourselves pops up in a Socratic dialogue between the professors. "In heaven's name," Kittridge pleads, begging Jameson to share the secret of eternal life. But the alchemist didn't pass along the formula. However unlikely it seems, Kittridge is lucky that he can't follow suit. Jameson hungered for eternity because he believed that death renders life absurd. In due time, experience taught him the opposite: Death is what endows life with meaning by qualifying every single moment precious. Jameson is worthy of limited empathy owing to his last words. Dying, he says: "Nothing lasts forever, thank God!"

Beat the Devil:

PRINTER'S DEVIL (2/28/63)

Beaumont based this episode on "The Devil, You Say?" (*Amazing Stories*), one of his early efforts. Entirely rewriting the piece for *Zone*, he provided yet another portrait of the auteur as not-so-young-man. The actor chosen for the lead looks like Serling, a comparison cinched by his name: Rob Sterling plays Douglas Winter. The character's name fits nicely; we meet him during his professional winter of discontent. Winter's traditionalist newspaper, the *Courier*, has after a long, honorable run lost readers to the *Gazette*, a superficial new tabloid. Winter's paper serves as a metaphor for *Zone*, in danger of cancellation owing to high ratings of superficial competition such as ABC's *77 Sunset Strip*. James Aubrey, then CBS president, scoffed at any commitment to the "prestige" show. Favoring mindless escapism (*My Living Doll*, etc.), he wanted *Zone* jazzed up, made profitable, or gone.

Similarly, from the moment we first see Winter in his office he resembles Serling not only in appearance, but in action (Winter chain-smokes and drinks from a bottle kept in his desk drawer to alleviate the pressure) and demeanor (intense, edgy) as well. His significant other, secretary Jackie Benson (Patricia Crowley), appears like Patricia

Breslin in *Nick of Time*, also modeled on Carol Serling: a stunning brunette with style and substance. They live in small Danzburg (the state is not identified), one more place that retains a sense of the past. But that's changing, owing to the junk that the *Gazette* churns out. This happens to readers in fictional Danzburg as, in real life, it proved the case for viewers exposed to *Petticoat Junction* instead of *Playhouse 90* or *Zone*. Linotype operator Andy (Charlie Thompson) regretfully leaves to work for the competition. He respects Winter but believes the *Courier* to be a losing cause. Likewise, longtime producer Buck Houghton, fearing that *Zone* would be cancelled at the third season's end, left to work for Four Star, thereafter producing superficial but successful shows like *Burke's Law*. Pushed too far, Winter heads for a bridge to commit suicide; director Ralph Senensky set up this sequence as an homage to that moment in Capra's *It's a Wonderful Life* when George Bailey (James Stewart), another decent small-town man who believes himself a failure, is about to end it all. And Bailey would have, were it not for the benevolent arrival of angel Clarence (Henry Travers). Likewise, Doug Winter halts as metaphysical figure Mr. Smith (Burgess Meredith) arrives on cue.

Smith, however, is a devil in the flesh, hoping to steal the hero's soul and reputation for quality. Able to light his cigarette with a finger that spouts flames, Smith offers to loan the editor enough money to continue while working the linotype machine and reporting. Soon, the paper begins to sell like hotcakes, thanks to early scoops on terrible things like honeymooners drowning in a lake. Yet Doug Winter is torn, loving the success (status and money) while sensing that what was best about his life's work is dissolving. Wouldn't it perhaps have been better if his paper, like *Zone*, were allowed to quietly disappear, doing so with dignity? The person who smells a rat is Jackie. It's she who says, as Smith (whom they've been talking about) arrives: "Speak of the devil!"

Likewise, Jackie articulates what the sweet life is doing to him: "You're different. You've changed!" Jackie so loves what Winter has always been that she'll break their engagement rather than remain with a lesser version. This would leave Winter, like screenwriter

Ernie Pandish (whose wife leaves him in *The Velvet Alley*), one of The Lonely. Cinching the parallel to Serling, friend Saul Marmer stated; "Carol saw it coming . . . she kept him on an even keel in Connecticut, but couldn't in California. She did threaten to leave him." Fortunately for Doug Winter (in this show) and Serling (in real life), each comes to his senses, hanging on to his woman and his personal integrity.

The contract Smith has fashioned for Winter (like the one in *Escape Clause*) allows him an out: Winter can terminate the working relationship if he agrees to surrender his life, his soul already gone. "What good is a soul, anyway?" Smith asks of the modern man. "It's kind of an appendix *these days*." Again, **Zone** emphasizes spirituality (or the lack of it) in an ever more scientific world. The linotype apparatus has been endowed with black magic—Smith is able to type in any terrible occurrence which will then come true—here's one more infernal machine like the ones already encountered in *The Fever* and *Nick of Time*. When Smith types in that Jackie will die in an automobile accident, her fate appears sealed. Winter is left with an hour and fifteen minutes to help her, one more variation on the Time Limit. Rather than seize the gun Smith has left for him to commit suicide, Winter believes free will can yet counteract fate. Winter types in a story in which Jackie survives the crash, and so she does.

Doug Winter also writes that Mr. Smith has left for another job; the devil is gone. But owing to the signed contract, there's one unanswered question: Though he will live a nice life with Jackie, what will happen to his immortal soul (which he signed away) when, eventually, he does die?

Mountain Music:

JESS-BELLE (2/14/63)

Earl Hamner Jr.'s *Jess-Belle* caused Serling to sum up his ambition for the show: "*The Twilight Zone* has existed in many lands, in many times. It has its roots in history, in something that happened long

ago and got told and handed down from one generation to the other."
These were ancient legends and myths that defined mankind's hopes
and fears, now retold for a modern audience requiring new variations
on old themes. "In the telling, the story gets added to and embroidered
on, so that what might have happened in the time of the Druids is
told as if it took place yesterday in the Blue Ridge Mountains." A
sense of continuum, essential to the series, was now formalized.
Jess-Belle is the only episode that does not feature closing remarks
by Serling (instead, we hear a final ballad of the episode's folk-like
song), suggesting that he had at last said all there was to say.

An updating of Val Lewton's *Cat People* (1942), *Jess-Belle's* title
character (Anne Francis) cannot accept that her beloved, Billy-Ben
(James Best), will marry respectable Ellwyn (Laura Devon). Jess
hurries off to witch Granny Hart (Jeanette Nolan) for a love potion
to enslave Billy-Ben. The consequences: Jess's soul is lost forever and
she will turn into a deadly leopard at midnight. Now Jess cannot
marry Billy-Ben for fear that when they retire, she'll tear him to
pieces. Basic to this story's power is that the title figure (like Sim-
one Simon in *Cat People*) is sympathetic. Despite a reference to evil
queen Jezebel, Jess (while hardly a heroine) never appears a clear-cut
villainess. She has been used (for sex) by Billy-Ben and, as a big cat,
could easily kill Ellwyn, but chooses not to.

If nothing else, Jess understands unconditional love. When it
comes down to a choice between enjoying Billy-Ben in her arms or
denying herself pleasure so he can live, Jess chooses the latter. The
title implies a Biblical dimension. When Ellwyn feels threatened
by a force of evil, Billy-Ben hands the girl a Bible, saying: "Trust in
The Lord; hold His word in your hand!" Sight is important, as the
potion will cause Billy-Ben to love (i.e., desire) what he sees, though
his heart belongs to Ellwyn. Jess is another ***Zone*** denizen who gets
what she wants and lives to regret it, defying fate by attempting to
create her destiny via free will. The notion of immortality (a witch
can't die), as well as death as a release from the pains of life (re-
embracing her human side Jess does expire, as a falling star makes
clear), reveals that this excursion into a unique rural subculture has
allowed for one more passage through Serling's highly personalized

fifth dimension. Hamner is the author; Serling remains the auteur, the primary artist behind *Zone* and its ongoing vision.

"The Devil, You Say!":

OF LATE I THINK OF CLIFFORDVILLE (4/11/63)

This episode opens with a view of that ongoing *Zone* villain, the raw capitalist. Or, as he will be described by a sexy-and-silken female Satan, Miss Devlin (Julie Newmar), "one of the few remaining rugged individualists of our time!" Her tone is ironic, condemning, though the target of her verbal attack is too self-satisfied to (initially) grasp that. William Feathersmith (Albert Salmi) owns a network of business interests, headquartered in New York. Like Martin Sloan, he has moved to Manhattan from a small town he now recalls with nostalgia. But whereas the early-middle-aged Sloan retained some of that place's values, the elderly Feathersmith is corrupted beyond hope of redemption. When he runs into the sexy devil and offers to sell his soul to go back in time, she laughs. She had that years ago! No, it's hard cold cash "they" want . . . and that's all Featherstone has left to give.

That concept is new to *Zone*. How does one dramatize a character who has fallen so low that his soul is already gone? Featherstone is bored. And, if incapable of admitting it, he is lonely. He misses the thrill-ride of getting to the top and wants to start over, not only to make his fortune once more, but to acquire a greater one owing to what he now knows: A piece of property found in 1937 containing oil pockets. He'll return to 1910, buy that land from its owners, banker Gibbons (Guy Raymond) and businessman Dietrich (John Anderson) for loose change, and then develop it. Only after Featherstone owns the marshlands does he realize that the technology doesn't yet exist to bring up black gold—that won't be possible for years. Until then, he'll be land poor, unable to buy a meal.

"The devil, you say," Featherstone exclaims after he finds himself on an old-fashioned train that grinds to a halt at the rural hamlet. This episode emerged during the same season in which Serling encouraged

Reginald Rose to write *The Incredible World of Horace Ford*, approaching nostalgia with a bitter tone. Buildings in Cliffordville are identical to those in Willoughby, but all resemblance ends there. The streets are unpleasantly muddy; people are confined to their homes with typhoid; the banker's daughter Joanna (Christine Burke), recalled as a beauty, is anything but. You can't go home again because each of us romanticizes the past in our mind. Actuality can never measure up to such an ideal.

Of course, Willoughby must also contain mud, typhoid, and unattractive people. In that episode, though, Gart Williams is so pure and innocent that he focuses only on the good he finds. Bill Featherstone, approaching just such a place with jaded values, notices only the ugliness. Taken together, the two tales restate the theme of *A Nice Place to Visit*: heaven and hell are one and the same; we impose subjective mindsets onto any situation we find ourselves in. Featherstone begs Miss Devlin to return him to 1963, though she requires a forty dollar "adjustment." Without funds, he sells the deeds to the oil-rich land to the first person he meets, a rube named (appropriately, if hardly subtly) Hecate (Wright King). Returning to New York in the present day, Featherstone finds everything reversed. In the opening, he sat behind a big mahogany desk, waited on by old Hecate; now, their positions are reversed. Presumably, Hecate made money, if only after a long wait, on the fields once the technology was invented and the land finally paid off.

Earlier Time Element episodes insisted that, try as we might, we can't change the major aspects of history even if we may alter minor, personal elements. That theme continues here. Featherstone clearly has re-charted the course of his own fate owing to the free will he exerts, inadvertently turning himself into an old pauper rather than a financial prince. On another (greater) level, though, the history around them remains identical; the name of the company's owner may be different, but that, in the larger scheme of things, seems minor. More important is a darkening of Serling's view of human nature. In the past, there were good people and bad. The final dialogue here belies that. Featherstone, entering the office to clean up, is as humble and sweet as old Hecate in the opening. On the other hand, Hecate says the same vicious, insensitive things to his lackey that, before the tables were turned, Featherstone spat at him. The implication is that good and bad are not written in the cement of individual character; power corrupts absolutely. That's a bleak new dramatic road running through the fifth dimension, one that would reach full fruition during the show's final season.

Return to the Velvet Alley:

THE BARD (5/23/63)

Here Serling had the opportunity to poke fun at the TV industry and, to a degree, himself. Our "little guy" antihero, Julius Moomer (Jack Weston), sets fire to pigeon feathers and ants (substituted for those of a falcon and spider's legs) on a pile of sand. Having acquired a book on the black arts, Moomer hopes to summon up a spirit to guide him in his profession, writing. The landlady's daughter, Cora (Judy Strangis), peeks in and caustically asks: "So tell me, *Faust*—to what end?" The devil is never seen here, neither as a horrible man (Burgess Meredith in *Printer's Devil*) or a tempting woman (Julie Newmar in *Cliffordville*). The spirit raised is benign: a god to all writers, the immortal Bard of Avon, William Shakespeare (John Williams).

Earlier, Moomer, a former streetcar conductor bitten by the writing bug, had pitched his latest ideas for upcoming TV shows to a blasé agent, Gerald Hugo (Henry Lascoe). These included concepts for stories about a heavyweight champ, a top gun in the west, and a science fiction piece about rocket men, all similar to ideas Serling employed for *Zone*. "I never heard so many variations on the same story," Hugo sighs, voicing criticism often raised about the recurring themes (travel through time and space, etc.) on *Zone*. "You will never be a writer," the agent insists, not unlike the journalist who tried to talk Serling's father into convincing his son of just that (See Introduction). Like Serling, Moomer does not quit, for the simple reason that he can't. Writing is a calling, a kind of secular religion understood by those who hear the muse's seductive voice and can't resist.

Julius Moomer is Serling's least likely autobiographical character. Serling mostly created approximations of himself and cast the parts accordingly. Plump, unattractive Moomer appears so utterly different from the show's creator that we might at first assume he couldn't be Serling's spokesmen. Perhaps that was a self-defense mechanism, since Serling will prove as unsparing toward himself as the industry that rewarded and limited his "God-given talent." Like Serling, Moomer hungers for the financial gains of a successful career. Though he does desire critical recognition (the Pulitzer), he spends more time talking about various material goods (a stretch limousine).

There were occasional lawsuits Serling had to deal with as other writers, professionals, and novices accused him of stealing ideas, however inadvertently. (For example, close friends pointed out that the teleplay *Grady Everett for the People* (1950) bore more than a passing resemblance to the novel *All the King's Men*). Here, Moomer is so eager to enjoy success that he can't see what we notice: He's not "collaborating" with Shakespeare (though that's what Moomer believes that he's doing) but handing in Old Will's work as if it were his and reaping the rewards. Even when accolades do come, Moomer can't truly enjoy them, so concerned is he that he doesn't really have it. In this light, John Frankenheimer's summing up of Serling's insecurities strikes home: "He never believed in himself as a writer. He always had doubts, and he could never solve that demon in himself." That was one of Serling's demons; another was that he'd sold out, allowing what talent he had to be compromised by censors and sponsors.

That happens here. Mr. Shannon (John McGiver) demands that one script be rewritten so there'll be no conflict with the best interests of his soup company. A pair of network suits arrive, suggesting that a *Romeo and Juliet* balcony scene isn't hip enough; the young lovers ought to meet in a subway. Moomer tries to defend the changes to Will, who grows furious at the corruption his "collaborator" refuses to acknowledge. Serling objectifies his inner conflict by breaking the two sides of his psyche into separate characters. Moomer is the half that hungers for financial success, even if that means compromising values; Shakespeare is the serious talent who wants only to create something of quality. The danger, in Serling's words, for any writer who steps into Tinseltown is that "everything's all whipped cream and marshmallows, mink coats and swimming pools"—style without substance, sweet but superficial, dangerously seductive.

Commenting on Serling's *Rank and File*, critic Harriet Van Horne noted that the protagonist arrived at "a moral crossroads" he couldn't escape from. Though well-intentioned, "Ultimately, gross ambition devours the gentle idealist." That play focused on organized labor; many observers sensed that Serling was writing about himself. "I am frightened," he told Edward R. Murrow about their industry (1958), "by striving to reach the largest possible audience for everything." That's satirized in *The Bard* when the self-important sponsor tears a great script apart, eliminating anything that might offend anybody. Yet it isn't easy to walk away from success when it turns one into a rich and famous man. You're "addicted," someone tells the lead character, Sammy, in *The Comedian*, to "adulation, the love of forty million people."

Not to de-emphasize cash. "It's money, ain't it?" Maish asked Mountain when the former heavyweight recoiled from the idea of professional wrestling. The ever-conflicted Serling gave us differing endings for his two versions of that play. For TV in 1956, Mountain rejects that proposal and goes home again to a simple, but better, life. That was before Serling lived in Beverly Hills. Following that life-altering experience, he provided a different finale for the 1963 movie. Mountain sadly nods his head yes, dons an Indian costume, and hops into the ring. Dirty money, he decides, is better than no money at all. Serling experienced that firsthand. "They give you a thousand dollars a week," a character in *The Velvet Alley* (about the dangers of becoming a commercial hack to sustain one's lifestyle) says. "And they keep giving it to you until you can't live without it." The tragedy is, having enjoyed the taste of honey, "there isn't anything you won't do to keep that thousand dollars a week." Including, we might guess, sell one's poetic soul to the devil of commercialism. This helps us understand why *Twilight Zone* contains so many Faustian fables: that effectively describes how Rod Serling saw himself.

9

HOW THE WEST WAS WEIRD:
Two Genres at a Crossroads

WHAT DID THE New America, created by a postwar economy and devoted to middlebrow values, find fascinating about the Old West? Peter Biskind claims that citizens of the 1950s stressed "conformity and domesticity" in their daily lives. Yet any suburbanite could finish off his TV dinner while slipping off into a televised fantasy about a bygone world in which rugged individualists refused to settle down and forever rode off into the sunset. However little of that had to do with the actual American frontier, this vision served as the basis for our romantic myth. The Western show was, according to Richard Schickel, part of a greater "popular nostalgia" for "an imagined past" that "informed much of the new popular culture." This widespread phenomenon extended even into the fifth dimension. No wonder, then, that Rod Serling felt comfortable working within the Western genre, which took our emergent nostalgia craze a step further back in time from the early twentieth century small towns he admired. But for Serling, even cowboys must have a cosmic bent. The result was a postscript to a form that was, even as *Zone* premiered, quickly reaching the end of its TV trail.

How Dry I Am:

MR. DENTON ON DOOMSDAY (10/16/59)

The opening shot, as set up by director Allen Reisner, presents a forlorn landscape, identical to what we might see on *The Rifleman*: Distant hill country forms the backdrop to a prairie that leads into a small, isolated town. A lone man steers a buckboard down the dusty main street. The first physical action: rowdy cowboys toss a pathetic drunk out of the saloon. Deconstruction of this typical situation begins as we realize that he's our protagonist. Al Denton (Dan Duryea), once a fast gun, has gradually become a joke and the butt of cruelty from a black-clad young gunslinger, Hotaling (Martin Landau), an ugly take-off on the similar dark-dressed but morally upright character played by William Boyd on *Hopalong Cassidy*. Hotaling openly bullies this shadow of a man, to the chagrin of a sympathetic saloon girl Liz (Jeanne Cooper) and the bartender, Charlie (Ken Lynch). Liz recalls Miss Kitty (Amanda Blake) on *Gunsmoke*; Charlie evokes Sam (Glenn Strange). Later in this *Zone*, Doc (Robert Burton) shows up, offering a parallel to Milburn Stone's Doc Adams. The only missing characters are likenesses of Marshal Matt Dillon (James Arness) and deputy Chester (Dennis Weaver.) That's appropriate since, in comparison to Dodge, this unnamed town exists without law and order.

Recurring themes appear—the issue of alcoholism most obvious—resulting in death and nightmares. Denton, Serling informs us, has "begun his dying early" via the alcohol addiction he cannot lick, in part because of "bad dreams that infect his consciousness." Destiny appears here as an allegorical figure, Henry J. Fate (Malcolm Atterbury). This tinhorn peddler appears cryptic, observing all that occurs from a distance. Yet he reveals himself as benign, allowing Denton his Second Chance.

This occurs through the fantastical device of a special six-shooter, though ultimately Serling rejects gun violence as an acceptable answer to social problems. Fate drops a pistol in front of Denton. When Hotaling forces the ruined man into a showdown, the gun's magic allows Denton to win, achieving the redemption he, typical of *Zone* heroes, hungers for. Even the title hints at this: following a victory over Hotaling, "Al the Town Drunk" is once more referred to as Mr. Denton. He glows with self-respect. Quickly, euphoria evaporates. Now, every fast gun in the West will drift in, hoping to make a reputation by killing "The Man Who Shot Hotaling," a theme that dominated Westerns beginning with *The Gunfighter*

(1950). The "young punk" here is played by Doug McClure, who shortly would star in such TV Westerns as *The Overland Trail* and *The Virginian*. Duryea was a veteran of Westerns, both on TV and in the movies.

Serling raises this cliché to undermine it. The rules of the Western dictate that these two will shoot it out and one (or both) must die. Not here. With his strange smile, Fate (knowing that Denton is nervous) provides the forlorn man with a potion (at no cost) that will make the old-timer unbeatable for ten seconds after he swallows it. But when Denton faces off with Pete Grant in the bar, the tired man realizes that Fate has played a cunning trick: The youth also has been handed the potion, leveling the odds. However demonic this may seem, it offers further evidence that there are angels in America. When the two men go for their guns, they prove to be equals. Instead of killing one another, Denton and Grant shoot one another's hands. The guns fall to the ground; though no one is dead, neither can ever gunfight again. Each is freed from the stigma of violence to find a better life. That's where free will comes in; Fate's role was to intervene, giving each his Second Chance at a decent existence. Religion is present, as indicated by what Denton says to Grant before they part company: both have been "blessed."

The Way West:

A HUNDRED YARDS OVER THE RIM (4/7/61)

When *Denton on Doomsday* aired in 1959, *Gunsmoke* still ranked as the highest-rated Western on television. Shortly, NBC's *Wagon Train* would usurp the top spot. It made sense that the conventions of this series, about a caravan slowly moving west, would also be undercut. In the opening shot we see Conestogas cross a stretch of desert as a harmonica plays melancholy music. Then comes our first glimpse of the wagon master, Captain Chris Horn (Cliff Robertson). That he's meant as a reference to *Wagon Train*'s pivotal character is made clear by his name. Following Ward Bond's death, the role of wagon master (now called "Captain Chris Hale") was played by John McIntyre. In comparison to the typical cowboy hat worn by that actor, Horn dons a stovepipe hat worthy of Abe Lincoln. Deconstruction of any expected cowboy costuming prepares us for the eventual breakdown of a persona.

On *Wagon Train*, the wagon master (as much a fantasy figure as the perfect lawman on *Gunsmoke*) always proved infallible. We encounter the opposite here, for Horn manages to get the train sidetracked. Headed for California, they instead find themselves somewhere in New Mexico. Horn's small band, lost and without water, cannot long survive. Worse, Horn's little boy, down with fever, appears doomed. Many pioneers want to turn back. Horn requests that they allow him a "second chance" to find salvation: He'll climb up over the far rim in hopes that something—anything!—may be there. No sooner does Horn disappear from their sight than he finds himself in modern times. Staggering onto a highway, he's nearly run down by a passing truck. But human kindness still exists in 1961's world: Horn is nursed by Joe (John Crawford), the owner of a diner, and his sympathetic wife Mary (Evans Evans). She hands him penicillin tablets, explaining their "miraculous" healing powers to the astounded man.

Here, we should to consider another aspect of the hero's name. Though everyone in the drama refers to the man as "Chris," in both his opening and closing narration, Serling invokes his full name—not Christopher, but Christian. Chris Horn will take ideas espoused by Jesus and carry them into the secular arena, making the real world a better place. Serling himself fully subscribed to the values proposed by Jesus and, on more than one occasion, half-kiddingly described himself as "a christian with a small 'c'." *Zone* was created by a Jewish author who did not absolutely accept the rising of Jesus on the third day after crucifixion. On the other hand, he fully subscribed to the values—peace, love, and forgiveness—preached by Rabbi Jesus. As to the Resurrection or Virgin Birth, such events for him qualify as "miracles" even as in *Zone* (*A Hundred Yards* included) events are indeed miracles for you, if you believe them to be precisely that.

In the diner in 1961, Horn flips through a reference book and notices an entry about his own son who, in time, would be a doctor specializing in childhood diseases. Horn realizes that Joe and Mary (can anyone not take their names as indications of a religious allegory?) have called the police out of concern for him. Horn hurries out to the desert and over the ridge, slipping back in time (arriving a split second after he left), rejoining the pioneers. Or, as they often choose to call themselves, pilgrims. Given the penicillin, Horn's son survives. As he must, to fulfill his destiny as written in the book at the diner and in the greater book of fate in which history is predetermined. Yet this couldn't have happened if Horn hadn't exerted free will and wandered over the rim. God helps those who help themselves.

The train continues, hopes raised. Horn's wife believes that the saving of her feverish child was a miracle, while we know that it was the result of medicine. Then again, penicillin had originally been hailed as a "miracle drug." That term, and the two differing words that compose it, summarize Serling's point of view. In the *Zone*, science and spirituality are in no way at odds. Rather, they complement one another; are alternative language systems, employed by people with varied levels of sophistication to describe the same thing. No wonder then that as a characteristic *Zone* hero, Horn (while still in the diner, attempting to grasp what's going on) states: "I know that I was put here for a reason." Serling's show continually reasserts during the late 1950s and early 1960s that, even in an era when traditional beliefs were being tested by technological breakthroughs, there is reason to believe (as George Lucas would insist) in the ultimately positive—if often incomprehensible—Force.

Justice, Guilt, Retribution:

EXECUTION (4/1/60)

In a highly stylized tableau of the Old West at its bleakest, circa 1880, members of a lynch mob slowly ride over a hill's crest. They guard Joe Caswell (Albert Salmi), about to be hanged for killing an unarmed man. Serling does not, in his opening narration, refer to Caswell as an "outlaw," nor does anyone else in an episode adapted by Serling from an unpublished story by George Clayton Johnson. Instead, he calls the man a "cowboy," a term ordinarily reserved for the hero, resulting in a deconstruction of the romanticized TV myth. A Reverend (Jon Lormer) with the posse provides a framing device for a story that begins on the frontier but soon enters the domain of science and technology. That religion (and a metaphysical theme) will serve as the central issue here is further underlined. "When the Good Lord passed out a conscience," we learn, Caswell "missed out." We also realize this is a legal hanging following a trial; Caswell was found guilty of a crime he did commit. If anyone, anywhere, deserves capital punishment (an issue raised often on *Zone*), it is he.

A distinct *Zone* touch follows. We learn that Caswell lacks "a heart" and has "no feeling for fellow men." The Reverend offers to pray for Caswell's immortal soul; the doomed man cynically replies that he's more interested in his mortal neck. More than an effective gag, the interchange sets up *Execution*'s moral paradigm. At that moment when Caswell's horse is slapped, leaving him dangling in mid-air (here suggested by shadow-play), the intended victim disappears. Not surprisingly, it is the Reverend who reacts, in close-up: "Oh, my dear God!" This decent nineteenth-century religious man, unaware of anything we think of as modernity, can't comprehend what he sees (the vision theme again) as anything but a metaphysical event. A miracle, seemingly, though Divine Intervention would hardly infer "justice" for this man.

Even as the scene switches to a scientific laboratory in New York, 1960, references to God disappear. A perfectly logical explanation for what's happened is offered: well-intentioned Professor Manion (Russell Johnson) randomly plucked a person from the time-space continuum and drew him into the present. Considering that the first writer, this actor, and a member of the lynch mob share one name, there are almost as many Johnsons in this Western as in Mel Brooks's 1974 genre-spoof *Blazing Saddles*. Manion guesses that this is no honest trail boss (though that's what Caswell claims to be). The professor has inadvertently "taken a nineteenth-century primitive and placed him in a twentieth-century jungle." Caswell murders Johnson, then runs off into New York's mean streets. Again ahead of its time, *Zone* presents the first televised depiction of noise pollution: Caswell clasps his hands over his ears to drown out the cascade of honking cars, rock 'n' roll, and loud voices around him. Such a situation invokes the nostalgia theme, this time featuring a less sympathetic lead than in *Walking Distance* or *Willoughby*.

Other motifs include the wrinkle in time and, if less obviously so, the notion of The Lonely. Though we can hardly sympathize with brutish Caswell, in *Zone* this malaise can overcome a villain as well as a hero. Ultimately, though, this episode can best be described as a "moral tale." It's not that there's an obvious message, but that the underlying meaning coexists with mass entertainment. "Some things don't change," Manion insists before dying; "ideas, concepts, right and wrong, justice!" Caswell scoffs, but at the end he'll receive his just deserts. Such poetic justice implies that we do inhabit an ordered universe, a traditionalist vision that survives into our scientific age. Caswell kills Manion. Simultaneously, *Zone* deconstructs not only our then-dominant notion of the noble cowboy, but its own medium as well.

This deconstruction takes place during an inspired sequence as Caswell enters a New York City bar. Up on the elevated TV, a Western plays. In it, a marshal talks directly into the camera, ordering an off-screen outlaw to draw. Caswell, stunned, yanks out the pistol he stole from Manion and shoots at the television; considering the order in which episodes originally played, this is the first of many *Zones* in which TVs, particularly when offering conventional junk, are violently destroyed. Earlier, a phone booth sequence (in which Caswell recoils from a disembodied voice on the other end) brought that recurrent motif into play. Other key concepts are raised by Caswell and Manion during their philosophical debate, an early example of the form Serling learned at Antioch and would employ often.

The issue here is whether justice and retribution exist in a modern universe. Caswell embodies William Butler Yeats's "rough beast," the anti-Christ (religiously speaking) or a throwback to our animal origins (scientifically), lumbering toward a contemporary Bethlehem to be born. For the decent Manion, justice and retribution remain real. Such forces will, however unlikely it momentarily appears, eventually be visited upon the guilty. That occurs as Caswell, desperate to slip away from this weird world, hurries back to Manion's laboratory, hoping to return to the past while a common crook named Paul Johnson (Than Wyenn) sneaks in. Marc Scott Zicree dismisses this as a "contrivance." If *Execution* were an attempt at realistic drama, he would be right. But like so many *Zones*, this one fits Aristotle's definition of true tragedy: drama on a metaphysical plane. If we interpret Johnson's arrival as fate (he represents Caswell's destiny, though neither man yet knows it), the situation is no more contrived than the constantly crossing paths of characters in *Oedipus Rex*.

In the ensuing brawl, Johnson strangles Caswell with a window cord. A man who was supposed to hang does indeed die in such a manner. Nor does Johnson escape his preordained punishment. Stepping into the glass compartment with plans of stealing anything valuable, he's propelled back in time, hanging out West in Caswell's place. Though a seeming "accident" instigated by Manion's experiment, two villainous figures are eliminated. Without Manion's exercise in scientific free will, the fate of both guilty parties would not have occurred.

Serling improves on George Clayton Johnson's original. In it, Caswell, through utterly ridiculous circumstances, is himself propelled back to the hangman's noose. Johnson's version was clever, and Serling's, philosophic. Now, the Reverend and his companions gaze on in wonder as the body of an unknown man in strange clothing appears:

> **REVEREND:** What kind of devil's work is this?
> **MARSHAL:** I don't know if it is "devil's work."

As the marshal implies, this is the "good Lord at work," something even the Reverend fails to grasp. We know what the posse cannot: A seeming "metaphysical transformation" (by God or the Devil) happened because of a modern machine. Just because we know the logical explanation, however, doesn't mean that this was not part of a Master Plan. Perhaps that Force inspired Manion to operate his time machine so that the larger destiny could be fulfilled.

REVEREND: Did we hang an innocent man?
MARSHAL: I hope not. I pray to God not!

Even they suffer. Perhaps this is their punishment for engaging in capital punishment, never taken lightly in *Zone*. Still, morality of an old-fashioned order has been served (rather than challenged) by the machinery of a modern age. Scientific technology fulfills rather than dispels our traditional religious values . . . in the fifth dimension.

A Good Day for a Hanging:

DUST (1/6/61)

Execution focuses on justice, guilt, and retribution; in *Dust*, Serling concerns himself with what Shakespeare called the quality of mercy: a man's essential imperfection and eventual redemption. This will be one of the grimmer *Zones*, posited by director Douglas Heyes's visualization of the Old West in contrast to genre series. *Bonanza* then rode high in the ratings, with its sugary, sentimental vision of decent folk inhabiting a picturesque frontier. *Dust*, on the other hand, recalls adult Westerns of the late 1940s and 1950s with their bleak portrayal of windswept towns surrounded by barren prairies. This unnamed town, says Serling, was "built of crumbling clay and rotting wood, and it squatted ugly under the broiling sun like a sick and mangy animal waiting to die." Like Shakespeare's Elsinore, we sense there's something rotten at work in this state. "The village had a virus, shared by its people." Not only has draught caused a once flourishing trade to disappear; squalor gave way to "hopelessness, a loss of faith." Whenever such social malaise strikes (this isolated cow-town, the suburban neighborhood in *The Monsters Are Due on Maple Street*, America itself during the era of McCarthy red-baiting), people "destroy themselves." Do these dark lines imply that Serling now offers an indictment of mankind? The citizens we meet here (and in such similarly inclined scripts as *The Shelter*) do provide worst case scenarios of moral degeneracy. Yet *Dust* is not submitted as a universal portrait of humanity; rather, it contrasts with other episodes in which people, however flawed, rise to the occasion and do the right thing. Such stories provide images of humanity at its best. For verisimilitude they need to be balanced by reminders of what we can stoop to at our worst.

Dust's dark story begins as Sykes (Thomas Gomez), a humble tinker, guides his frayed carriage into the sullen hamlet where a lonely crowd awaits the hanging of Luis Gallegos (John Alonso). He's been found guilty of killing a little girl when, drunk, he rode wildly down the street. The execution will be carried out by Sheriff Koch (John Larch) who despises this part of his job, particularly since Koch understands that such a stupid yet unintentional incident might have been forgiven if the perpetrator were white. Ethnicity, in which this Latino caused an Anglo to die, provides an element of racism in the demands for execution. Recurring themes are invoked: an implied warning as to the dangers of alcohol; the fear of a once-decent community degenerating into a mean-spirited mob; any sort of prejudice as the worst aspect of mankind; the role of death in our lives; the secular city, a place devoid of faith; and the anti-raw capitalist theme as, for Serling, the man whose only interest in life is to make money is the one we should indict.

In this case, that's Sykes, who sold the rope that will be used. Far worse is what Sykes does next. When Gallegos' old father (Vladimir Sokoloff) begs for his son, the townspeople rudely shove the elderly Mexican away. Sykes agrees to sell Gallegos's father a packet of magic dust that he can sprinkle over the mob, resulting in a miracle. People will turn from hate to love and (mercifully) set Luis Gallegos free. As Old Gallegos hopefully rushes off to borrow money, Sykes cynically laughs as he scrapes ordinary dust off the street and slips it into a little bag he'll shortly sell to the naive father. Sykes represents the devil in the flesh. He laughs out loud at the sheriff's concerns, then insists Gallegos "got stinking drunk" and deserves death. Hypocritically, Sykes shouts this while uncorking a bottle for himself.

We view Sykes in contrast to the sheriff, he the flawed but worthy opposite aspect of man: aware of his potential to, like Luis, unintentionally do a terrible thing if he happened to be in the wrong place at the wrong time. To be truly human, in Serling's moral universe, is to see one's own potential for a momentary failure in others less fortunate, and to express compassion, not condemnation, for their failures. Koch also drinks, though he refuses to touch the bottle opened by Sykes, "a midget." Here is Serling's recurring little people theme. Actor Gomez (a Mexican playing an Anglo!) is anything but small in stature. Yet many *Zone* heroes are short. The sheriff's harsh condemnation here refers to Syke's inner character.

Sykes then suggests that the sheriff should not shed tears over Gallegos because of the youth's race. This angers Koch, who serves as the moral epicenter, unable (owing to his badge) to stop what he knows will be a great wrong, yet suffering from the realization that, of all people, he must perform the vengeful act. "When was it (that) God made people?" Koch muses at the episode's midpoint. "The sixth day? He should have stopped on the fifth!" It's difficult not to read this as proof of growing pessimism on Serling's part. Such darkness will dominate the show's fifth season (see Chapter 12). Yet to take this line out of context is to misunderstand it. For Koch (who now brings religion into this episode's mix) speaks his mind at this moment, when all others appear ready to allow the boy to die. All the same, Luis Gallegos maintains his own faith, even as the hour of doom draws near.

When a small Anglo child calls through a barred jail window, asking if Gallegos will be hanged, the sad-eyed victim insists that this will happen if it is "God's will." As the tale moves toward denouement, we see sparks of evidence indicating a benign aspect to man—and a metaphysical element, allowing for Gallegos's resurrection in every sense. As Gallegos's father rushes up with a handful of coins, stunned Sykes grasps (as do we) that the poor *peones* pooled their money to save the boy. Then Old Gallegos desperately rushes to the sight of the gallows. Though every other element of the town has been displayed realistically, this spot conveys (like the hanging tree in Wellman's *Ox Bow Incident*) an other worldly quality, shrouded in a bizarre light from above.

This out-of-the-way hillock in an unnamed town serves as the area's Calvary. Gallegos's death, if it occurs, will take on aspects of a crucifixion. Gallegos's father tosses the dust about. At first, all but the humanistic sheriff laugh. As Gallegos chants his plea for love to replace hate, one by one the gathered multitude falls under his aura. Many chant along with him. Goodness, Serling suggests, will always win out over evil. At that moment, the sheriff does what he must do, but the rope breaks. Luis Gallegos lands on the ground beneath the gallows, shaken but essentially unharmed. So far as the sheriff is concerned, only the parents of the dead child have a right to demand the hanging be repeated. But Mrs. Canfield (Dorothy Adams), who possesses more of the quality of mercy than her vengeful husband (Paul Genge), convinces her spouse that enough is enough. If what Sykes claims was a new rope broke, this had to be the hand of "Providence" at work in the world. An act of God turns everyone around. The mob dissipates; in its place we see what they once were, a respectful community of good men and women that existed before they caught "the virus" of hopelessness.

If one chooses to believe, a miracle has occurred. If not, accident and coincidence ruled the day. Either way, a catharsis has taken place in this mini-tragedy, closing with Serling's insistence that most people will ultimately do the right thing, no matter how deep into darkness they may have momentarily drifted. "Why?" Sykes asks, confused. Then he (like the sheriff) smiles broadly. This is not the cruel smile he earlier displayed. Sykes no longer relies on liquor. A change has come over him; the worst person on view comes back in touch with some long-lost relic of decency, the potential for good that once existed within him. And, like Wordsworth's primal sympathy, it always remained there despite being dormant too long. Gallegos has been resurrected; as a result, Sykes is reborn. "It must have been magic," he sweetly says. If even he can be salvaged, everyone has a second chance to embrace the Light. One's fate, ironically, becomes a matter of free will. Do you reach upward to the stars or remain mired in the cave? That's the moral choice *Zone* presented to viewers beginning with its first installment, also proof that as dark as this episode may be, we have witnessed cautious optimism rather than an indictment of mankind.

The Man Who Shot Pinto Sykes:

THE GRAVE (10/27/61)

The Grave appeared six months before the theatrical release of *The Man Who Shot Liberty Valance*, the final John Ford film to deal with the pioneer community that this master of the Western so poignantly painted in classics like *My Darling Clementine*. Now in place of one more tribute to the frontier at its brightest and best, Ford mounted a bittersweet analysis of our westward movement's dark side. Lee Marvin was cast as a victim, a vicious outlaw finally laid to rest not by one heroic individual but by a collective including James Stewart, John Wayne, and Woody Strode. Lee Van Cleef and Strother Martin played cowboys; in *The Grave*, they likewise assume such roles, Marvin cast as yet another gunslinger. In this tale, however, he's not the legendary shootist (that's Pinto Sykes, assassinated by the town at large) but a hired gun who was supposed to, but did not, track down and kill that dangerous man. Here's yet another 1960s acknowledgment that the code of the west, so present in films and TV shows of the past, would not survive long in a new decade, which would conclude with Sam Peckinpah's *The Wild Bunch* (1969).

Once again, **Zone** got there first. Montgomery Pittman's script and George T. Clemens's noir-like direction (almost the entire episode takes place at night) allows for unique variations on recurring **Zone** themes. A minute after the episode begins, Pinto lies dead on the main street. What occurs next develops the death theme as well as that undiscovered country to follow. As Conny Miller (Marvin) drifts in (this is also his hometown), guitar-strumming wiseacre Johnny Rob (James Best) derides the apparent tough guy for taking their money then avoiding Pinto rather than facing him off in a traditional gun duel. Miller protests, perhaps too much. The more he insists he tried to catch up with Pinto, the more the townspeople (as well as viewers) wonder if he's lying, even to himself. Where does courage end and cowardice begin? Many **Zones** pose that question, and make clear that if an answer is possible, it's difficult to determine one or the other.

Then, Pinto's sister Ione (Ellen Willard), a witch-like beauty, appears, all in black. She assures Miller that what Rob and the others already told him is true: Before dying, Pinto left word that he still waits for Miller to approach, if he dares. Rob bets Miller that he lacks the nerve to visit the graveyard at the stroke of midnight and stand over Pinto's grave, for with his final words Pinto swore that he would reach out and yank Miller down. When Mothershed (Martin) and Steinhart (Van Cleef) want in on the bet, Miller feels cornered. He agrees to walk up there alone. He will stick a Bowie knife into the fresh grave, then return. When the others (too spooked to go with him) head up there in the morning, the knife will prove that Miller went all the way. This is his Second Chance, a shot at redemption. But Miller never returns. When the others approach by daylight, there he is, dead, as if he was pulled down by an inexplicable force.

Arguably the most elemental through-line in *Zone* is the relationship between the rational and the illogical, the limits of the real world in contrast to the vast spiritual infinity of space and time. If *The Grave* ended with the discovery of Miller's body, this would be nothing more than an effectively haunting ghost story. But Steinheart offers an acceptable analysis of what likely happened, based on evidence. Miller shoved the knife not only into the ground but, accidentally, also through his duster. That allows for "a perfectly rational explanation." Terrified, Miller did not notice that the wind had whipped the tail of his jacket under his legs or that he more or less nailed himself to the ground while driving down the knife. When he tried to rise and couldn't, Conny assumed that the curse had come true; he was held tight by Pinto. At this moment, his already tested heart gave out; Miller was scared to death. That makes sense. Then Ione appears, cackling as she dances in her dark robe. The wind, Ione points out, had been blowing from the south the previous night. That means it would have carried the tail of Millers's duster away from the grave, not closer toward it.

Serling's conclusion does not present us with a "lesson to be learned in *The Twilight Zone*." He refuses to say whether there was a ghost or if Miller's death resulted from "shadow or substance." This, Serling whispers, "we leave up to you." At its best, *Zone* did not tell us what to think. Instead, Serling's series forced us to think for ourselves.

Night of the Living Dead:

MR. GARRITY AND THE GRAVES (5/8/64)

Serling's finest fifth season episodes play as a bitter epilogues to previous themes. Among them is this return to the Western that flourished during *Zone's* early years. Here, the wild frontier has passed. Our antiheroic title figure (John Dehner) travels into a town once known as Satan's Stage Stop. Recently, that's been changed to Happiness, Arizona, though the people Garrity encounters seem less joyful than apathetic, drinking their days away in the local saloon. At least no one shoots up the town anymore; all the outlaws and many good citizens (128 to be precise) are buried up on boot hill. But along with violence, the spirit of the surviving townspeople has seeped away. Garrity, though, brings some incredible news: He can raise the dead! The mayor's wife, the bartender's brother. . . . At first, no one believes him, so Garrity displays his skill by bringing a dead dog back.

As darkness descends, Garrity works his magic, which he (a modernist) refers to as "the application of scientific principles." Sure enough, a figure wanders down through the mist. The bartender, however, is not certain that he wants to see his brother again. Though a huge wall portrait plays tribute to the man, he was in truth a horrid drunk. So the bartender pays Garrity to send his brother back; the figure disappears from sight. In rapid succession all the townspeople cut deals with Garrity. However mournful each appeared, they will reward Garrity to keep the dead away. An apparently heroic sheriff, Gilchrist (Norman Leavitt), fears the outlaw he dispatched; he (like Pat Garrett with Billy the Kid in actuality, if not movie mythology) shot the man in the back. Collecting his wages, Garrity heads out of town, joined by the "dead" dog (a well-trained pet) and professional actor who impersonated the bartender's brother. Off they go to the next town, where they'll work their clever (and profitable) ruse again.

In each American outpost, they figure to encounter more "solid citizens," once the image of civilization is scratched. Serling's script (from an unpublished story by Mike Korologos) recalls Mark Twain's *The Man Who Corrupted Hadleysburg*, about a similar fleecing of frontier types who present bright smiles to the world but are inwardly ugly. In later life, Twain deserted the idyllic adventures of Tom and Huck, his tales (like his view of man) darkening. Likewise, Serling left those barefoot boys (whom he had earlier revived in *Willoughby*) behind as he moved into murkier terrain. But if the finale sounds cynical, Serling pushes beyond that superficial emotion to full (and profound) pessimism. After Garrity has driven away, the dead rise and begin their procession toward town, where they will wreak havoc. Serling's final words emphasize his ever-bleaker worldview: "Respectfully submitted from an empty cemetery on a dark hillside that is one of the slopes leading to *The Twilight Zone*."

An Epitaph on an Emotion:

SHOWDOWN WITH RANCE McGREW (2/2/62)

By 1962, the golden age of the TV western was over. Those who wanted action turned instead to the small screen's imitations of the newly popular James Bond films: *The Man From U.N.C.L.E.*, *I Spy*, and *Secret Agent* among them. Shortly, only the most durable oaters would still ride high: *Gunsmoke* and *Bonanza*. Gone were the days when a simple hero in a tall white hat would always defeat the bad guys; such an appealingly simplistic coda became ever less acceptable once America moved into the era of political assassinations, a controversial war in southeast Asia, an emergent angry youth movement and, in time, Watergate. At this juncture in our social history and the pop-culture that reflects our ever-changing zeitgeist, Rod encapsulated the altered tenor of the times. Playwright George Bernard Shaw once noted that a joke is an epitaph on an emotion.

Showdown, one of *Zone*'s comedies, allowed audiences to laugh at the cowboy caricatures they had taken seriously only a few years earlier, providing a postscript to the entire TV Western genre.

The conception of Serling's scenario allows us insight into the manner in which any story idea for the series eventually bore the stamp of the man who created *Zone.* Fred Fox came to Serling with a plot idea about a contemporary cowboy, living in the modern west, who passes through a time tunnel and finds himself back in the wild days. Likely, Serling would have put that premise into production had it been submitted in 1959. What Alvin Toffler called "future shock" changed everything. Serling bought the concept, transforming it into a statement about the fading Western genre. Rance McGraw (Larry Blyden) is a faux cowboy star who rides on to the set in a white Cadillac convertible. He can't stomach alcohol nor can he twirl, much less shoot, a gun. Whenever there's to be a staged barroom brawl, McGraw screams out for the stuntman to take his place.

In one scene, he must shoot it out with an actor (Robert Kline) playing Jesse James. The script calls for James to try to shoot the hero in the back, but the actor playing the outlaw notes that Jesse James would not violate the Code of the West. Nonetheless, the onscreen director (Robert Cornwaite) proceeds with the inaccuracy. At that moment, Rance McGraw (the name of both the actor and his character, as was the case with such TV heroes as Roy Rogers and Gene Autry) finds himself back in the real west. There, the actual Jesse James (Arch Johnson) calls him out for a face-to-face duel. A key *Zone* theme is recapitulated as reality comes into conflict with the false images the public learned (in the worst sense of that term) from TV. Also, James is aware of how he and his fellow heroes and villains of the frontier are being misrepresented on TV, and has come back from the grave to clear his "good" name.

Showdown begins with a precise redux of *The Grave*'s opening from only a few months before. Here, though, Serling brings up the idea of a showdown—townspeople wait for a fast gun to arrive—to deconstruct it. In *The Grave,* everything appeared grim and dirty, as it would in the real West. When McGraw arrives to shoot it out with several fellows at *Showdown*'s opening, the scene is as brightly lit as anything in a typical TV Western. When Serling chose to do a Western, he always insisted on a noir quality missing from the routine shows then on the air. But when he mounted an epilogue on western emotions, it was necessary to revive the now bygone style of those shows. We never know for certain if McGraw was dreaming (a *Zone* motif) or was actually transported into the old west. Or, if on the set he was somehow visited by members of that "motley collection of tough moustaches (who) left behind a raft of legends." When McGraw snaps back to his current reality (his job of creating false myths) the audience, like him, must assume that right you are as you think you are. At least, though, the real Jesse James—dressed in a business suit, as he would have been, rather than the arch black costume the actor playing Jesse James had worn—has apparently impressed on Lance the need to move away from such obvious falsehoods.

As we laugh along with Serling's premise, we also come to a realization that we, as a people, had begun to change. When cowboy dramas disappeared, they were replaced by rural comedies: *The Andy Griffith Show*, *Beverly Hillbillies*, *Petticoat Junction*, etc. Likewise on *Zone*, cowboy heroes gave way to country rubes. With *Jess-Belle*, Earl Hamner Jr. joined the ongoing fold of writers and set into motion a future for television that would in time include everything from his own *The Waltons* to *Hee-Haw* and *Petticoat Junction*.

For better, as Rod would say, or worse—that call is ultimately up to the individual viewer.

10

"LOOK TO THE SKIES":
Close Encounters of the Zone Kind

PEOPLE FROM ANOTHER planet invading Earth is an idea that can be traced back at least to the ancient Samarians who recorded the arrival of the *Annanaki*, a race of super-humans descending from the stars. Some historians believe that these mythic tales concern visiting gods; others view the stories as realistic recordings of close encounters of the third kind. Though such "sightings" have continued through the centuries, a virtual obsession with aliens developed during the postwar years, due in large part to rapid advances in aviation during WWII. Now, jet planes flying high and fast came into contact as never before with heavenly (in every sense of that term) bodies. Widely circulated reports from flyers led to close scrutiny of the skies by normal people, who began seeing things "out there" as never before. First the movies responded; and then, with *Zone*, television.

Fifth Columnists from the Vast Beyond:

THE MONSTERS ARE DUE ON MAPLE STREET (3/4/60)

Serling's first "invader" story begins in bright daylight only to end in the bleakest of nightscapes. A predecessor of the noir *Zones* to follow, we here witness one of Serling's harshest portraits of mankind. The time is late summer, the most mellow of seasons in suburbia. Men wash their cars on a quiet Saturday afternoon as kids enjoy ice cream. An object passes overhead, momentarily casting *Zone*'s Death Light over the area. When it's gone, nothing works as before: Not only is the electricity "dead", but radios don't work, cars won't start. As Charlie (Jack Weston), an unpleasant fellow in a loud hawaiian shirt, exclaims: "It's as if everything stopped." Calmer and more logical, Steve (Claude Akins) suggests that this might be the after-effect of a passing meteor. One neighbor heads over to the next block to check on the situation there but never returns. In a split second, modern civilization, seemingly solid and impregnable, collapses.

Dramatizing the old adage that a child shall lead them, teenager Tommy (Jan Handzlik) adds his two cents. The boy warns Steve and Charlie not to try to leave. He believes that the bizarre occurrences are the result of aliens intent on conquering the world, beginning with this neighborhood. At first, everyone laughs, though the boy's next words prove disturbing: The Martians would likely have sent a seemingly normal family ahead to pave the way. That might be any of those gathered close. The majority gives little credence to this until the car belonging to Les Goodman (Barry Atwater) inexplicably turns on. Why, Charlie wonders, did Les not run out to look up like everyone else? Other neighbors now note that Les and his wife always appeared "different," then move en masse toward the stunned Goodman family as a once-positive American community transforms into a mob.

No other *Zone* more effectively employs the mechanics of imaginative fantasy to comment on then-contemporary malaise. There is no mention of politics, yet the scenario presents a case study of Americans turning on each other owing to guilt by suspicion. This is precisely what triggered the Hollywood blacklist and national Red-baiting during the McCarthy era. At this episode's end, all order breaks down after midnight and "good people" kill one another. Director Ron Winston slowly pulls back his camera to reveal a pair of aliens, calmly watching Maple Street degenerate into chaos. See? It isn't necessary, one Martian convinces the other, to invade earth with death rays for a war of the worlds. All they need do is snap off the electric lights, then sit back, relax, and watch as Earthlings destroy each other. "Throw them into darkness for a few hours," the first alien smirks, and "they pick the most dangerous enemy they can find. It's always themselves." Merely go from one street to the next . . .

To make certain that we don't miss the message, Serling's final narration leaves no uncertainty: "And the pity of it is that these things cannot be confined to *The Twilight Zone*." This, as a flying saucer (via stock footage from *Forbidden Planet*) glides back to its planet with, no doubt, plans to return soon! "Fifth columnists from the vast beyond," the sensible Steve chuckles when his neighbors grow as concerned about an invasion as they would have been about nuclear confrontation with Soviets. Steve is the conscientious liberal, believing the best about his neighbors until one by one they join reactionary bigot Charlie, who actuallty looks like Senator Joe McCarthy. Their arguments constitute one of *Zone*'s early Socratic dialogues as extreme views on a subject are stated while the masses try to pick sides. The tragedy is, their common "fear of the unknown" causes people with no firm political beliefs to fall in behind rabble rousers and be manipulated by demigogues with strong prejudices but weak minds. Making the episode all the more chilling is that it was filmed not in a real suburb but on the old *Andy Hardy* street on the MGM back lot. Here is Serling's approach in a nutshell: revealing the dark underbelly of Norman Rockwell's America.

Teenager Tommy proves analogous to Serling's storytelling, himself a storyteller within the story. His ideas concerning creatures from the stars, which he relates with frightening intensity, come from comic books and B-movies kids delighted in during the fifties. Perhaps unconsciously on Serling's part, Tommy can be also understood as a representative of the young people who provided a large share of *Zone*'s audience. When the neighbors turn on Tommy (he is a strange-looking boy!) and chase him down, this becomes a video equivalent of Shirley Jackson's story "The Lottery." That's enhanced by cinematographer George T. Clemens's use of straight-on shots for the first half, then oblique angles when night falls.

"As God is my witness," Les cries out, hinting at the metaphysical theme, "you're letting something begin here that's a nightmare." This statement is made while the sun still shines; a dark dream in broad daylight. Neighbors singled out for persecution are those secretly considered "oddballs," a criticism of the era's conformist mentality. Serling creates ironic distance between suburbanites at home watching and their alter-egos onscreen. When Pete (Ben Erway) strolls off to find help, a close-up identifies the hammer in his belt. Later, when Maple Street's residents believe that a monster approaches from out of the dark, a similar close-up lets us know that this is Pete, whom panicked Charlie will shoot. A distinction between audience and characters, despite their similarity, allows Serling to employ suspense (we know more than they do) rather than mystery (we are at one with the confused characters). As such, we take a critical stand against ourselves (or alter-egos) at our worst.

Somehow, optimism prevails. Serling can at least hope that we may be wise enough to learn from the mistakes of those others who resemble us in this cautionary fable.

Famous for Fifteen Minutes:

MR. DINGLE, THE STRONG (3/3/61)

Two Martians descend to Earth and play havoc with human affairs, with comic results, in this whimsical fable. The antihero (Burgess Meredith) is another "little man," smaller in stature (Dingle is the same height as the bullies who pick on him) than in self-image. And another variation on the mind's eye; since Dingle views himself as a victim, that's what he is. Dingle is initially situated between a bookie (Edward Ryder) and a bettor (Don Rickles) as they argue in a bar. The sports in question are two of Serling's favorites, boxing and baseball. Dingle becomes a punching bag because he, in a passive-aggressive way, asks for it. Shortly, Dingle will, like that forlorn alcoholic who discovers he's actually Santa Claus, enjoy his own night (day, here) of the meek.

These Martians, their high foreheads recalling *This Island Earth*, (1953) are bound together by one mechanical body. Believing is seeing: everyday people here have no idea that invaders are in their midst, so the creatures remain invisible to all but us. Dispassionately, the visitors amuse themselves by "blessing" Dingle with strength, then stand back to watch. As in *Maple Street*, the people around Dingle go mad, here not with fear but another of **Zone**'s deadly sins, greed. Everyone wants to make money off Dingle's sudden surge in strength as he's offered everything from a boxing contract to a TV show.

An interviewer (James Millhollin) leads a camera crew into the bar for a live TV news spot. Important stories that affect everyone occur nearby, but the interviewer assumes they'd be of no interest to his audience. Here is a freak show, something he (and TV) can exploit. This allows the uncomprehending Dingle what Andy Warhol would shortly refer to as fifteen minutes of fame. When the Martians grow bored and remove Dingle's super-powers, everyone loses interest. The announcer attempts to spin the situation by suggesting that he unmasked a fraud. Then a pair of diminutive Venusians (Donald Losby and Greg Irvin) arrive and bless (again, this word not casually chosen) Dingle with intellectual power. No sooner does the small man spout knowledge than avaricious people argue as to how they might best exploit this gift. Serling's vision transforms what initially appears to be light escapism into an early example of black humor on TV.

The Good Ol' Boy Who Cried Wolf:

HOCUS POCUS AND FRISBY (4/13/62)

Fear of an unknown potential of aliens overpowers the protagonist (Andy Devine) in this comedic piece, adapted by Serling, from Frederic Louis Fox's unpublished concept. *Frisby* plays as a companion-piece to *Denby*, turning all that occurs there inside-out: Instead of a big city, the fable begins in a general store located in a small Midwestern town. Called Pitchville Flats, it's a charming caricature of the Homewoods we've already visited and a reminder that, nostalgia aside, there are such simple enclaves still to be found in America. Frisby himself is the polar opposite of Denby: Instead of listening while everyone else talks, Frisby transfixes his fellow rednecks with tall tales that always posit himself as a heroic figure. If Frisby is to be believed, he won both world wars almost single-handedly, helped

Ford develop the automobile motor, and wrote a scholarly treatise on meteorology. None of the gathered folk believe a word of it. But Frisby's a spellbinding storyteller and unlikely autobiographical figure. So all take delight in his exaggerations.

The invaders pull up in a contemporary car to purchase gas and overhear all Frisby has said. As they hail from a planet where lying is unknown, they can only assume that Frisby really is the greatest man on Earth and tempt him aboard their UFO. He observes that the complex machinery resembles "movie props" from sci-fi films he's seen, referencing the entire genre that includes, of course, *Hocus Pocus and Frisby*. Frisby even references *Zone*, expressing fear that, after returning to the distant planet with these creatures, they'll "put me in a cage," precisely the hero's fate in *People Are Alike All Over*. They admit that this is the case; Frisby escapes by whipping out his harmonica, on which he had appropriately played "Red River Valley." To the aliens, the five-note tune Frisby improvises is as painful to their ears as microscopic germs were to Martians in *War of the Worlds*.

The final irony: Back with his friends, Frisby now has an amazing story to tell, but because of all his lies, no one will believe. Frisby is the good ol' boy who cried wolf. Serling mentions Aesop, heightening the connection between his contemporary social education via the moral fable and that of his inspiration. The term *hocus pocus* (in the title) never appears in this episode. Yet as with magic in *Mr. Dingle*, *Frisby*'s aliens offer a rational explanation for things that would otherwise appear beyond human conception. Always in *Zone*, a miracle exists less in its reality than in our inner perception of an event.

Small People Got No Reason to Live:

THE INVADERS (1/27/61)

In this Richard Matheson classic, a lone woman (Agnes Moorehead) is visited by a pair of visitors from the stars, arriving to set the pace for invasion. The use of sound, as employed in *Dingle*, has its counterpoint here: When the star travelers initially arrive in their spacecraft (that saucer from *Forbidden Planet* again) at an isolated farm, the noise of a landing on the roof so pains the ears and brain of The Lonely (that recurring theme) person that she shrieks, as did *Frisby*'s aliens. This at first seems an inverse of what occurred there. When at the end we learn that she exists on a far planet and they are members of the U.S. Air Force space probe, we realize that what happens is identical. The earlier episode that *Invaders* reverses is *Third from the Sun*.

The approach to making such a turnabout work without dishonestly misleading the audience is the same here as in that earlier show. The farmhouse, as Serling informs us in the opening, exists in one of those "out-of-the-way places" where electricity, radio, and other modern devices aren't present. "A house untouched by progress" so, as this lack of contemporary conveniences allows the woman's situation to turn into a nightmare, *Invaders* plays as an anti-nostalgic piece by writers who provide the other side to Serling's story. The woman tosses various objects (apparently food items, though they look nothing like what a typical American farm might produce) into a gigantic pot. This and other elements of the setting allow a hint of what's to come so that we don't feel unprepared at the final revelation. A noir, this story takes place entirely at night. The drama, without dialogue until the final minute, provides a tour de force for Agnes Moorehead. She performs in a style that occupies a middle ground between the realistic approach we expect and a mime-like effect to convey emotional reactions and thoughts through exaggerated body language. The way in which this "person" reacts to what happens is not as a normal human would. We don't need to hear the woman speak in a foreign tongue to grasp that she's not of this Earth; we can see it in her mannerisms, close enough to an Earthling's that the ending isn't given away, yet slightly stylized so her every odd gesture helps to legitimize the revelation.

The shadow-play that lent another episode its title works here because of that lack of electricity. Everything we see is lit by a candle (inside the house) or stars (when the woman crawls up on her roof). Her opening and closing of the trap door and tendency to, during moments of panic, drop her candle allows for expressionistic lighting. That the aliens are small introduces the relativity concept; they are "little" if we contrast them to the woman. After she attacks them and a dying astronaut tries to warn Earth not return to this planet ("a race of giants"), it's clear that Serling's fascination with size dominates even those episodes he did not personally write.

Playing God:

THE LITTLE PEOPLE (3/30/62)

Serling provided this follow-up to *The Invaders* three years later. Here, one more ship carrying two more star travelers lands on a distant planet. We note that the craft is shaped like a needle, suggesting these are Earthlings. Then again, as the flying saucer from *Forbidden Planet* has been employed on *Zone* for both Earthlings and invaders, we can't assume here that a needle-like rocket necessarily signifies an earth ship. Still, Captain William Fletcher (Claude Akins) and his co-pilot Peter Craig (Joe Maross) do speak of Thanksgiving turkeys and Yankee Stadium, at one point mentioning "the Earth." Adding to our sense of uncertainty, *The Little People* was filmed in Death Valley, which in other *Zones* has been the Earth, a distant planet, or a parallel universe.

No question though that the men landed in a cave (or, as they call it, "canyon") which resembles that animated one from the first-season opening. The surroundings are symbolic for Craig, who descends into the pit of man's ignorance. He's one of Serling's little men, not in physical stature (he's as tall as his companion), but in personality:

> **FLETCHER:** What do you hope for most? A thick steak? A blonde?
> **CRAIG:** I'd like a whole lot of people at my elbows. I'd like to give the orders.

Craig suffers from a smallness of spirit, which finds full release when his pathetic dream comes true. He discovers a race of people the size of ants. We still can't be sure if the astronauts or the natives are Earthlings. The point is, it doesn't matter. What is essential is the implication: power corrupts; absolute power corrupts absolutely.

One more of Serling's humanists, Fletcher is horrified when Craig steps on a small mound of civilization as if he were a nasty child crushing an anthill. Fletcher first spots the title characters when he gazes through a microscope, another variation on the limits of human perception. *Little People* develops the religious theme fully. "A God," Craig calls himself, claiming these little people have "been created in my image!" Out of fear (rather than love or respect), the little people build a life-sized statue of Craig, which they then worship. For any race of man, any planet in our solar system or a parallel universe, fear of the unknown leads to a false belief that this force is all-powerful because it's more powerful than those who fall under its shadow. Fletch, knowing how small a man Craig was in the context of their world (there had to be a reason why Fletch was in charge) understands what the natives do not: Here is a hollow deity.

Dismissing Craig as "a sick, scared little man full of delusions of grandeur," Fletch boards the ship and heads for home. The theme of madness resurfaces, as Craig becomes so carried away with power that he rolls around on the ground, out of control. He speaks of a "new age," making clear that he's one of Serling's despised fascists, insisting on "discipline above all." The twist Serling has in store for Craig satisfies not only on a dramatic level but a thematic one as well. Another ship lands with another pair of space travelers inside—giants in comparison to Craig. The theory of relativity applies here: size is not objective. These new invaders are large children who kill the ant-like Craig without conscience. Here we find poetic justice and something more even than that. In one of director William Claxton's final shots, the little people yank down the statue. God (or at least this false one) is dead.

Garbo Lives:

THE FEAR (5/29/64)

Like everything else, fear is relative. That point is driven home at this episode's conclusion. This fifth-season fable might best be described as a "reverse noir" in that it opens at night, in darkness, but concludes as a sun rises, revealing that the fate in store for the humans in *Monsters on Maple Street* is avoidable, though only if mankind embraces the better side of our nature. State Trooper Robert Franklin (Mark Richman) drives up to an isolated house. In *Invaders*, we had no idea why the old lady chose to be in such a place. Here, though, Franklin (and we) understand why beautiful Charlotte Scott (Hazel Court) embodies The Lonely: She fled her job as a Manhattan fashion editor for peace in the country. That romantic dream soon soured: There's a UFO flying over her house. In terror, she has called the state police . . .

Serling's opener features total darkness, punctured by two gleaming lights that glide toward the camera. We aren't certain whether they will belong to an ordinary car or a descending space craft. The closer they come, the more we get a fix on the image and guess that it's the former. Later, we again see a pair of lights, though these turn out to belong to a flying saucer. This visual paradigm, like many others, impacted on young Steven Spielberg, who employs just such a reversal in *Close Encounters* when Neery (Richard Dreyfuss) stops at a rural crossroads to figure out where he is, first mistaking a car behind him for a saucer, then a saucer for a car. Here, Franklin steps out of his vehicle and we get our first good look at him. Though Mark Richman is tall, with a lengthy face, he nonetheless resembles Serling; his voice is all but identical. This adds if not an autobiographical element (Serling never worked as a trooper), then a personal one. When the two people debate, we assume Franklin to be the author's spokesman, particularly when he quotes *Hamlet*: There are more things in heaven and earth . . . than are dreamt of in your philosophy.

If Scott is the skeptical Horatio-like realist, Franklin grasps there's also an "irrational" element to the universe. Garbo-esque, Scott claims that she wants to be alone; the rubes and rednecks in town (presumably like those in *Frisby*) interfere with her motivation for living here. An amateur psychiatrist, Franklin realizes that this is her cover.

Scott felt isolated even back in New York, surrounded by those of her own ilk. If her character arcs during the narrative, then this allows Scott to become a humanist. Her change is revealed by her commitment to another person. Now, they are haunted by the Death

Light, which appears just outside the window. As in *Monsters*, the aliens here cut off all power so the couple cannot listen to the radio, much less call for help. Worse still, these aliens have the power to move mountains. We see what the characters do not: A giant shadow is cast over the isolated house. In the morning, Franklin discovers that his car has been picked up and dropped by some invisible giant that left fingerprints on the vehicle's sides. In *Little People*'s first half, Earthlings found themselves to be giants on another planet; here, some extraterrestrials apparently experience the same thing on Earth.

Scott splits in two, psychologically speaking; her inner panic is reflected in a Mirror Image. In that shot, we see only one of Franklin, Serling's spokesman: "Being afraid is a normal function." What separates heroes from cowards is not the presence or absence of fear, which is universal, but the way a person processes it. We can hide under a bed (which is what Scott initially wants to do) or, like the woman in *The Invaders*, fight back. Scott is not yet ready to do that, so Franklin must take the ladder up to roof. "Maybe it's just a little imagination seeping into the both of us," he reassuringly whispers. Or "maybe the loneliness." The pressure of their inexplicable situation is precisely what Scott needed: She begins to relate to him not as a functionary, but as a person. When they venture out the next day and confront a gigantic robot monster (with one Cyclopean eye, recalling the perception and reality theme), Scott transforms. Though Franklin is willing to try to hold the thing off while she runs, Scott insists on standing by her fellow man. Buoyed by each other's courage, he dares to fire; to their surprise, the thing (a balloon) deflates.

"That's it?" she laughs. "Is that what we've been afraid of? A fugitive from a Thanksgiving day parade?" As always, what we fear most is the unknown. Together (in a relationship capable of dismissing fear) they notice a small saucer. Two miniature aliens cower at the sight of the giant Earthlings and radio their planet, warning their fellows not to come here. The fingerprints, we learn, had been painted on the car, which they moved with a power source. Aliens were defeated by the "Earth man's failure to be frightened." Referencing *The Little People*, Franklin turns to Scott: "Maybe the next place they land, they can be giants."

Here is a reversal for the end of *Maple Street*: All we need do to survive is embrace the best in ourselves, rather than surrender to the worst. Serling then quotes President Roosevelt's advice, which saw their generation through the Depression: We have nothing to fear but fear itself.

Them!:

WILL THE REAL MARTIAN PLEASE STAND UP? (5/26/61)

On a snowy night, an elderly lady calls the police to report that a UFO passed over her remote area. Two state troopers (Morgan Jones and John Archer) discover that a saucer did crash into the pond at Hook's Landing. They find tracks that indicate a survivor crawled out and headed toward a local diner. There, a bus is stranded; with the blizzard closing off the roads behind it and rumors that the bridge ahead isn't safe, the driver (Bill Kendis) and his six passengers wait inside for the storm to abate while a genial short-order cook (Barney Phillips) whips up chili and coffee. There's one problem: seven people are in the diner, which suggests that the odd man (or woman) may be the extraterrestrial. This allows Serling and Montgomery Pittman to develop one of *Zone*'s telling themes: Normalcy is a myth; under close scrutiny, seemingly everyday people all at once appear "suspicious."

This comedy contains elements from diverse sources—*Invasion of the Body Snatchers*, *The Monsters Are Due on Maple Street*, even William Inge's *Bus Stop*—all played tongue in cheek, allowing for self-referential gags. "I don't like science fiction," one person complains, noting that their situation is "a regular Ray Bradbury!" As the troopers interrogate each present, one man sits at the counter, back to us, putting off the revelation of his face for as long as possible. We assume that he'll be revealed as the visitor when, after he finally turns, the man appears "different" from the others: an over-the-top old timer (Jack Elam) whose wild behavior makes him suspect. But assumptions are dangerous in Serling's world; this man turns out to be the most normal (more correctly, least abnormal) of the bunch.

Two married couples are among the stranded, one elderly (Bill Erwin and Gertrude Flynn), the other young (Ron Kipling and Jill Ellis). We might guess that they could verify each other. The opposite happens: Closely scrutinizing one's life-partner for the first time, each of the marrieds wonders if this really is that significant other or a reasonable facsimile.

As in *Maple Street*, the electricity switches on and off. But the phone works, so the troopers receive a call from authorities telling them that the bridge is safe. This turns out to be one of those Long-Distance Calls that lead to no good, probably placed by the visitor's compatriots. All on the bus, along with both troopers, are shortly killed when the bridge gives way. We learn this when the one survivor (John Hoyt), who struck us as the most normal (if least pleasant) man present, wanders back and joins the cook at the counter. While relating what happened, he lights a cigarette, a third arm protruding from under his jacket. Cryptically, he admits that he's the Martian. If he suspected panic on the other's part, he is mistaken—the cook yanks off his low-slung cap, revealing a third eye on his forehead. He's a Venusian; his people have already begun to colonize Earth, and woe to those Martians who think they are welcome here.

Lolita Conquers the Martians:

THE FUGITIVE (3/9/62)

A gentle, whimsical episode, this "Cinderella story" adds a disturbing subtext to what initially seems easygoing enough: A twelve-year-old orphan, Jenny (Susan Gordon), living with an unpleasant aunt (Nancy Kulp), competes at sports with the boys despite her lame leg. Occasionally, Jenny wonders why Old Ben (J. Pat O'Malley), the only adult who plays with the children, hasn't cured her deformity. He can create what the kids call "magic," events the adults might refer to as "miracles": Ben makes baseballs fly off into the stratosphere or, when children play alien games, transform into a monster out of a bad B-movie. This doesn't frighten his charges, for they know that underneath the scales it's gentle Ben. What they don't yet realize is that Ben himself is a benign visitor. As to the parents, they've heard the children talking about Ben's "gifts," but assume that this is only a product of youthful imagination. Too busy with their own "important" things to visit the playground, they neither see nor believe what's obvious to the kids' eyes—or minds, where all magic and miracles ultimately exist in *The Twilight Zone*.

Writer Charles Beaumont, in collaboration with director Richard L. Bare, includes a proto-feminist theme. Jenny must educate not only the neighborhood boys but also Ben about her right to be team captain based on ability. Shortly, we learn why Ben hasn't used the full extent of his god-like-powers (compared to anyone on Earth, though ordinary where he hails from) to cure Jenny: Two men in suits (Wesley Lau and Paul Tripp), mistaken by Jenny's aunt for policemen, are emissaries from his planet who have been detached to bring Ben back. The aura of an old man is one Ben assumed to hide (appearance and reality), so they aren't sure if he is the fugitive. But a miracle as great as the curing of lameness (quite Christ-like, of course) would give him away.

Though spiritual issues openly raised in Serling's scripts aren't articulated here, by implication this is one of the most religious pieces. The premise is based on the need for faith (the ultimate form of love in its pure unconditional form). "Suffer the children," Jesus said. Jenny's situation (in a wonderful touch, she expresses no self-pity) and Ben's situation (he must choose between loyalty to the child over concern for himself) allow for a dramatization of that concept. Likewise, the Bible insists that the "visitor" will be a "King"; Old Ben was king of his planet.

"Don't leave me, Ben," Jenny cries. Even with all his powers, Ben can't come up with a solution to that one. But Jenny does, in a twist that resurrects the doubling theme. Ben can take any form he chooses, so Jenny whispers that Ben should make himself look precisely like her. Not knowing which of the two is really Ben, the celestial policemen must bring both back. As in any good fairytale, Ben and Jenny will live happily ever after . . .

However, this turn of events raises a disquieting issue. If this is a love story, then haven't a twelve-year-old girl and an eighty-year-old man just become a couple? Yes—but we must recall that Ben is not actually the way he appears on Earth. Still, that wouldn't make any difference to Jenny. She loves what he is inside. In Serling's epilogue (he appears at the end as well as the beginning of this episode, a rarity), the host shows us a photo of what Ben (whom Jenny is about to marry) really looks like: a handsome teenage boy.

Still, we note that Serling shares this happy news while he sits on the bed Jenny and Ben have shared throughout. While on a bed, Ben often embraced, tickled, or petted her. When the two weren't on a bed, Jenny was often seated on Ben's lap, with her arms around him as they discussed their devotion. When they walked together he openly flirted with Jenny, referring to her as his "best girl" and "only true love." Jenny considered Ben her "boyfriend." That he's actually young perhaps assuages any awkward feelings. Then again, we should note that if we logically follow the progression the story outlines for us, a nineteen-year-old boy will now marry a twelve-year-old girl. Thanks to the genre of fantasy *Zone* came closer to realizing the implications of Vladimir Nabokov's *Lolita* than did the Stanley Kubrick film (in which the title blonde was a fully developed teenager), which was released a few months after this episode's broadcast.

The Second Coming:

THE GIFT (4/27/62)

If an ability to subtly suggest ideas was primary among Beaumont's gifts, Serling's own talent might be thought of as complimentary. A comparison of their different approaches in handling relatively similar stories could not be better served than by contrasting *The Fugitive* to *The Gift*. In the latter, one more benign alien visits Earth and is as misunderstood by adults, though a beatific child appreciates the visitor's savior-like qualities. Serling draws his Biblical redux in the clean, clear lines that the more subtle Beaumont chose to only suggest.

In a small Mexican town, where ravens congregate on the desolate stucco walls, word spreads that a UFO has dropped from the sky. The alien on board has escaped and is considered dangerous. Labeled "a monster in the darkness" though no one knows what it looks like (the human perception theme), the creature (Geoffrey Horne) turns out to be handsome and soft-spoken. Only the town's intelligent, educated doctor (Nico Minardos) and a radically innocent child (Edmund Vargas) see that as the alien claims, "I come in peace!" Little Pedro is not considered "normal," so he (like Henry in *The Big Tall Wish*) can believe, devoid of prejudice toward another who is clearly as "different" as he. As in other *Zones* that posit young and old as equally perceptive in contrast the main, an elderly guitarist (Vladimir Sokoloff) senses the visitor's goodness. Blind, he's a Mexican equivalent of Old Tieresias in *Oedipus Rex*. Insight is more important than an ability to see things in a superficial way, a point that connects *The Twilight Zone* to ancient tragedy.

Ultimately, though, this episode is more Biblical than Greek. The stranger requests wine, precisely what Jesus most often asked for while wandering into unknown villages. His hands are bloody and, the moment before he's killed by an uncomprehending mob, he extends them outward and upward in a symbolic crucifixion. Earlier, he fell down, seemingly dead, only to rise again (in this case three hours rather than three days later). The bartender Manuelo (Cliff Osmond) betrays his visitor for a handful of silver coins, causing the doctor to dismiss him as "Judas!" The dying alien's promise to Pedro: "I will come back, some time." Such a second coming would be welcome, as in their abject ignorance (i.e., irrational fear of the unknown), the villagers burned the title object (a book), fearing that it was "the devil's work," even as opponents of Jesus accused that rabbi as hailing from Satan. They destroyed what this visitor brought for mankind: A cure for cancer.

The charge has been leveled that *The Gift* is, however unintentionally, racist, owing to stereotypical depictions of the Mexican people as a superstitious, fearful lot. More fairly, we could compare the Mexicans here to the white suburbanites in *Maple Street*, all but identical to these people in words and actions. One good liberal who opposes the mob appears in each story; otherwise, the people (Anglo or Latino) are ignorant, bigoted, and (as always in Serling) fearful of the unknown. In *Zone*'s context, Serling has not singled out people of color for such a harsh treatment, but offers an inclusive, if grim, view of a human stain that cuts across all barriers of race and religion.

From Dust to Dinner:

TO SERVE MAN (3/2/62)

As if sensing the necessity for a strong antidote to all his invasion episodes written in a *Day the Earth Stood Still* tradition, Serling scripted (from Damon Knight's story) this unsettling piece in the more menacing style of *The Thing*. A flying saucer lands. The star creatures, called Kanamits (nine feet tall, all played by actor Richard Kiel) insist, like so many other *Zone* aliens, "we come in peace." By making them giants (in Knight they were of average height), Serling invokes his little people theme; all on Earth now feel small, because large and small are based on relativity. Documentary footage of New York City's U.N. building allows for realism, adding to the power of the legendary punchline. As famine is banished, life on Earth changes. War becomes unnecessary. Hero Chambers (Lloyd Bochner) brings up the Bible, noting that the world has been restored to a Garden of Eden. In *The Twilight Zone Companion*, Zicree notes that the Kanamits "resemble angels gone to seed, with full-length robes" and "high-domed heads," the latter recalling *This Island Earth* (1953); here as there, higher intelligence does not imply higher morality. People worldwide experience the new friends on television—one more reference to Serling's medium of choice.

As for Chambers, he and assistant Pat (Susan Cummings) decode a Kanamit book, *To Serve Man*. Unfortunately, as Chambers boards the saucer to visit the aliens' world, Pat runs up, her translation complete: "*To Serve Man* is a cookbook!" If we were unprepared for this line, the episode would remain superficially entertaining. But

Serling allowed numerous hints as to what was coming. The open-ing displays Chambers, on his bunk, smoking in a Serling-like way. Director Richard L. Bare sets up a diagonal image, suggesting that while things seem calm, something's wrong with this picture.

From outside the cubicle, a Kanamit asks Chambers if he's hun-gry, which causes the human to lash out in anger. Why? At the end, Chambers's fury at this attempt to fatten him up makes sense. He lunges up and confronts himself in one more Mirror Image. He wants to know what the hour is on Earth, evoking the Time Element. Chambers whisks us back to the beginning of our end, noting that Earthlings were as "frightened as farm animals" of the Kanamits. They admit that they want to be "good shepherds," eventually making clear that we are their mutton. Their name should (but doesn't) give it away: Kanamit "evokes the word cannibal." Despite such preparation we are surprised; that's the genius of the piece.

To Serve Man is to the invader-oriented episodes what *People Are Alike All Over* was to space travel, if darker still; instead of specimens in a zoo, people are headed for the kitchen as pieces of meat. (No wonder CBS brass refused to rerun this installment!) Here too is a reversal of all previous invader *Zones* that had ignorant masses react in fear to anything new, while the educated elite were open and accepting of change. That turnabout causes *To Serve Man* to work, in the series context, as a strong conservative answer to Serling's own earlier liberal statements (see Chapter 11). For once in *Zone*, the reactionaries are proven to be right. There is (pardon the pun) no free lunch, *To Serve Man* says: Santa Claus (invoked twice in Serling's script) is not real, and to believe in him (as *Night of the Meek* hinted we should) is to be dangerously naive. Beware not only Greeks, but anyone bearing gifts. Fortress America expands to Stockade Earth; the progressive's dream of "peace and prosperity" will, if it ever actually occurs, in truth destroy man, transforming us "from dust to dessert." As to the finale: Here is the only time in *Zone* that a protagonist looks into the camera, directly addressing the audience: "All of us," Lloyd Bochner shouts, recalling Kevin McCarthy doing the same thing at the end of the 1956 feature film *Invasion of the Body Snatchers*, telling the audience: "You're next!"

RIGHT TURN/LEFT FACE:
Politics in the Zone

DURING HIS LIFETIME, Rod Serling was always identified as a liberal. He campaigned on behalf of nuclear disarmament and civil rights, and was among the first celebrities to oppose the Vietnam War. Still, the term "liberal" fails to fully describe this iconoclast's complex politics. Media expert Louis Giannetti noted that a preference for a real or imagined "golden age" rests at the heart of conservative thinking; for a true liberal, the best is yet to come. Serling, obviously, was a nostalgist. Also, something old-fashioned underlined Serling's personal manner. At a time when other middle-aged writers donned tie-dyed jeans, flowered shirts, and love beads, he kept his hair short and continued wearing natty suits. What, then, were his politics? In 1963, Serling had publicly blamed the assassination of President Kennedy on "Leftists and Rightists," the "Absolutists" on both sides. "The Enemy," for Serling, existed on the fringe to either side of our moderate middle, that consensus with a conscience he so appreciated. Serling most admired the Greek golden mean he'd studied at Antioch, believing that a delicate balance between the two political sensibilities might serve as our salvation.

Now, Voyager:

JUDGMENT NIGHT (12/4/59)

The opening image presents the S.S. *Queen of Glasgow* passing through a foggy stretch of the Atlantic, circa 1942. Serling informs us that "*Glasgow* is a frightened ship, and she carries with her a premonition of death." Director John Brahm contrasts sight with insight. On the deck, peering through thick fog, stands Carl Lanser (Nehemiah Persoff), one of half a dozen passengers. As the camera tightens on the man's face, Lanser appears jittery. The camera then continues to push forward, focusing tightly on the man's eyes. This episode will chronicle Lanser's attempt to truly see for the first time. Capable of physical sight, Lanser lacks insight. This he will gain by the conclusion.

Here is a hint that in *Zone* politics and religion will always interrelate. A man's (any man's) political philosophy in the world expresses in words and deeds his spirituality, or lack thereof. Any person's fate in Serling's universe is tempered by free will. Destiny places each character in an awkward moral conundrum. What he does (or does not do) under such stressful circumstances determines whether he's a humanist. Lanser possesses the capability of being a decent person; this is established as he steps inside the cabin. A child drops her doll. Among the adults present, only Lanser notices, pausing to pick it up. *Judgment Night* then is something other than a simple morality play with clear-cut heroes and villains. Good and bad, the potential for both or either, exists in everyone. Lanser must decide whether he will be Dr. Jekyll or Mr. Hyde. The influence of that film, viewed in a Binghamton theatre by the young Rod Serling, fully asserts itself here.

Present too is nostalgia for a romanticized past. When another passenger, Barbara (Diedre Owen), asks Lanser if he's heading to or away from home, he wistfully replies: "away!" We sense that all aboard are Flying Dutchmen after we learn that the *Glasgow* has lost touch with its convoy; now, all feel separated from the greater human community. A hint of what's to come occurs when Captain Wilbur (Ben Wright), amazed by how much Lanser knows about German submarines, comments: "You sound rather like a U-Boat commander." Like many other inadvertent visitors to the *Zone*, Lanser becomes confused about the key details in his life, one more victim of Identity Crisis. Lanser knows only his name (though that turns out to be false) and a vague sense of home; he admits that he hails from Frankfurt to the surprise of his fellow travelers, all Allies.

Déjà vu sets in as Lanser realizes that the others seem familiar. He's been here before, but can't remember where or when.

Sleep, Shakespeare's gentle nurse, proves impossible. Lanser fears (like the characters in *Perchance to Dream* and *Shadow Play*) that he may already be asleep. If he is dreaming, the other passengers are figments of his unconscious. When he admits "it's as if I'm in a nightmare," Lanser speaks for all visitors to the fifth dimension. Others on board fear that a U-Boat may be trailing them; Lanser states: "I know it's there!" A steward (Richard Peel) discovers the MacGuffin, that object capable of unlocking the truth: In Lanser's cabin sits a U-Boat captain's hat with the owner's German name embroidered inside. The Time Element appears: Glancing at a ticking clock as it strikes midnight, Lanser realizes that the *Glasgow* will explode at 1:15. He rushes about trying to warn the others, but they have mysteriously disappeared. Lanser might well, like Mike Ferris in *Zone*'s opener, call out: "Where is everybody?" Then another recurring symbol appears. Over the bar, Lanser spots a Mirror Image of himself and knows at once that he is not the person he believed himself to be. Lanser exists as a doppelgänger aboard this ship for his twin: the Kapitan of the approaching U-Boat.

As Lanser gazes over the deck (spotting the approaching submarine's beam, which recalls the Death Light), he locks eyes with a fellow across the way who is ready to give the order to fire. What Lanser spots is the insensitive (willing to kill all aboard) side of himself. Lanser then briefly glimpses ghostlike images of his fellow passengers. Without warning, they're gone. Were the ghosts there, or did Lanser imagine them? It doesn't matter; reality exists in the eye and mind of the beholder. The final detail is the girl's doll in close-up, floating in the water. This image had an impact on Steven Spielberg, who employed a variation (a teddy bear) as the ending of his first film, *The Sugarland Express* (1974).

Up to this point, nothing appears implicitly (much less overtly) political. Then comes the finale aboard the U-Boat. The Kapitan (Persoff) sits at his desk, satisfied that he's done a good day's work. A distraught young officer, Lieutenant Mueller (James Franciscus), stumbles in.

LT.: There were people on board that ship. Women, too.
We gave them no warning! Makes me wonder if we're
not damned men.
CAPT.: (laughing) In the eyes of the British admiralty, we're
all damned men.
LT.: I meant (whimpering) in the eyes of God!

Religion has entered the equation.

And, if less obviously, so has politics. This lieutenant is a Nazi.
Unlike the smug Kapitan, he comes across as . . . difficult as this is to
admit . . . sympathetic. Significantly, the Jewish Serling had previously been accused of anti-Semitism with his final script for *Playhouse
90*. Set in the Warsaw ghetto, *In the Presence of Mine Enemies* (CBS;
5/18/60) featured Charles Laughton and Susan Kohner as Jewish
heroes. Young Robert Redford (in his TV premiere) played a surprisingly decent-minded Nazi. This so outraged fellow Jewish-American
author Leon Uris (*Exodus*) that he described the piece as "the most
disgusting dramatic presentation" in TV history.

A fair charge or not? The answer is relative. As an iconoclast,
Serling could not compromise his individual vision to render the
work more acceptable to some preexisting group-think mindset.
Again, Shakespeare: "This, above all, to thine own self be true."
Serling remained precisely that. He knew the truth (or at least his
truth) and stuck with it, consequences be damned. On *Zone*, first
in *Judgment Day* and later in *He's Alive* (discussed below), Serling
took the concept of the sympathetic Nazi to its limit. This author's
job, as he saw it, was to communicate his own vision in the form of
televised drama. This qualifies him TV's first true auteur.

So *Judgment Day*'s lieutenant wonders if there might be a "special
fate for people like us": those who unnecessarily took lives. They easily
could have warned those aboard the *Glasgow* to abandon ship at once
before they sunk it. The Kapitan feared that this might allow the
Glasgow an opportunity to escape, and refused to do so. A "special"
(and horrific) fate would cause the perpetrator of such an inhumane
act to "suffer as they suffer" and "die as they die," for "we'd ride the
ghost of that ship every night . . . for eternity!" The guilt-stricken

lieutenant's employment of the plural turns out to be his only mistake. The implication here is that those who were "just following orders" will escape such an ongoing hell. The U-Boat's crew members were, from what we've seen, not aboard the ghostly *Glasgow*. Only the Kapitan (the man who gave the orders) is doomed. A controversial position, to be sure. Nonetheless, this is Rod Serling's position—his personal philosophy as expressed in public drama.

The people on board the *Glasgow* "could die once, only once," the lieutenant continues. "But we could die a hundred million times, every night, for eternity!" The smug smile disappears from the Kapitan's face. On some level he grasps that this will happen. To him. Perhaps the reason why (in Serling's moral paradigm) the lieutenant is spared derives from his willingness to assume personal responsibility for what did happen, though he would never have given such an order. The Kapitan (who disclaims responsibility) pays the piper. For Serling, the man who misuses power (military here, political in other episodes) experiences eternity in hell, and does so as The Lonely. Clearly, Serling believes in judgment day, although in **Zone** the apocalypse likely will occur at night, and on a one-on-one basis for each human rather than as a single event. Final judgment ultimately rests in the hands of a greater power, a Force (of good) in the universe. Serling's belief is hammered home in the closing lines: "This is the comeuppance awaiting every man when the ledger of his life is opened and examined, the tally made, and the reward or penalty paid."

No wonder, then, that the Kapitan was endowed with some positive traits, including sensitivity to children. *Judgment Night* isn't the indictment of Nazism that Leon Uris hoped it would be (explaining his disappoinment), but an Everyman play: a cautionary fable insisting that a potential for evil exists in each of us, as does a capacity for good. For Serling, everything boils down to one's individual choices. The lieutenant may not make it to heaven, but the worst to befall him would be purgatory. As to the Kapitan's fate, we've witnessed that. In **Zone**, such a man does not enter into a group-hell out of Dante. He (and, should we fail to do the right thing, we) encounters a hell specifically fashioned for him, every detail arranged to fit the unique missteps of an amoral individual living in what ultimately proves to be a moral universe.

The Devil's Disciple:

HE'S ALIVE (1/24/63)

THE HOWLING MAN (11/11/60)

Thematically speaking, *He's Alive* (one of the fourth season's hour-long episodes) picks up where *Judgment Night* left off. Rather than portray the show's central character, a "bush-league Führer" (Dennis Hopper) in a simplistic manner, Serling transforms Peter Vollmer from what he first describes as "a sparse little man who feeds off his self-delusions and finds himself perpetually hungry for want of greatness" into a complex figure. This in-depth portrait of a destructive man's confused psyche reaches such a rich level that even the most anti-Nazi viewer might at moments find Vollmer, unworthy of sympathy, at least empathetic.

First, already-established motifs reappear. Money, or the absence of it, is invoked when the American fascist stands on a street-corner soapbox, preaching to those sad souls desperate enough to be drawn in by his rhetoric of hate. Jews are not specifically mentioned, though it's obvious that Vollmer plays on the frustration of people in poverty by unfairly blaming this minority. Jews are less often the subject of Vollmer's tirades than Catholics, blacks, and Asians. Such an inclusive approach broadens the impact. As Serling stated in 1967: "I think the singular evil of our time is prejudice." In his writing, Serling damns "man's seemingly palpable need to dislike someone other than himself." If Serling's status as a Jew made him particularly sensitive to anti-Semitism (in high school, he was denied entry into a top fraternity due to his ethnicity), it's important to note Serling would not focus exclusively on this prejudice, which had been directed at him personally.

A generalist in ideas, even as he was a populist in approach, Serling mounts convincing literary attacks on a more universalized concept. Leon Uris could concentrate on the specific evils of anti-Semitism; no less Jewish but far more American, Serling attacked all prejudice, which partly explains his wider, broader appeal. Serling condemns what hate-mongering does to all people, to those who hate as well as the hated. Never in this episode is the number of Jews killed during the Holocaust, six million, mentioned. Yet the number of all casualties attributable to the Nazi regime, twelve million, is. Vollmer's grotesque ravings about a vast international "conspiracy" contain anti-Jewish insults ("Izzy," he howls). But they aren't limited to this; nasty nicknames are also verbalized for every other ethnic or racial minority. Yes, Serling hates those who hate Jews. What uniquely characterizes his work is hatred of those who hate any minority group.

Despite the subject matter, cautious optimism abides. The vast majority of those who pass Vollmer spit out insults (a few even throw objects) at the neo-Nazi, suggesting that the American man grasps how dangerous this nonsense is. Two policemen, one white and one black, protect Vollmer from an escalating mob. No sooner is it dispelled than the policemen make their loyalties clear: They agree with the protestors. In rescuing Vollmer, they merely observed the code of their profession. All mobs, even anti-Nazi ones, are scorned in a Serling script. This all takes place in summer, ordinarily Serling's season of tranquility. Dialogue mentions the heat that drives residents out of their tenements. Even during Rod's favorite time of year, the potential for evil exists. Also, *He's Alive* takes place entirely at night, when mankind, without natural light, proves vulnerable to moral bleakness.

Vollmer screams out that "the communists did this," referring to his humiliation. Even the least enlightened viewer will grasp that this was not the case. Those who reject neo-Nazism onscreen offer role models to the audience of how, if they follow their best thoughts and don't surrender to ugly instincts, they will treat a spokesman for evil: rebutting his absurd arguments, hurrying on without inflicting bodily damage.

Vollmer wanders over to "Building 13," shuffling up the stairs to visit the one person he truly cares about: A concentration camp survivor, Ernst Ganz (Ludwig Donath). Likely Ganz is Jewish; true to his singular approach, Serling never insists on this. Ganz represents not only the Jews but all people victimized by Hitler. A smart, well-read, gentle soul, Ganz allows Vollmer to enter his humble apartment, providing a washcloth for the beaten man. This unexpected turn of events raises *He Lives* above the level of anti-Nazi diatribe. As does what appears next: Serling creates a sense of sorrow for Vollmer on the part of Ganz and, via that character's concern, within the audience. If the wonderful Ganz has any weakness, it's his Christlike inability to turn any person away, even one as offensive to Ganz's sensibilities as Vollmer. In Serling's vision, though, this doesn't constitute a weakness. Ganz might be thought of as charac-teristic of all *Zone*'s heroes. His savior-like quality derives not from extending a hand of friendship to admirable people (easy to do!) but to the worst. No person, however horrific, exists completely apart from the community of men. There is no question that Vollmer is as bad as a person can be. Even he can't grasp why Ganz remains a loyal friend, despite Vollmer's condemnation of Jews as stereotypical Shylocks. And Vollmer knows from firsthand experience that this isn't true; he's been extended the most wonderful of all human gifts by Ganz: unconditional love.

He's Alive is a play no one but Rod Serling could have written. "I only see the boy," Ganz sighs, "not the man." We learn during their conversation that as a child, Peter Vollmer experienced abuse at the hands of his parents. Regularly beaten and nearly starved, he found comfort and friendship only with this elderly gentleman. At first such a revelation appears to suggest some gross contradiction. If this were the case, how then could Vollmer possibly grow up to be a Jew-hater? He's a lost man-child who, if raised with the decent values Ganz lives by, might have turned out differently. A victim of his environment, Vollmer is not a bad seed. Conservatives hold that, to the contrary, "biology is destiny." Serling's belief, as implied through the drama, is liberal: If Ganz had only been blessed with an opportunity to reach Vollmer earlier, the results might have been different.

But to invoke the Bard, "What's done cannot be undone." Vollmer is what he is: a monster. Even Ganz knows and admits this. We sense, too, that on some level the Peter Vollmer who might have been (the sub-microscopic element of the innocent boy that remains alive inside this corrupted man) knows it, too. That, in the final analysis, represents the truest tragedy. If the last vestige of any decent instinct beating within Vollmer draws him to Ganz's apartment, the bigot cannot escape what sordid experience has made of him. He must walk out the door, descend again to the street and, once there, articulate an ideology of hate he knows to be false.

The weakest dramatic element appears to be a shadowy figure (Curt Conway) who pushes Vollmer to horrifying deeds, ultimately insisting that he murder old Ganz. Toward the episode's end, this monster steps out of the shadows and is revealed to be none other than Adolf Hitler. Critics carped that virtually every viewer guessed this twist before Serling chose to reveal it. Still, the situation rates as a script flaw only if we assume that Serling didn't want us to guess this. Yet the title could refer to no one but Hitler.

The episode works because we do grasp the shadowy figure's inevitable identity. Vollmer's metaphysical confrontation with the devil/Hitler may take place only in Vollmer's mind. None of the other neo-Nazis, including Frank (Paul Mazursky) ever notices him. Vollmer's stalking and killing a man he considers to be his (spiritual) father adds a mythic dimension.

Our empathy for the child Vollmer is now so strong that we hope for a denouement in which he'll come to his senses and do the right thing, reject Hitler. If that force of evil can be exorcised, perhaps the innocent child will afterwards reemerge, with Ganz now acting as his righteous shepherd. Since this is a tragic drama, that does not occur. When, after murdering Ganz, Vollmer is shot down by a police detective, we react as Ganz might have were he still alive, and as the author's voice clearly does, with pity rather than hatred. This episode has made humanists of us all, Serling's intention for *Zone*.

In Serling's view, individual human beings can never be absolutely evil. That status is reserved for a mob or for Hitler himself, similar to the title character (Robin Hughes) in Charles Beaumont's *The Howling*

Man. A naive fellow, David Ellington (H.M. Wynant), discovers a seemingly harmless victim imprisoned by an apparently deranged monk (John Carradine). Out of pity, Ellington sets the man free, but discovers that, as the not-so-crazed monk insisted, this is Scratch himself, loosed upon the world. When after years Ellington recaptures Satan, his equally well-intentioned, if misguided, housekeeper (Ezelle Poule), fearing that Ellington is deranged, considers freeing this "poor" man. Does this imply that Ellington or the monk has failed? No! In *Zone*, those who fight the good fight every day of their lives can never be so dismissed. A realist who grasped that perfection can never be achieved, Rod Serling believes we can (indeed, must) fight the forces of evil—and continue to do so, even if what his narrative voice says about the metaphysical figure of Old Scratch holds true for his all-too-historical counterpart, Adolf Hitler: "You can catch the devil, but you can't hold him long." Still, the epic heroes among us (including those who inhabit the *Zone*) must be admired, for they will never cease trying.

If I Were a Carpenter:

THE OBSOLETE MAN (6/2/61)

Serling's *Obsolete Man* is set in an unidentified country in some unspecified age, Kafka's *The Trial* re-imagined for TV. Director Elliot Silverstein self-consciously allowed himself to be influenced by the German expressionist films of Fritz Lang, including *Metropolis* (1927) and *M* (1931) so bizarre camera angles and a shadowy mise-en-scène are in evidence. An angular intro presents the Chancellor (Fritz Weaver) high atop a jutting podium, his Subaltern (Joseph Elic) seated below. Eerie lighting effects suggest a distant galaxy, though that doesn't stand in the way of this episode serving as a metaphor for what we might become, a point driven home in the narration. Serling insists that this "is not a new world (but) simply an extension of what began in the old one."

As in Huxley's *Brave New World* or Orwell's *1984*, we encounter a near-future cautionary fable: The most horrible elements just beginning to appear in our own world are purposefully exaggerated so we can see (and hopefully avoid) the likely consequences. Such a presentation invokes a sense of optimism: There's still time for us to change the future if we heed the warning inherent in this strange story about a little man with a big heart. That would be the effectively named (after Serling's favorite romantic poet) Romney Wordsworth. Dragged before a merciless court, the sad-faced fellow is accused of a heinous crime against The State: He's become obsolete. Wordsworth was a librarian. As in Ray Bradbury's *Fahrenheit 451*, this is a world in which books are banned and burned. Essential to the success is the casting of Burgess Meredith. Earlier, he played Henry Bemis, book-obsessed bank clerk in *Time Enough at Last*. His return as yet another small-of-stature fellow (little people a recurring motif) "whose passion is the printed page" creates a connection between the episodes. Rather than a repetition of the earlier show, *Obsolete Man* provides its reversal.

The reason Bemis ultimately had to be punished had less to do with strong feelings for literature than his lack of love for people. Books insulated Bemis from others, always a sin for Serling. Conversely, Wordsworth does not horde books, though plenty are on view in his apartment. Wordsworth most enjoyed sharing books with others; he is a humanist who views reading as merely a means to end, enlightenment of the masses—essentially Serling's own view. The enemy is a totalitarian state, symbolized by the dictator in charge. Here then is the episode in which Rod's political views are rendered clear. In *The Twilight Zone Companion*, Zicree incorrectly assumes that what we witness is a right-wing society: "a neo-Nazi super state." Serling never employs those terms. When the evil Chancellor mentions his personal heroes, fascistic Hitler is included, but so too is Stalin, the latter Russia's communist dictator. Like Hitler, Stalin ordered millions of his countrymen put to death. Serling despises neither left nor right, only extremes of either. He condemns not conservatives or liberals but "absolutists." Villains on either side are unwilling to do precisely the same horrible things as their political opposites. Rod's refusal to identify the Chancellor's political position is not due to a failure of nerve, but is his basic point.

Serling's singular vision is enhanced when we learn that in addition to books, religion has been banished. Wordsworth and the Chancellor heatedly debate the value of reading, but their voices never rise to a fever pitch until spirituality is brought up. The Chancellor shouts "there is no God!" to which Wordsworth shrieks, "there is a God!" The Chancellor paraphrases Karl Marx; all religious faith is but the opiate of the masses. Of all Wordsworth's books, the Bible remains his favorite. This is hardly the position we expect from a hero created by a party-line liberal. Then again, Serling reaches far beyond conventional politics. Progressive on social issues, he expresses an abiding belief that we must continue to believe in something larger and greater out there, beyond the realistic boundaries of time and space. Were he alive today, Serling would despise the religious right, with its implied condemnation of liberals as godless. On the other hand, he would be a founding father of the emergent religious left, which insists that true liberalism can only derive from a faith-based value system.

A deconstruction device brings the medium we watch into the message conveyed as Serling addresses television. With 48 hours left to live, Wordsworth sits in his room, reading the Bible. He has chosen to be executed live on TV. A monitor, installed on the wall, will shortly share Wordsworth's last moments with the public. Here, Serling inserts a comment on the lowest level to which TV could descend. When the Chancellor pays a visit only to find himself locked in with the doomed man (a bomb has been set to explode when the ticking clock reaches midnight, invoking the Time Element), Wordsworth reads the Twenty-third Psalm to his terrified companion. He pauses on those words about the valley of death, reminding us how significant "passing" (particularly in cases of premature death) is to *Zone*. The Chancellor finally leaps up, begging for his life. As Wordsworth anticipated, his nemesis blurts out the required words for Wordsworth to unlock the door: "Let me out in the name of God!" Having won his victory, Wordsworth allows the Chancellor to go, then calmly submits to an ersatz crucifixion by contemporary technology. Anyone requiring internal evidence to prove Wordsworth was intended as a Jesus figure need look no further than his secondary profession: carpenter.

In the final moments, Serling asks us to empathize with the Chancellor! As with *Judgment Night*'s Kapitan, Serling dares insist that even the worst among us constitute a part of the human race. If we do not feel something for them (bad as they may be), we are no better. Returning to the courtroom, the Chancellor discovers his Subaltern in charge. The Chancellor had escaped by assuming the role of Everyman and admitting that he clings to the hope that there is a God, at least during those moments when we face our mortality. Since the Chancellor's statement was televised, he too is rendered obsolete. Momentarily, we are delighted as the villain gets his just deserts. Yet as others crowd in, we recall the residents of Maple Street—how the "good" people there turned evil the moment they degenerated into a mob.

The progressive side of Serling believes in the innate goodness that can derive from a human community. But he also empathizes with any person about to be (wrongly or in this case rightly) destroyed by a group gone mad. Here is Serling the traditionalist. Now, that person happens to be the Chancellor, so our hearts go out to him, even if our heads tell us he isn't worthy. Here then is the vision of a humanist—the only way in which Serling could end this drama.

Grand Illusion:

ON THURSDAY WE LEAVE FOR HOME (5/2/63)

In individual episodes, Serling made clear his distaste for vicious dictators on the left or right. What, though, did he think of benign dictators? That issue would result in this parable about would-be pilgrims, stuck on a distant planet for 30 years. To survive while out of contact with Earth, they required a strong leader, one able to endow them with hope, courage, and discipline. The only choice was William Benteen (James Whitmore), a Moses-like figure who treats his flock as sheep, offering guidance. Thanks to him, the colonists did not fall into nihilism. Benteen insists that they pray daily (religion and politics here go hand in hand) for deliverance. Then Earthlings locate the lost colony and launch a rescue ship, captained by Sloane (Tim O'Conner).

Upon its arrival, every space pilgrim understands that they truly were blessed (that word not used randomly) with level-headed Benteen. Yet things quickly go awry. Benteen resents the degree to which Sloane assumes command of "his" people. Worse, Sloane addresses him as "Mr. Benteen" rather than as "Captain," the honorific title the 187 pilgrims had conferred on him. (187 is the precise number of Texicans who died at the Alamo on March 6, 1836; Captain Benteen was among the cavalry officers who failed to reinforce George Custer in Montana on June 25, 1876. Coincidences or intentional parallels? We may never know. Still, Serling did pen an episode about the Little Big Horn, *The 7th is Made Up of Phantoms*. And the Western genre is often incorporated into *Zone*.)

Now, none of the pilgrims cares that Benteen believes that they shouldn't play baseball with the rescue ship's crew in the midday heat. When he suggests that they settle together after returning to Earth, maintaining the sense of community (and identity) that sustained them here, his flock openly rebels. Each individual wants to be free. Stunned that his era of power is over, Benteen attacks the ship. Beaten off by Sloane, he vows to remain alone. As the ship ascends, Benteen barks orders to an imaginary following—better to be the benign dictator of make-believe people than an ordinary citizen on Earth. Absolute power has corrupted Benteen absolutely.

The dramatic arc we witness here might be described as *He's Alive*'s character transformation played backwards. There, we met a terrible leader who misguided any potential followers, yet came to grasp the evil within once he discovered his potential for goodness. Here, we encounter a fine political leader and spiritual guide, a positive influence on all around him, whose dark side is revealed. If a humanist like Benteen might be subject to egomania, then the potential exists in everyone. If we fall in love with power, no matter whether from the left or the right, and no matter if we employ it for ill or good, we are doomed. Benteen's tragedy: he's left alone, realizing too late his mistake. "I want to go home," he cries in solitude, now The Lonely, desperate to recapture a past he has lost. No wonder then that Benteen makes his home in a cave, *Zone*'s ongoing metaphor for the pit of man's superstitions, the dark side we must escape from.

During his tenure, Benteen positioned himself as a modern day Moses. Before the rescue ship's arrival, when a woman chose to hang herself out of despair or the rebellious Al (James Broderick) asked why they must wait in line for water ("There shouldn't be any rules!"), Benteen tellingly shouted: "Blasphemy!" As was the case with Moses, to rebel against any law he establishes is to rebel against God. He's an Old Testament patriarch, utterly unforgiving. He carried a Bible, holding it while inspiring the crowd, creating for them a Promised Land, an idealized Earth of milk and honey. His vision resembles what French writer-director Jean Renoir tagged a grand illusion: a fantasy, yes, but one necessary to sustain mankind, vulnerable and weak, during such strife. If ever the pilgrims gave up hoping and praying, they would have been doomed. The many who had already taken their lives did so because they lost faith, choosing to surrender to the abyss rather than continue a meaningless existence. Benteen offered positivism by way of exaggeration and myth-making.

Benteen was, like the author who created him, a supreme storyteller. Throughout the first half, he rates as a role model. That Sloane can replace him is clear when we realize that Sloane, too, is a religious man, telling the colonists that Earth is much the same as when they left it, noting sadly that wars continue to occur; by the "grace of God, we never had the Hydrogen war" that Earthlings feared. As loyalties turn toward this savior from the sky (a gentle New Testament figure), the flock one by one turn away from Moses who, by his own admission, held them together thanks to rock-like willpower. Benteen retires to the depths of his cave, even as Moses did on the far side of the Jordan. His one-time followers, still incapable of fending for themselves, instinctually turn to Sloane, who appears as appropriate for their second coming to Earth as Benteen had earlier proven for survival (if not forty years, close to it) on a planet resembling the harsh Sinai.

Too sympathetic to be written off as a villain, Benteen is an anachronistic figure who has outlived his usefulness. "When you pray to God," Sloane noted while reeducating the people, "his name should not be Benteen!" Sadly, the man who for decades warned these pilgrims against false idols has become one himself. "May God help you all," Benteen warns the departing multitude. There is a degree of truth to what he says. After all, Benteen conditioned them to believe in Earth as a Garden of Eden, which of course it isn't. "You think you'll be on the way to paradise," but "you're going to hell!" If these voyagers, in a state of disappointment after arrival because of the disparity between their ideal and the reality that they encounter, choose to emphasize the negative, they will suffer. If they consider the ways in which Earth is preferable to the desert planet, they will fashion a heaven out of what they discover upon their return. Like everything else in the *Zone*, heaven and hell exist in the mind; in the way in which we perceive our surroundings.

One final image: Benteen is alone on his planet, happy so long as (in his own mind) he imagines his flock remains there, and he is still in power. Then he hears the ship depart and Benteen's grand illusion falls apart. He's dictator over nothing—the sad fate of even a decent man when he changes from one who hoped to empower his people into a tragic figure who cannot survive without exerting power.

Waiting For Goldsmith:

THE OLD MAN IN THE CAVE (11/8/63)

On Thursday concludes with a once-revered leader off in a cave like the animated one on view in *Zone*'s first title sequence. Conversely, *Old Man* begins with a similar person stepping away from such a place. In a small nearby post-nuclear-apocalyptic town, the few remaining survivors patiently wait for Goldsmith (John Anderson) to bring back The Word from The Old Man who lives beyond a huge metallic door, hiding the identity of their God. None doubt that who or whatever the Old Man is, he speaks, however deep in the earth, from the summit of man's intelligence. When Moses-like Goldsmith returns, everyone does precisely as he tells them to, keeping their covenant. They won't eat "unclean" food after Goldsmith tells them that this is the Old Man's command.

Everything alters with the arrival of Major French (James Coburn), a fascist dictator who scoffs at all such concerns. The "contaminated" canned goods can, and should, be consumed. Only Goldsmith rails against any departure from their invisible father. In retaliation, French and his squad of armed followers decide to unmask the Old Man as a fraud. Politics in Goldsmith's view insist that right makes might; those who follow French hold that might makes right. The people, sensing that the time has come to make a political and, by implication, religious choice, head for the cave. French blows up the barrier and, with anxious citizens following, steps inside to see (sight in place of insight) what's there. The Old Man turns out to be a computer, spitting out information. French roars with laughter while the people grow disenchanted.

As always, familiarity (particularly of a visual order) breeds contempt. Goldsmith's followers join with French's uniformed thugs to form a detestable mob and destroy the computer. No one actually shouts "God is dead," though Nietzsche's words underline the situation. Feeling free for the first time in years (if not grasping the distinction between freedom and chaos) they (like the ancient Hebrews, celebrating while Moses remained high on the mountain) revel in alcohol, food, dance, and (by implication) sex. A lap-dissolve carries us to the final shot: All lie dead in the streets, except for Goldsmith. Like a Moses without any followers left, he (a humanist) wanders off to hopefully find some Promised Land. Goldsmith has become The Lonely. His eyes express pity for those of little faith who listened to a false savior, accepting an easy answer rather than to continue to follow Goldsmith's strict self-denial.

The Old Man, scripted by Serling from Henry Slesar's short story, serves as a fitting conclusion to all that had gone before. In the opening, we seemingly see a man driving a car until director Alan Crosland, Jr. glides his camera back to reveal a horse pulling the automobile, confronting us with *Zone*'s appearance/reality theme. Goldsmith looks cold and reserved, whereas French smiles and exudes charm. Yet he (if unknowingly) is the devil in the flesh; Goldsmith represents those harsh but wise Hebraic rulers who speak for a Yahweh demanding absolute obedience based on unquestioning faith. Like Moses, Goldsmith understands that this can only continue so long as the source remains unseen. "Only God knows how many will die" because of the revelation that their "Lord" is but a machine, Goldsmith mournfully states.

They needed their grand illusion. Goldsmith turns out to have been correct when his one-time followers perish. Perhaps there are more people out there somewhere whom Goldsmith can save. If that's so, he likely will do this as a New Testament figure, a point driven home when, as Goldsmith trudges out of town, an immense cross leads the way.

Here, too, we encounter *Zone*'s last great anti-nuke statement. Even in this episode from the fifth season, during which stories grew darker than those that preceded them (see Chapter 12), Serling manages to eke out at least a little optimism. This is "not a prediction of what is to be"; he—acting as a kind of video rabbi to people of all faiths, *Zone* his electronic age pulpit, morally educating us through entertaining fables—reassures us, "just a projection of what could be." There is still time, brother! This is a possible fate but one that can be divided if we only use our free will correctly. Might never makes right; right, if we have faith, always makes might. In a nutshell, that's the political and religious position of Rod Serling—and, once we grasp his meaning, the ultimate reason for not only *Zone*'s immediate impact, but for the ongoing appeal of the series this writer-producer created.

12

VIDEO NOIR:
The Dark Side of the Small Screen

HOWEVER MUCH *ZONE* reflects the 1950s, only the first six shows were broadcast during that decade. Others constitute an end-product portrait from a new perspective: the Kennedy era, marked by heady transition as the middlebrow mendacity of the Eisenhower Age gave way to youthful exuberance. Here was an era known as Camelot, an epithet as drenched in nostalgia as the supposed "happy days" that preceded it. *Zone*'s fifth and final season began in late September, 1963, two months before JFK's assassination. Episodes that followed mirrored the current mentality of confusion, fear, and even despair. As always on TV, Rod Serling got there first and with the most. The already discussed *In Praise of Pip* (9/27/03) introduced the Vietnam War to a mass audience via imaginative fantasy. In *Come Wander With Me* (5/22/64), Gary Crosby played the first Bob Dylan-style "folkie" to appear on the small screen. Not surprisingly, Serling offered audiences an early understanding of our emergent world as the American dream shattered. In fact, such a dark strain, if not dominant until now, had long been present pretty much from the onset.

Big Brother Is Watching You:

EYE OF THE BEHOLDER (11/11/60)

Serling's opening places the viewer "suspended in time and space," on a planet with similarities to and differences from our own. The latter are kept under wraps till the denouement, like the face of Janet

Tyler (Maxine Stuart), a hospital patient hoping that the staff may succeed in altering her hideous appearance. *Eye* takes place entirely at night, unfolding in real time. Director Douglas Heyes sustains a Hitchcock-like mood while cinematographer George Clemens relies heavily on Hitch's bird's-eye-view shot to keep us disoriented. Bernard Herrmann's *Vertigo*-like score proves eerily unsettling; William Tuttle's make-up is uniquely strange. Serling's script? One of *Zone*'s uncontestable masterworks.

Originally titled "A Private World of Darkness," the piece opens as Janet emerges from deep sleep. Once again, what occurs may be the character's dream. The Time Element appears as we realize that Janet can't grasp where or when this occurs. Her surgeon (William D. Gordon) also attempts to get his bearings, glancing down at a wristwatch, one of *Zone*'s symbolic timepieces. A nurse (Jennifer Howard) reminds this doctor that he's becoming too involved on a personal level, establishing that he's a humanist. Everyone is hooked on cigarettes, Serling's own weakness. Constantly rising smoke adds to the macabre atmosphere, making it difficult for us to grasp what's going on. That *Eye* is, on one level, a variation on the limitations of a human perception theme supported by the hazy mise-en-scène. Adding to the impact is the fact that this is the only *Zone* in which the protagonist can't see.

Inspired by this, the collaborators created *Zone*'s most complex visual scheme. Act One, in which the situation is introduced, was shot in a subjective style. We do see Janet, but aren't allowed a good glimpse of the others because the bandages that make it impossible for her to see dictate that what we perceive remains in shadow. More than just "clever," this proves a functional style at the rightly famous pay-off. Act Two begins when the doctor cuts away the bandages. Here the majority of shots are from Janet's point of view; we see what she sees. We are Janet; she is us. As the bandages are cut, we experience the most stunning sequence in *Zone*. Her point of view, and ours as well, remains stationary, focused on a ceiling light. With each layer of mummy-like material removed, that light grows brighter, resembling the Death Light. Aurally we can't be sure if a palpitating heart is Janet's, the sympathetic doctor's, or our own. TV's equivalent of the proscenium arch has been removed; we are utterly at one with everything that occurs on screen.

Bandages removed and the medical crew in shock, we are plunged into a brief third act, the camera now objective. We see Janet as the doctor and nurses do and finally get a good look at them. Janet (now played by Donna Douglas) is a Monroe-type beauty; they are pig-like creatures, as hideous to us as the blonde is to them. In the epilogue, Janet runs into Walter (Edson Stroll), leader of the "deformed" community to which she will be banished. The approach might be described as super-objective: The camera assumes a distanced quality as Janet converses with a man we perceive as handsome, though she must try to adjust to his "hideous" appearance.

In addition to the subjectivity of perception, *Eye* is rich with themes, including a nightmare-scenario of 1950s style conformity. Janet's key statement, "I want to be like everyone else!", begs for consideration. A giant Orwellian TV screen (self-referencing Serling's chosen medium) allows Big Brother to watch you. He speaks of "glorious conformity"; the image appears as a screen within a screen, positing us as among the citizenry. Janet's loathing of him implies the metaphysical theme: "The state is not God," she cries. The doctor earlier admitted that when scientific efforts are finished, only a "miracle" helps. By having two actresses play Janet, *Zone*'s Mirror Image is implied. Janet asks to be eliminated, re-introducing death as something not to be feared. A sense of fate prevails; when Janet rushes into the arms of Mark, the doctor notes, "oddly, you've come right to" your "destiny." Unconditional love is offered by Mark. *Eye* even attacks the myth of normalcy. Striving to achieve a false standard of perfection destroys what Serling loves most and best in people: their individuality.

Dr. Spock Was Wrong:

IT'S A GOOD LIFE (11/3/61)

This classic indicates a change in attitude toward young people. Anthony Fremont (Billy Mumy) serves as a prototype for Serling's revised view of the post-Dr. Spock generation, a gross exaggeration of every child whose parents opted for appeasement of their offspring's whims. That *Zone* was, at least by implication, about the changing face of America is inherent in Serling's opening to the script he fashioned from Jerome Bixby's short story. Standing in front of a large map of the U.S., Serling points out the small town of Peaksville, Ohio, a mid-American enclave with old-fashioned buildings and cornfields, one more Homewood. Now, though, we witness its dark underbelly. It is not the adults who have soured the place, but (surprisingly) a child.

Inexplicably, Little Anthony (a reference to the rock 'n' roll star?) has acquired a power to mentally transform anything around him. He has banished the town's cars, isolating Peaksville from the outside world. Everyone (adults, other kids, even dogs) must appease Little Anthony, knowing that, if angered, he will "wish them away into the cornfield." Not even friendly behavior toward the diminutive "monster" works, as he reads minds. Any time a person thinks negative thoughts, Anthony dispatches the transgressor. His parents (John Larch and Cloris Leachman) and neighbors must insist that Anthony has acted well even when he destroys someone. "That was a good thing you did," people less-than-convincingly tell him. How striking an irony that the American scribe who predicted the youth movement would insist that, if allowed absolute freedom (which, like absolute power, corrupts), young people would turn out worse than the previous generation.

One memorable sequence has Anthony controlling the TV, imagining a battle between table-top dinosaurs, which the adults pretend to enjoy. Movie brats (Spielberg, Lucas, et al) would soon take over Hollywood and institute what critic Pauline Kael decried as an "infantilization of our culture." Such a coming climate is here foreshadowed by director James Sheldon's image of Anthony, surrounded by long-suffering grownups, imposing childish tastes instead of being told, in the traditional manner, what to watch. Perhaps Anthony's ultimate statement is the line he shouts loudest: "I hate anybody that doesn't like me!" Here is a nightmare vision of the era's upcoming youth movement gone out of control.

One unique element is the manner in which Serling and Sheldon employ music. Though Anthony loves to listen when guest Pat Riley

(Casey Adams) plays piano, he can't stand it if anyone sings. That's the easiest way to annoy him, as Dan Hollis (Don Keefer) learns when he gets drunk and plays an old Perry Como record, reviving a key *Zone* theme: this child is a bad person because he can't stand the human element. The title offers an sardonic put-down of the name Frank Capra chose for his best-loved film. No wonder this episode (like *Monsters on Maple Street*) helped institute *Zone*'s noir element—stories with no sense of hope at the end.

There isn't even a denouement! Angrier than ever, Little Anthony transforms a lovely summer day into a winter storm. That this represents a coming darkness to the show and to society is evident in Serling's refusal to hint at what all this means. "No comment here," he tells us. "No comment at all." What a shock these words provide in contrast to the typical "lesson to be learned," that earlier approach implying that drama can make better citizens of us all. The ending here? As close to nihilism as *Zone* can come.

The End of the World:

THE SHELTER (9/29/61)

ONE MORE PALLBEARER (1/12/62)

The darkest of Serling's early scripts dealt with the end of the world. Here he could express his anti-nuke position as cautionary fables and case studies, collaborating with director Lamont Johnson on two particularly strong episodes.

First to appear was *The Shelter*, a virtual rewrite of *Monsters on Maple Street* with nuclear weapons substituted for Martians. The first image reveals a typical suburban neighborhood. In the home of Dr. Stockton (Larry Gates), neighbors at his birthday party toast this beloved fellow who took good care of their children. Then the TV snaps off and the radio (the two media Serling best understood) informs them that atomic bombs are headed for the U.S. Everyone hurries off while Doc, his wife Grace (Peggy Stewart), and son (Michael Burns) rush downstairs to their bomb shelter.

GRACE STANTON: Why is it so necessary to survive?
DR. STANTON (indicating their son) *That's* why.

That Stanton cares more about the survival of his child than him-self establishes him as a heroic humanist. This fine quality is tested as never before when Jerry Harlowe (Jack Albertson) shows up, begging that he and his kids be allowed to join them. Doc refuses. There's only enough food, water, and air for three people; when he built this refuge, Doc begged the neighbors to create bomb shelters of their own. All laughed. To allow them in now would not help the others, and would only succeed in dooming his family. Are we to accept or reject Doc's decision? That's up to each viewer; as Serling insists, "No moral, no message." Again, no lesson to be learned . . .

The power derives from a new complexity in Serling's scripts. Here we find no easy dichotomy between between humanists and the less enlightened. A selfless hero must choose between loyalty to blood ties and to the community of man, including innocent children. The conflict is no longer between good and bad, but addresses the socio-political duality of America: rugged individualism vs. community loyalty. Doc is in a no-win situation, new to *Zone*. Civilization in postwar suburbia is a sham; when push comes to shove, people do just that, preparing a battering ram. But do adults do this for their own survival or concern for their children? Motive, apparently, is now everything to Serling.

The metaphysical theme intrudes on this meditation on personal responsibility: "God help you," Doc firmly (but not coldly) informs Harlowe. "It's out of my hands." Desperate as he may be, Harlowe senses that the others do wrong when they bash down the door: "You're acting like a mob and a mob doesn't have a brain," he says, here serving as the author's spokesman. The shelter appears as a contemporary version of Serling's recurring "cave," now fashioned from concrete. Doc bears more than a passing resemblance to Ibsen's "enemy of the people," as he is also a doctor who transformed in the public perception from hero to villain. Yet Serling goes Ibsen one better: As the intruders storm in, the radio informs all that the objects above were only harmless satellites. Under pressure, seemingly average people found "out what we're really like." Including Doc! He delivers the most poignant line in this episode and, perhaps, *Zone*: "I don't know what 'normal' is."

This growing complexity is further expanded in *One More Pall-bearer*. This Serling script also involves people who believe the world is about to end, though it is not. There's also a man, Paul Radin (Joseph Wiseman), who owns a bomb shelter. But Radin is as cruel as Doc was kind. Radin throws his doors open to virtual strangers, inviting Colonel Hawthorne (Trevor Bardette), Reverend Hughes (Gage Clark), and teacher Mrs. Langford (Katherine Squire), all elderly and retired, to his hideaway. We know what they don't: Earlier, Radin paid electricians (Joseph Elic and Robert Snyder) to install an elaborate TV/radio center; as in *The Shelter*, Serling acknowledges the power of his media. Monitors are rigged to falsely convey "government messages" proclaiming that an atomic war has begun. Radin assumes that each invitee, who long ago insulted him, will beg, scrape, and apologize for past indiscretions to remain inside and so save their lives.

Yet the opposite happens. The "mean" schoolteacher who flunked him asserts that she was right; he cheated on a test. The Reverend won't apologize for accusing Radin of a "lack of character"; young Radin drove a naive girl to suicide. The colonel did order Radin's court martial, but only because Radin's lack of courage in combat caused thirty men to die. (This last is a reference to Serling's earlier realistic plays). Bravely, each begs to be let out so he or she can die with friends and family; Radin has neither. When they hurry off to their presumed deaths, Radin is left alone (one of The Lonely).

Pallbearer concludes with a merging of two key *Zone* themes. Radin wanders up out of his self-made prison and discovers that the world has come to an end. If that initially seems an irony, it's the setup for a greater irony still: The post-apocalyptic world exists only in his mind; though true for Radin, it isn't for others. Like many *Zone* villains before him, Radin has gone mad. Other themes also reappear. The Reverend summons up the metaphysical, with references to the gospel and his final "Amen!" Radin was involved in one of those Long-Distance Calls that fail to communicate when the trio entered. He glances at his watch throughout for the Time Element. Radin's giant TV screen reflects his Mirror Image when at the end he destroys it. The concept of death obviously runs through both these noir-ish episodes.

Night Gallery:

THE MIDNIGHT SUN (11/17/61)

Here the world does end, though nuclear weapons, or any of man's other shortcomings, do not cause the holocaust this time. Inexplicably altering in its elliptical orbit, the Earth draws closer to the sun. Serling and director Anton Leader offer something no previous *Zone* presented: death en masse without hope of reprieve. How do people relate to others in such a situation? Young Norma (Lois Nettleton), living in a Manhattan apartment, reveals her heroism through humanism, offering her own water to a little girl who lives upstairs, then sharing a precious bottle of juice with her landlady, Mrs. Bronson (Betty Garde). They constantly check watches and clocks, knowing that the Time Element is pitted against them.

Norma is an artist. Since this crisis began, she's been painting variations on a theme: the sun as our enemy. Mrs. Bronson loses control while considering them. "Please, Norma, paint something cool today." Mrs. Bronson stands in for the TV audience, eager for the form to provide escapism. Norma represents Serling, hungry to create images that force people to reconsider reality. The characters keep in contact with the outside world through radio broadcasts. Recidivism to an animal state looms large when Mrs. Bronson fears that she's acting like a beast. A need to balance rugged individualism with community loyalty is expressed by Norma: "We've got to start living with one another now."

Madness makes itself felt when a frightful man (Tom Reese) breaks in. Though initially he appears threatening, the women grasp that he's decent, but "acting crazy" owing to harsh circumstances. The religious element appears; Mrs. Bronson spreads her hands, suggesting a crucifixion. As Norma bends down to embrace the body, Leader structures the moment as a Pietà. In one memorable image, water in the "cool" painting Norma prepared appears to pour downward as increasing heat melts the paint. This image foreshadows a device employed in Serling's *Night Gallery* (NBC) series in the early 1970s.

Midnight Sun reverses *Zone*'s earlier notion of summer as a charming season. The ironic turnabout occurs when Mrs. Bronson, still alive (at least for the moment) stands by the window, watching a snowstorm. Norma wakes from a nightmare, a twist prepared for when Norma stated that this was what she half-expected would happen. But as this is a noir, her (and our) relief proves short-lived. Norma's dream was an inverse of the true problem: The earth is orbiting ever further away from the sun; everyone will shortly freeze to death.

The Shape of Things to Come:

LITTLE GIRL LOST (3/16/62)

KICK THE CAN (2/9/62)

SPUR OF THE MOMENT (2/21/64)

Richard Matheson's *Little Girl Lost* spins a bizarre fable about a child named Tina (Tracy Stratford) who, on a seemingly normal night, rolls off her bed and onto the floor, passing through an invisible passage into another dimension. The frantic mother, Ruth (Sarah Marshall), hears but can't see her daughter, one more case of the limits of human perception. Director Paul Stewart sets up the mother as the subject of a Mirror Image shot when her challenged sanity (another recurring issue) appears in her looking-glass. Then the father (Robert Sampson) must crawl through a black hole into an alternative universe to retrieve Tina. Things conclude happily, thanks to the family's faithful dog dragging the child to safety. "Man, what a mutt!" a neighbor (Charles Aidman) proclaims. As a physicist, his final words disquiet us: "Junctures between dimensions are freaks of nature that happen" and can appear in any of our ordinary abodes as unpredictably as here.

Earlier, George Clayton Johnson presented a notably different father-child relationship. The son, David Whitley (Barry Truex), is a grown man dealing with his elderly father, Charles (Ernest Truex), who hopes to leave Sunnyvale Nursing Home. Charles enjoys watching neighborhood children play kick the can, a game that lends this episode its title. Roommate Ben Conroy (Russell Collins) resents kids; shortly the two engage in one of *Zone*'s Socratic dialogues. "It's a special summertime ritual," Charles claims, echoing Serling's sensibility. "You don't believe in magic?" he asks Ben, who has lost his primal sympathy. Here is the romantic-realist dichotomy: Charles explains that if one returns to the "grass" and finds splendor there, he'll be young again.

An old adage insists that you're as young as you feel. *Zone* insists we feel as young as we think, because reality exists in the mind. When Charles and the other old people slip out to dance in the moonlight, they appear to middle-aged caretaker Cox (John Marley) as small kids. The darkness occurs before dawn for Ben, who realizes that by doubting his friend, he's lost his Second Chance to find glory in the flower. Forlorn, Ben returns to the building alone while the others play.

Matheson returned to the parent-child relationships in *Spur of the Moment*, the most brightly-lit of all noirs. *Spur* begins as a daughter of privilege, Anne Henderson (Diana Hyland), leaves her palatial home for an afternoon ride. As her white horse approaches a hillock, Anne spots a frightful image: An elderly woman, dressed all in black, seated on a dark horse, staring down. Terrified, Anne hurries home, the figure in pursuit. Anne's father (Philip Ober) calls the police, but the horrified teenager believes that this was a force from beyond. Her fiancé, Bob (Robert Hogan), jokes that perhaps the death-like figure appeared to warn her against going through with their upcoming marriage. Roguishly handsome David (Roger Davis) forces his way in and begs his lover Anne to run off with him. Anne must now make the decision of a lifetime: marry Bob according to her parents' wishes and live a conventional life, or run away with her great love, David.

At the episode's midpoint, our point of view shifts. The black-clad woman, also Anne, rides up to the mansion. Twenty years have passed and her father is dead. Inside, Anne's mother (Marsha Hunt) wastes away in the ruins of the glorious lifestyle we glimpsed earlier. Bitter, nasty Anne castigates her mother and deceased father for ruining her life. What's happened seems obvious: The vulnerable girl did as told, and lived to regret it. Then, in a satisfying turnabout, her alcoholic husband wanders in. To our surprise, it's not Bob, but Dave: A

At the beginning of Season Two, Rod began appearing in the opening and closing shot (here, *Nervous Man in a Four Dollar Room*), making him television's best known celebrity author.

The Serling home in Binghamton, New York, on a quiet, pleasant, upper-middle-class neighborhood; the fictionalized yet obviously accurate equivalent in an early **Zone** episode, *The Monsters Are Due on Maple Street* was modeled on this photograph.

Unlike such Beat writers as Jack Kerouac and Allen Ginsberg, Rod Serling liked to have his cake and eat it too. This created a contradiction in terms: Here, TV's "Angry Young Man" spends a conventional evening in the suburbs with wife Carol and daughters Jodi and Nan.

Individual images were consistently framed to suggest the small television screen as a potential escape from the Eisenhower era; Gig Young (back to camera) wanders toward his beloved Homewood, reflected in a vending-machine mirror in *Walking Distance*.

A sense of identity emerges as the wanderer (Earl Holliman) finds a memory rekindled by a movie poster in *Where Is Everybody?*; he rates as the first, if hardly the last, *Zone* visitor to do so.

Zone relied on implication rather than didacticism to make anti-capital punishment statements; Dennis Weaver awaits execution in *Shadow Play.*

An open door and a shadow serve as two of *Zone*'s most significant recurring symbols; they are combined in the opening sequence of *A Passage For Trumpet.*

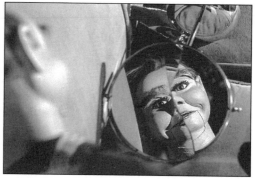

Shattered glass represents the identity crisis of many *Zone* characters, including the title non-human figure in *The Dummy.*

Difficult relationships, internal and external, are expressed in this image from *The Dummy*: The most complex single shot in the history of TV drama up to that point in time, directed by Abner Biberman.

As **Zone** was shot at the MGM studios, settings from their legendary sci-fi film could be used as a backdrop for distant worlds: Here, Roddy McDowall cautiously disembarks from his spaceship in *People Are Alike All Over*.

A human (Roddy McDowall) learns how animals feel on Earth when the superior beings of a far away planet put him in an observation cage in *People Are Alike All Over*.

The great world of literature, including the finest examples of the science-fiction and imaginative fantasy genres, has always dealt with man's desire to conquer time: In *Time Enough at Last*, Burgess Meredith falsely believes he has done precisely that—momentarily!

As revolutionary as **Zone** may have been, its morality was in many regards traditionalist: In *A Nice Place To Visit*, Larry Blyden and Sebastian Cabot mount celestial steps to check the former's "record."

As in Arthur Miller's "realistic" play, Rod's script for *In Praise of Pip* deals with the need to extend parenthood beyond the biological; Jack Klugman in the present treats Russell Horton with the respect he failed to show his own boy in the past, thereby redeeming himself.

In a hall of mirrors *Zone* had been leading to for five years, *In Praise of Pip* presents a father (Jack Klugman) worthy of ancient tragedy attempting to reconcile with his beloved boy (Billy Mumy) when fate allows him a second—and final—chance.

The title character (Burgess Meredith) writes the history of the future in *Printer's Devil*.

Having passed through a time-tunnel, the confused wagon master (Cliff Robertson) marches to meet his destiny in *A Hundred Yards Over the Rim*.

Serling brought the advice of Franklin D. Roosevelt, his hero from the 1930s, into the Eisenhower era with his indictment of mob mentality in *The Monsters Are Due on Maple Street.*

Beat the Devil? . . . that's not so easy to do, as the hero of *The Howling Man* discovers after he inadvertently frees Old Scratch (Robin Hughes).

A seemingly deranged passenger (William Shatner) explains to a stewardess (Asa Maynor) there's a gremlin on the wing while his wife (Ruth Wilson) sleeps in Richard Matheson's *Nightmare at 20,000 Feet.*

In *Zone*, the merry-go-round consistently represents a melancholy middle-aged man's lost youth, which he desperately wants to recapture: Jack Klugman attempts to mentally experience the fun he should have shared with his son (Billy Mumy) *In Praise of Pip.*

During *Zone*'s early years, Rod took a hands-on approach to the show; here he meets with actors Beverly Garland and Ross Martin between takes on *The Four Of Us Are Dying.*

flashback reveals that Anne followed her heart, rather than her head. Anne blames her parents for not forcing Bob upon her, and spoiling her so that she, at age eighteen, wasn't mature enough to make the right decision and do as her parents commanded!

In a series that so often posits the romantic attitude that emotion should take preference to logic, *Spur* unfolds as a late cautionary fable against such an immature approach. If *Zone* more effectively played to a youthful audience than any other TV drama of its time, that did not mean that Serling and company couldn't offer a harrowing anti-romantic warning against self-indulgency, portraying wondrous first love as unlikely to last. The kind of angry young man who serves as a perfect object of a girl's early affections is best left as the man she loved, lost, and forever remembers; the reality of such a person on a daily basis likely turns that wondrous dream into a bleak nightmare. The black-clad rider was, of course, an older, wiser Anne trying to warn her young self against the disaster of marrying Dave, though this turns out to be precisely the opposite of what, in youthful naiveté, Anne believed. As Serling pronounces, "Her desolate existence once more afflicted by the hope of altering her past mistake—a hope which is, unfortunately, doomed to disappointment." In this, as in most other fifth-season episodes, decent characters do not receive a Second Chance.

Zicree argues that the episode fails because of "close-ups in the teaser which clearly show that the girl and the middle-aged pursuer are one and the same." Director Elliott Silverstein does offer a tight shot on the pursuer, leaving no question that this is an older Anne. But because of this, audience involvement works on a profound level. What we experience upon finally realizing who Anne did marry then plays as a perfect final twist rather than a simple trick.

Ruthless People/Wasted Lives:

UNCLE SIMON (11/15/63)

Don Siegel, whose *Invasion of the Body Snatchers* served as *Zone*'s predecessor, vividly brought this Serling script to small-screen life. Uncle Simon (Cedric Hardwicke) reveals himself to be a mean, verbally abusive old man. He orders his niece, Barbara Polk (Constance Ford), around in the mansion they share. Clocks stare down as they argue from the far ends of a Hitchcock-like staircase, suggesting that the Time Element hovers over them. As Simon's own time on Earth is running out, he embodies oncoming death. Barbara has wasted what might have been a good life by spending it here and caring for the unappreciative old codger because she wanted his house after Simon's passing. Each existence is a living nightmare, her greed and his cruelty a sado-masochistic yin and yang. For Zicree, this represents a failure of imagination. "It's a sordid story about two sordid people," he claims, dismissing the piece because "neither is terribly likeable." If it were true that the leads in a play must be likeable (it isn't); Serling achieves a new complexity by not presenting us with a conflict between one "good" and one "bad" character.

As the world around Serling darkened, his artistic vision necessarily responded in kind. This hardly implies Serling grew superficially cynical about man, no longer believing that the good people exist. Rather, Serling surrendered to profound pessimism: the bad outnumber the good. With Simon's death (whether Barbara killed him or he died accidentally is left ambiguous), she inherits everything. Then, black humor: this includes an android (played by Robby the Robot of *Forbidden Planet*) whose personality has been modeled, by the tinker of an uncle in his lab, in his own emotional image. Barbara is doomed to spend eternity with an immortal Uncle Simon, as a clause in the will insists that should she destroy the mechanical man, Barbara forfeits all. Her grim acceptance during the final moments suggests that the hoped-for heaven after Simon's death has turned into an even worse emotional inferno.

As I Lay Dying:

THE MASKS (3/20/64)

Death is now omnipresent: Terminally ill Jason Foster (Robert Keith) summons his four closest blood relatives for the reading of his will.

The one qualification for dividing his wealth equally is that, this being New Orleans and the first night of Mardi Gras, they all wear masks during the countdown to midnight. Then, the wheelchair-bound codger plans to expire, fulfilling his Time Limit. Cryptically, he mentions that the masks were "created by an old Cajun," implying the metaphysical theme. This is heightened by several references to a Higher Being; Jason's doctor says "God willing" when the elderly man insists that he'll survive until the witching hour and Jason himself hisses "May God pity you" at his offspring before dying. He also references the Bible, sarcastically calling hypochondriac illusions of his middle-aged daughter Emily (Virginia Gregg) Job-like.

Serling's script cites the Bard when beautiful Emily (Brooke Hayward), obsessed with her Mirror Image, snorts to critical Jason: "He laughs at scars who never felt a wound." Wilfred (Milton Selzer) is a money-oriented businessman; his son Wilfred, Jr. (Alan Sues) is a coward who inflicts cruelty on others. The group represents *Zone*'s four deadly sins: self-interest, vanity, greed and inhumanism. Director Ida Lupino creates abject horror at the denouement, when all remove the masks and realize that they'll forever look like what they truly were: hideous creatures resembling the pig-people in *Eye of the Beholder*. Even here, though, Serling includes a patina of his old guarded optimism, coupled with the civil rights theme: as a foil to all these petty types, there's Jeffrey (Bill Walker), the black butler who truly cares for Jason Foster. However few in number, good people still exist.

Through a Glass Darkly:

LIVING DOLL (11/1/63)

NIGHTMARE AT 20,000 FEET (10/11/63)

Though the Charles Beaumont/Jerry Sohl script *Living Doll* opens in the afternoon, we're shortly guided through a long day's journey into a bleak night. Director Richard C. Sarafian opens with an oblique angle on what should to be a pleasant scene: A mother, Annabelle (Mary La Roche), leads her daughter Christie (Tracy Stratford) into their handsome home. The girl clutches a new doll, Talking Tina. But these females must contend with the husband and stepfather, Erich Streator (Telly Savalas), who resents the diminutive version of *Zone*'s earlier mannequins. When he's alone with Tina the doll no longer warbles pleasantries, but threatens him. This halts whenever anyone approaches, so again we wonder if the doll's nasty statements exist only in Erich's mind.

An anti-humanist, Erich denies Christie the father-daughter bond the child craves. Happily, Erich is no simple rendering of evil, but a psychologically ill man: Insecure because of his inability to conceive children, Erich perceives the doll as an intended slight on his wounded masculinity. He's allowed a Second Chance after realizing how deeply he hurt Christie. This, after Erich received one of those Long-Distance Calls, presumably from Tina. Like Gibbs in *The Fever*, Erich wakes at night in a sweat, heading downstairs, tripping on the doll and breaking his own neck. Annabelle hurries down, terrified. Tina turns her evil eye on the good lady, threatening: "You'd better be nice to me!" This, despite the fact that Annabelle has never been anything but kind. At this point in *Zone*'s development, even living as a humanist no longer protects people from the dark side.

Matheson turned to a more traditional form of noir for *Nightmare at 20,000 Feet,* about a late-night flight (the ongoing aviation theme) on a commercial airliner. As Bob Wilson (William Shatner) and wife Ruth (Christine White) board, we notice the handsome (and normal looking) Bob displays slight, subtle nervous ticks and that Ruth shows great concern for her husband, who has been recently released from a hospital following a nervous breakdown. The two are "going home," presumably to some Homewood-type town from the big city. A chain-smoker, Bob recalls Serling. Bob accuses himself of "cowardice," recalling many WWII tales.

While his wife sleeps (one way of interpreting what follows is that it's all her dream), Bob notices a gremlin (Nick Cravat) on the wing, tearing up a cowling plate. When panicky Bob tries to inform a stewardess (Asa Maynor), the creature disappears. Is it all in his mind? Possibly, if we recall Bob's "problems." Lightning strikes, depicting the Death Light. Eventually, Bob steals a gun from a snoozing guard and attempts to save everyone by killing the gremlin before he can dismantle the engine. If that sounds like a positive finale, nothing could be darker than the double-twist: first, that the humanist willing to sacrifice himself so others might live (another Christ figure) is forced into a straightjacket rather than rewarded. Second, we learn that he was right as director Richard Donner's camera pulls back to reveal the half-dismantled flying apparatus. Perhaps there is a bright side to this dark fable. The strain disappears from Bob's face. In time, the disabled wing will be noticed by others. Better still, he knows that he is not mad. Thanks to pain and self-sacrifice, Bob's catharsis is complete.

The Sun Also Rises?:

I AM THE NIGHT—COLOR ME BLACK (3/27/64)

For some, this episode aimed for ambitiousness though it slipped into pretension. It is true that Serling reveals none of his earlier desire to achieve a balance between popular entertainment and personal expression. Yet it's important to keep in mind when *I Am the Night* appeared: near the end of *Zone*'s final season. With nothing to risk with CBS and much to gain, Rod seized a lame duck's opportunity to employ TV for a radical statement. The omnipresent darkness in *I Am the Night* serves as a metaphor for an emotional darkness then settling over our country.

The story takes place in an eternal night that has descended on a spot Serling describes as an "inconsequential village." The bittersweet tone of earlier seasons has given way to bitterness, so the following tale contains not a single sweet character. Here is the work of a humanist who, at this moment, feared that there might be no decent humans left on Earth. This town, another Homewood, reveals only wicked elements, a total turnabout from the way things were on *Zone* (and the country) in the good ol' days of 1959. It's 7:30 AM on the day Jagger (Terry Becker) will be executed. Newspaperman Colbey (Paul Fix), and the sheriff, Charlie Koch (Michael Constantine), huddle in the lawman's office. Both are deeply concerned because the sun has not risen.

Can this impossible situation have been precipitated by decent men corrupting themselves? The journalist failed to report that the man Jagger shot was covered with powder-burns; he'd attacked Jagger, so the act was self-defense. The sheriff wondered about this but, as in Ibsen, Jagger was an enemy of the people. They hate him because, as a local civil rights activist, he shot down the man who led the Klan. Colbey and Koch, each with a conscience, were done in by capitalism and conformity. The sheriff hungers for reelection; the editor didn't want to lose advertising. They allowed the lies of a mean-spirited deputy, Pierce (George Lindsey), to ensure that Jagger would be found guilty and hanged. As the world around them darkens, they have second thoughts. Still, neither will stand up to Pierce or to the mob.

That *I Am the Night* is intended as a pro-civil rights piece is heightened when an African-American minister, Reverend Anderson (Ivan Dixon), arrives. Jagger refuses to speak with him; the victim has not only lost faith in man, but in God as well. But Serling does not feel the same. "Do you believe there could be a theological reason" for the darkness, the editor muses. "Praise God," the sheriff mutters, with no trace of irony. What we witness is an abandoned universe as the Force leaves these horrid people, to borrow from Kurt Weill, lost in the stars. A new maturity dominates Serling's vision: the reverend turns against Jagger once he grasps that the condemned killed not just to save a black person, but because killing gave him pleasure. This is not a cautionary fable against lynching an innocent man. Serling insists that guilt or innocence are unimportant; all capital punishment is amoral.

Director Abner Biberman cuts to clocks, reminding us of the Time Element. We may well recall that the episode's first image was of

Mrs. Koch sleeping, causing us to wonder if all that occurs may be her dream. After the execution the radio reports that the darkness no longer remains isolated. In Birmingham, Alabama, where black students were threatened while attempting to desegregate schools, a black cloak also descends, as it does in Vietnam, where a war that would shortly tear America apart at the seams had just begun to rage out of control and in Dallas, Texas, where the ugly new order of things began on the day Kennedy was shot. But what is the blackness? "Hate," one character concludes. "Don't return their hate," the reverend begs Jagger. But now, consumed with it, he lashes out. He was "the village idiot who tried to be his brother's keeper" and will be crucified for it. What can we do about such hate? "Only God knows." Now, Serling admits that, compared to five years earlier, he hasn't any answers.

Irony in the Ionosphere:

THE LONG MORROW (1/10/64)

"Not everything that meets the eye," Serling intones in the opening narration, "is as it appears." A distinction between seeming realities and actuality is developed here, with darker implications than earlier. The first image is of Commander Doug Stansfield (Robert Lansing) suspended in a box. He appears dead, but sleeps and dreams, his mind free to wander, bodily functions maintained by scientific equipment. Stansfield appears identical to Mike Ferris as we saw him in *Where Is Everybody?* This astronaut's dreams are as sweet and mellow as Ferris's were dark and depressing. Then again, he who laughs last laughs best.

If we detect something like a smile in the final shot, it's a bitter one indeed. Something has happened to him that likely would not have occurred in the earlier episodes: The finest humanist of all has been cosmically screwed. *Zone*'s Time Element pulls a nasty trick here, unlike any we have seen. In a double narration, Doug relates his story involving the most cruelly imperfect future Serling ever conceived. Forty years earlier, Doug met with Dr. Bixler (George MacCready), agreeing to travel to a distant solar system 141 light years away. Doug would spend 20 years traveling, six months exploring, and another 20 coming home. During flights, he would be frozen so that, on return, he would have aged less than a year. Before takeoff, Doug meets Sandra Horn (Mariette Hartley), an attractive space program employee. This makes Doug's launch more difficult. Sandra will wait for him, though she'll be an elderly woman waiting for the young man to return.

No sooner has Doug departed than Sandy has a sudden inspiration: she'll have herself frozen, with instructions to be awakened (still young and beautiful) when Doug returns. Bixler attempts to send that message up, but it's another of those Long-Distance Calls that fail to connect. Out of touch with Earth, Doug makes a decision as precipitous as Sandy's: He turns off the anti-aging device to be the same "age" as she upon return. The elderly man steps off the space craft only to find a beautiful young woman waiting for him. She is willing to spend the rest of her life with the old man. While he appreciates this, Doug will not allow it.

Finally, General Walters (Edward Binns) speaks to The Lonely man. What Walters earlier described as bitter irony in the ionosphere doesn't conclude the episode. We realize that this serves as Serling's ultimate statement on unconditional love; the final portrait of fine people, those who live by that all-important coda. Now, such humanists are destroyed. What occurs is worse than tragic if we accept one definition of that term: a serious drama unfolding under the constant vision of a deity. If God is not dead in *Zone*'s fifth season he has surely wandered away, no longer making sure that only the bad are punished. The Force is mentioned only once, swiftly and in passing: "God help me," Walters sighs, considering the reason Doug undid his anti-aging device, "I know why."

Other than that whimper in the cosmic wilderness, there is . . . nothing! The mission has been for naught, as no life existed in that star system. Doug was forgotten decades before returning with the "news" scientists have long since learned. Sandy's life is meaningless without Doug. In a *Zone* reimagined for the post-JFK-assassination era, the good suffer terrible fates once reserved for the evil. If there's any consolation, it exists solely in the mind of Walters. Nothing in his own life will come close to the distinction of having met Doug: "That I knew a man who put such a premium on love." The ability to feel deeply for another gives this military man the courage and faith to go on. The good news: Unconditional love remains Serling's conception of the best element in us. The bad? *Zone*'s creator no longer believes that this is likely to reap just rewards in the fifth dimension. Or, more tragically still, in the real world.

Conclusion:
WHY SHOULD WE TAKE
SERLING SERIOUSLY?

THE MIDWAY OF a sleazy carnival, erected just beyond the barriers of any supposedly safe city, has been a symbol for the darker aspects of our human imagination since *The Cabinet of Dr. Caligari* (1919), first of the great German expressionistic films. Forty years later, *Zone* would revitalize its pop iconography. And like that oddest of midway attractions, the shape-shifting funhouse mirror, Serling's series forced each passerby to momentarily perceive himself and his world closely: To truly see, perhaps for the first time.

At first glance, that funhouse mirror appears to skewer everything. We laugh nervously after overcoming our initial shock at the sight, then try to force the memory out of our mind's eye, pretending that this is some cruel temporary trick. Yet forgetting what we briefly acknowledged isn't so easy. We intuit that this monstrous vision reveals a terrible truth, one that in our ordinary lives we choose to ignore—likely because the human psyche cannot cope with such a frightful revelation of the greater, deeper horror all around. Whether we ordinarily notice or not . . .

Standing for a horrifying moment before the funhouse mirror, even the most oblivious citizen momentarily senses that our world can be twisted up into a dark doppelgänger. That's why these "distorting glasses" (as the ancients once referred to them) exist, and what they were created for. The funhouse mirror served as surrealism's predecessor a full millennium before Jean Cocteau and other avatars of the avant-garde created that term early in the twentieth century to describe a threatening type of art—edgy art that evokes the thrilling, yet terrible, tenets of a technological milieu in which the mind-bog-gling complexity of science challenges the reassuring simplicities of religion. People shudder at such admittedly awful images. Still, they want, expect, need those mirrors to be there, located on that well-trod path between the carousel and cotton-candy concession.

As to the limitations of a more conventional looking glass, critic Peter Biskind notes that in the 1950s the most popular films, those with the biggest budgets, the brightest stars, and the greatest impact, were movies like *Giant, The Man in the Gray Flannel Suit,* and *Rebel Without a Cause.* Yet they appear transparent, no more than windows on the world showing reality as it was.

In contrast were less prestigious pictures: *Invaders From Mars, Them!, Earth vs. the Flying Saucers.* Less realistic windows on the world than mirrors into the American psyche, these films offered a perspective never served up by middlebrow art. Conventional storytelling may initially strike us as more important, only to fade in a way that imaginative fiction, at its best, does not. For here is art (if rarely thought of in such lofty terms) that reveals a hidden nightmare behind everyday actuality. Providing what we now call the surreal vision, imaginative fiction, while seeming to distort, cuts away the shallow surface to reveal a grotesque truth below. "There is something evil in our midst!" the forlorn hero of *Caligari* shrieked forty years before *Zone* premiered. No one listened. Everyone assumed that he was crazy, which is precisely what those people driving by Kevin McCarthy at the end of *Invasion of the Body Snatchers* (1956) thought when he tried to warn them, "You're next!" And, shortly, many similar glances were directed by onlookers as the average passerby considered Serling's latest lost soul.

From 1959 to 1964, *The Twilight Zone* served as our national fun-house mirror. That in itself establishes Serling's show as the most important TV drama of its era. More remarkably, *Zone* still serves that purpose a half century later. Viewed on late-night cable TV or DVD boxed sets, here's something more than a glimpse of the way we were, explaining why *Zone* passes the test of time. While watch-ing, we come to better understand not just America at a past point of transition but America itself. Then and now. Not only who we were but who we are today—and what we may yet become.

How important to recall then that fairgrounds abound on *Zone*. There are carousels aplenty (*Walking Distance*). Ferris wheels, too (*Perchance to Dream*). One of each in *In Praise of Pip* (a funhouse mirror is there as well). Each classic *Zone* offered viewers a seemingly other worldly story only to comment on the hard truth of our existence, providing an electric shock to a shattered sensibility. Importantly, it did so at a time when TV otherwise floundered in Minnow's vast wasteland.

Rod Serling qualifies as the single most important author ever to work in such an unsettling genre on TV. And, some might say, he rates as the leading practitioner to appear since our country's founding father of the macabre, Edgar Allan Poe (1809–1849). A diminutive man and an enormous talent, Poe is recalled as wandering through nineteenth century Baltimore by moonlight, black cloak draped over his shoulders. A far cry from Rod Serling, relaxing by his pool, effortlessly dictating stories into a tape recorder. But the inner Serling, self-questioning, for reasons even he couldn't explain expressing his take on reality via wild fantasies, appears closer in spirit to the much-misunderstood Poe.

Understanding one, then, is to better grasp the other.

Poe's special genius, according to Baudelaire, grew from a "unique temperament that allowed him to paint and to explain, in an impeccable, gripping, and terrible manner, the exception in the moral order" as "all the imaginary world floats around a nervous man." Prefiguring the twentieth century antihero, that "nervous man" seemed strangely out of place when Poe envisioned him in an age of epic American poetry and prose by the likes of Longfellow (*Hiawatha*) and Cooper (*The Last of the Mohicans*). This strange sensibility would, however, be stretched further halfway around the world as fin-de-siècle approached, ushering in the age of modernism. Russia's Fyodor Dostoevsky (1821–1881) unveiled his underground man: caught in a complex web of mysticism and morality, outer conventionality and inner abnormality, social conformity and the fearful possibility of abject insanity.

This emergent figure would dominate our contemporary "serious" literature, most notably the works of Franz Kafka (1883–1924). In that Austrian-born, Prague-educated Jewish-German author's masterworks—*The Trial* and *Metamorphosis*–his central character wakes from an absurd dream to discover that life has become more bizarre than anything experienced in the recesses of his imagination. Kafka's characters grasp in horror that they've been transformed into cockroach-like creatures or forced into a shadowy courtroom to face some heinous crime no one will identify. Then again, could this be nothing more than another nightmare, a dream within a dream? Likewise on *Zone*, people find their ugly inner selves turned outward (*The Masks*), are forced into a bizarre trial (*The Obsolete Man*), or are lost in dreams (*In Praise of Pip*).

The most important recurring theme in *Zone*'s five-year canon, though, is death. This brings us back to Poe, whose groundbreaking work initiated the modern vision. Even as Europe's *belle epoque* faded and a less spontaneous, more mechanical world emerged, Paris-based artists seized on what they'd learned from that guilt-racked American during the new century's early decades. In its second half, Serling took what had until then existed as a cult art form for the self-contained *cogniscenti* to the people, offering a video counterpart to an aesthetic approach that began in painting and poetry, eventually motoring the birth of alternative cinema in 1929 with *Un Chien Andalou*.

The first surrealist film of major significance, that experimental collaboration by Salvador Dalí and Luis Buñuel, like so many *Zones* to come, prominently featured an image of an immense all-seeing eye, coldly staring down on our "normal" world, not unlike Dr. Eckleberg's advertisement towering over the valley of ashes outside New York City in F. Scott Fitzgerald's *The Great Gatsby* (1925). For 22 minutes (the running time of most *Zones*), Dalí and Buñuel offered an increasingly off-putting chronicle of one man's descent into an alternative realm on the edge of what we reassuringly refer to as "normalcy." When three decades later what had been a radical vision reached the masses, it did so via Rod Serling: "There's the signpost up ahead!" he warned viewers.

But back, at least momentarily, to Poe. A significant theorist as well as a superb craftsman, he wrote in the mid-1840s of the need to first choose some "novel" effect, through the power of words make it "vivid," and, finally, to convey a phantasmagoric impact via what began as "ordinary incidents," presented with an ever more "peculiar tone." In Poe's phrase, we encounter a perfect summation not only of *The Black Cat*'s impact but that of *The Monsters Are Due on Maple Street*. The initial image introduces an ordinary setting, everyday stuff soon interrupted by the unexpected arrival of the unknown. This leads first to curiosity, then concern, and finally to mass paranoia. All advance that sense of the "peculiar," and always end with a surprise resolution, one that satisfies because we sense, in that revelation, that this is what had been coming our way from the very first. "It is only with the denouement constantly in view," Poe continued, "that we can give a plot its indispensable air of consequence, or causation." True too of *Zone* at its best are the episodes that entered what Burt Hatlen calls "the myth pool," and for Jung constituted our "collective unconscious" in which familiar modern icons from King Kong to Superman serve as touchstones in our daily conversations.

As Serling was always quick to admit, the series had its share of losers. In the long run, that doesn't matter much. The whole was (and still is) more than the sum of its parts. *Zone* meant something back then. Yet so did many other shows, all but forgotten today. *Wagon Train* was the number-one rated series at the time. Other than nostalgists, does anyone recall it today? Earlier *I Love Lucy* rated at the top of the heap. For decades, that show remained strong in the syndication market. Now? Not so much. However dazzling its physical comedy, the show is mostly beloved today by aging baby boomers. Cable's *TV Land*, which used to showcase *Lucy*, now tends to run it at odd hours. Mostly, it pops up on minor local channels to fill time for older audiences.

Not that there's anything wrong with that! Still, the significance of *Zone* resides in its appeal not only to young people of the late 1950s and early 1960s but to each new generation that rediscovers it—and, more incredibly, spots something of themselves in Rod's world. In truth, *Zone* may mean more to us today than it did back then. Whenever ordinary life stretches into what feel like surreal directions, most people describe it in one easily understandable way: "I felt as if I was entering *The Twilight Zone* . . ."

Even that, however, fails to answer the big question: Why? What's the essence of *Zone*'s appeal? Quality drama? Sure, but that could be found elsewhere: *Douglas Fairbanks Presents, The Dick Powell Theatre.* Again: Why *Zone*? Just this question was asked of Mark Scott Zicree during radio, TV, and print interviews for his *The Twilight Zone Companion.* When he attempted to answer with any of the obvious retorts (high quality, memorable scares, etc.), Zicree noticed the interviewer's disappointment. Of course that was true. Still, this hardly answers the question. So in a *Note to the Second Edition* (1982), Zicree tried to come up with something more satisfying: During the postwar era, young couples moved away from small towns, buying tract houses in the recently built suburbs. With this, "the extended family became a thing of the past—and alienation the great dilemma of our age." Since *Zone* rated as "the first, and possibly only, TV series to deal" with such alienation, that qualified it as the one show to accurately mirror, if in the guise of weird fantasy (that funhouse metaphor again), a new reality.

Zicree's answer is good, so far as it goes. But he fails to take into account that by the 1980s, a second (and shortly third) generation had been born into the suburban life. Having never in their own experiences known small-town America firsthand, the loss of which Serling mourned with his Willoughbys and Homewoods, these new generations could hardly respond to that aspect of the show. Why, then, did they find Serling's series as appealing as their parents (or grandparents) had? Zicree does suggest the key, mentioning that he learned of "a pastor [in Washington] who shows episodes to his congregation in order to raise theological questions." The incident, passed over all too quickly, contains a germ of the full answer. *Zone*'s impact derives from its focus on the most disturbing issues raised by the advent of modernism. The writings of Darwin on evolution, Freud on the complexity of the human mind, Marx on the value of an individual in relationship to the mass trickled down from an intellectual elite to ordinary people. Then along came Nietzsche, influenced by those others and, as representative modern philosopher, he added a nihilistic view to all that preceded him: "God is dead!" More fully understood, Nietzsche wondered if ordinary people could continue to accept the Biblical explanation of creation (the Lord accomplished it all in six 24-hour days, on the last creating man in his own image; then he stopped, the task complete) after science revealed that our world is billions of years old. When in 1925 a teacher dared forward this theory in Tennessee, the religious right put him on trial for destroying their children's absolute belief in a higher power. Science and religion, they insisted, were antithetical. Science, even on a theoretical level, spread seeds of doubt. So they found the teacher, Scopes, guilty as charged, hoping to put an end to it. Ironically, the opposite occurred. As the trial was conducted by the era's great lawyers (conservative William Jennings Bryant prosecuting, liberal Clarence Darrow for the defense), the event would be covered by a then-new medium, radio, which carried the debate to every American home. People who had never heard of Darwinism were exposed. The conservatives won the battle only to lose the war.

Hollywood responded by turning out films that featured evolutionary subtexts. In Rouben Mamoulian's *Dr. Jekyll and Mr. Hyde* (1931), novelist Robert Louis Stevenson's concept of the murderous villain (a small gnome with a yellow-green complexion) was jettisoned. As Jekyll (Fredric March) takes the formula (now a scientific concoction) he devolves into the missing link. A seemingly fantastical movie (or, as Serling would eventually prove, TV show) can by implication deal with topical problems. The Scopes Monkey Trial reemerged in our public consciousness at precisely the same time that Rod was preparing *Zone*. First, a theatrical version, *Inherit the Wind*, appeared on Broadway; then message-movie producer Stanley Kramer mounted a big-budget film starring Spencer Tracy and Fredric March. The movie proved anything but an anomaly: By implication, *Inherit the Wind* educated the movie-going public about the need to accept science as (in the age of Sputnik) a valid area of study for youth.

Did that mean that was religion was now out, an intolerable concept to most Americans? Not at all. In the final scene, Tracy (a non-threatening moderate-liberal if ever there were one) seizes a copy of *Evolution of the Species* with one hand and holds the Holy Bible in the other. Carefully, lovingly, he brings them together, gently placing both books in his open satchel. Acceptance of science, the image implies, does not necessitate a rejection of religion. The two coexist; they are not polar opposite ways of viewing the world but alternative forms of saying the same thing. This was heartening to hear and, in that film's case, see. Still, a suggestion that all might yet be right with our world was not enough. We as a people needed a full series of examples, vivid dramas that would prove this point. Where, though, would we discover such an important storytelling venue?

On Friday, October 2, 1959, the *Twilight Zone* premiered. Week after week for nearly five years, Rod Serling and company assured us that miracles (for the Judeo-Christian mind) and magic (hailing back to pagan times) aren't forced out of existence by science—at least not for the open-minded, the truly liberal in the best sense of that term. Yes, the world likely was created by a big bang. Yet there remains what we cannot ever make sense of in technical language: Why did the big bang occur? What (or Who) caused it to happen? We can, if we choose, call that force God. Science now offered terminology to help a generation that no longer believed in miracles to accept them under a new name. Trace back through this volume's twelve chapters, take another look at each show; clearly, this was what Serling said to us, and what his audience needed to hear—otherwise they might have fallen into despair. To this day, works of imaginative fiction that reign supreme (George Lucas's *Star Wars* trilogy, Steven Speilberg's *E.T.*) borrow from what our current writer-directors, when they were young, were most impressed by: Rod Serling and *Zone*.

The *Zone* phenomenon assumed international proportions over the past half-century, hardly a result of criticizing temporal problems in our social discourse. Its spiritual aspects prove more powerful than ever. Not since the Scopes Trial nearly 85 years ago or the revival of such a crisis in the mid-1950s has a rift between chemistry and Christ been so significant or mean-spirited. Hard-core extremists on either side (such people damned as "absolutists" by Serling half a century ago) insist that the opposition be silenced. Most mainstreamers sensibly grasp the need for both spirituality and science. No wonder, then, they respond so overwhelmingly to *Star Wars* and *E.T.*, each film insisting that the two basic elements can (must!) come together if we are to survive other than on an animal level. We want—need—to believe that the Force remains with us.

No wonder, too, that recent generations, their appetites whetted by those films, are thrilled to discover the point of origin. Spielberg and Lucas often acknowledge the impact Serling's series had on them. Here is where they learned that the world can indeed be a frightening place. Yet as little Henry, a Wordsworthian child as swain in a Serling script, simply but beautifully said, we all "got to believe." Not that this constitutes anything new: There is special providence, Shakespeare assured his audience, in the fall of a sparrow. Greek tragedy said much the same thing 2,000 years earlier, when a newly founded scientific outlook caused citizens of Athens to question all the old ideas, including the very existence of their gods. Today, the right attacks the "secular humanism" of the left. The progressive in Serling believed in humanism, in an abiding sense that the good in man outweighs the bad. Yet the traditionalist in him insisted that all true humanism must be faith-based. In the polarized climate of the twenty-first century, the meaning of Rod Serling's work reminds us of our need for a center than can hold.

Everything old is new again. *The Twilight Zone* bridged a gap between what had come before and what would follow. Like all true tragedy, it was not depressing but uplifting, providing (as Aristotle claimed) drama on a metaphysical theme. *Zone* touches on what were the ultimate issues to the ancients, remain so to us, and likely will be for those who inhabit the future: What does it mean to be a man (in the generic, not machismo, sense), a question which can only be answered by adding yet another: What is our place in the universe? Today, young people who dismiss almost anything shot in black and white make one notable exception. The *Twilight Zone* remains alive and well and living on TV . . .

Prior to the series premier, Serling realized that he would face a difficult struggle because of a long-standing prejudice against imaginative fantasy. A week before *Zone* debuted, its creator appeared on

Mike Wallace's popular CBS interview show. Serling was aware that Wallace held a high opinion of his teleplays *Patterns* and *Requiem*. Yet, gruffly, Wallace snapped, "So you've given up writing anything serious for TV?" Following a double-take, Serling stumblingly insisted that "serious" was precisely what he was going for.

The pseudo-sophisticated have always laughed loudly at genre pieces, certain that they can't contain the lofty intent of realistic works. In truth, realism is nothing more than one more genre. TV soap-operas and paperback potboilers, if set in the everday world, may be labeled realism (in the most general sense of the term), even as are the masterworks of Hugo or Chekhov. The former are without serious ambition; the latter are brimming with precisely that. Imaginative fiction can likewise offer the enjoyable escapism of *Flash Gordon* and *Buck Rogers* or far more serious stuff: Orwell's *1984*, Huxley's *Brave New World*—or even Shakespeare's *The Tempest* as compared to his more realistic *Othello*. To rate a work according to genre is at best naive, at worst dangerous. What serves as a proper basis for judgment is what a single author does with the form—what he hopes to say through its conventions.

Exposure to **Zone** soon countered Wallace's glib remark, as would Newton Minnow's insistence, while decrying post-Golden Age TV, that **Zone** provided the happy exception. Yet this created another reason why a post-*Patterns* Serling did not receive the respect he deserved: a second prejudice, angled at TV itself. Such an argument runs more or less like this: If so much mediocrity existed on TV (indeed, it did!), didn't that mean TV is by its very nature a lesser narrative form than, say, plays, novels, or the movies? Yes, everyone concurred, **Zone** was the best thing on TV; still that wasn't saying much. But we should recall that Hollywood films weren't initially accepted as "serious" in the way tales appearing in print or on the legitimate stage were. Acknowledgment and acceptance of commercial film as an art form came slowly; eventually the intelligentsia, then the public at large, realized that *Citizen Kane* was not merely a superior work in a lesser medium, but a viable American classic. This acknowledgment proved that movies were as "legitimate" as the live stage—not better or worse but, as Rudolf Arnheim insisted, an original art form. Lest we forget, the early novel was not considered on a par with the "higher" art of poetry. Shakespeare never would have guessed that his plays would live on; if he enjoyed artistic immortality, he believed that this would have been through his verse. A false prejudice *Hamlet* helped to dispel.

Minor plays on Broadway, no matter how cleverly written and smoothly produced, aren't automatically superior to a heavyweight TV work like *The Days of Wine and Roses, Twelve Angry Men,* or *Patterns.* As a storytelling form, TV rates as neither superior nor inferior to any other. Recently, the higher quality of televised drama and comedy has legitimized the medium; *Zone* is now revered as a precursor.

Yet another roadblock to full respect has to do with TV's commercial basis. The good news is that, since *Zone* has remained in syndication, its finest episodes forever reach new audiences. The bad? That's true too for the weaker ones. *Zone* is a product. CBS (which owns the rights) perceives it as an ongoing source of revenue. Virtually all episodes are included in the package rented by cable outlets and local stations. If that doesn't seem like a major problem, consider this: The English poet Percy Shelley (1792–1822) was, for half a century following his death, considered a lesser talent than fellow romantics Wordsworth, Byron, and Keats. The reason? Their works were highly edited for republication so that only the best would continue to circulate. But Shelley's widow Mary so believed in her husband that she wanted everyone to experience every word he wrote, the mediocre alongside the gems. In Serling's case, it was not his wife, Carol, but CBS that allowed weaker (and in a few cases terrible) shows to enjoy equal opportunity. This, for half a century, has been Serling's fate.

Until now. This volume, by its selective approach, is an attempt to remedy that situation. My desire? To force a fresh focus on the best of *Zone.*

There's a final reason we should take Rod Serling seriously: he was television's first auteur. Not always the author (i.e., writer) of every episode, Serling was the single person who, while working in a collaborative endeavor, was always responsible for the show's vision. During the 1950s, French critics coined the term "auteur" to legitimize commercial movies not only as entertainment but as a true (and unique) art form, one related to preexisting ones (the novel, play, dance and painting) yet not merely a modern extension of any one. V. F. Perkins insisted not on film-as-electronic-age theatre or film-as-celluloid-novel, but film as film. Fine. But for the lofty status of art, we expect self-expression. In a process that obviously includes a team of craftsmen, that creates a problem: Who is the primary artist?

For critics ranging from Andre Bazin to his American counterpart Andrew Sarris, in movies that person would likely be the director, explaining why we refer to *Psycho* as a film by Alfred Hitchcock rather than one by screenwriter Robert Block. But how about television? The degree to which movies dominate TV schedules led to a widespread belief in TV as an extension of the movie medium, an alternate venue for viewing films. This seemed particularly true following the demise of live-TV, which had briefly characterized the medium as unique. Why, though, did great films like *Ben-Hur* seem considerably less impressive when viewed on a small TV? Television has to be understood as its own medium, far more suited to intimate stories. Needed was a new aesthetic; an auteur theory for TV that would validate this medium as an original art form.

Who, though, ought to be seen as the primary artist on TV? Writer? Director? Producer? All or none of the above?

If Rod Serling was far from TV's first author, he did emerge as its first auteur. Such a claim could not be made for Alfred Hitchcock, whose own series (premiering four seasons before *Zone*) was left entirely to others. Trusted assistants picked the scripts; he directed one or, at most, two shows a year. Likewise, Dick Powell occasionally acted in TV "theatres" featuring his name in the title but left the grunt work to others, and had little—if any—interest in expressing himself as to the society around him through TV. Powell set out to provide classy entertainment; he achieved precisely that.

Then along came Rod Serling and *Zone*. Here, we discover the very definition of a TV auteur, though likely Serling could not have known that at the time. He was not the director or writer of every episode but the creator of the series itself, a hands-on executive producer who may or may not also write individual episodes. As with a film or a live play, many people working together turn out a high-quality show. But what we're talking about now is authorship: Whose show is it? Here, TV differs from other collaborative media. On stage the writer rates as primary artist; that's why we call out "Author! Author!" following the debut of any fine new work. In films, a director "signs" his work with the final credit, as in *Stagecoach*; a John Ford film. Television? Norman Lear's *All in the Family* or Aaron Sorkin's *The West Wing*. In some cases, that person stretches even further by directing, too: Rod Lurie's recent (and vastly under-appreciated) *Commander in Chief.*

Here then is what was needed before TV could ever be seriously studied on the university level, as is currently the case. It all began with one show, one person: *The Twilight Zone*; Rod Serling. The terrible irony is, Serling died believing himself something of a failure for never having written in the pre-existing storytelling forms he held great respect for: live theatre and the novel. Nonetheless, his work outlives most of his then contemporary practitioners (Sloan Wilson, Leon Uris, William Gibson, William Inge) in those venues. Serling gave us something so much more important: the first proof positive that a filmed series, when its unique abilities were properly understood and fully employed, constitutes an original art form. Rod Serling was the visionary who paved the way. As a result, his own greatest fears and doubts can be set aside. No writer of his time possessed a greater imagination. And none turned out anything that comes close to his body of work in terms of lasting importance.

INDEX